BIRDS *of the* TEXAS HILL COUNTRY

NUMBER FIFTY   *The Corrie Herring Hooks Series*

BIRDS
of the TEXAS
HILL COUNTRY

MARK W. LOCKWOOD

Drawings by Clemente Guzman III

UNIVERSITY OF TEXAS PRESS ❧ AUSTIN

Requests for permission to reproduce material from this work should be sent to Permissions, University of Texas Press, P.O. Box 7819, Austin, TX 78713-7819.

♾ The paper used in this book meets the minimum requirements of ANSI/NISO Z39.48-1992 (R1997) (Permanence of Paper).

LIBRARY OF CONGRESS CATALOGING-IN-PUBLICATION DATA

Lockwood, Mark.
Birds of the Texas Hill Country / Mark W. Lockwood ; drawings by Clemente Guzman III.
    p.   cm. — (The Corrie Herring Hooks series ; no. 50)
Includes bibliographical references (p.   ).
ISBN 0-292-74725-X (hardcover : alk. paper) — ISBN 0-292-74726-8 (pbk. : alk. paper)
1. Birds—Texas—Texas Hill Country.   I. Title.   II. Series.
QL684.T4   L62   2001
598'.09764'87—dc21
                                           2001000939

For Cindy—*I can never praise or thank her enough.*

CONTENTS

Foreword by Terry Maxwell   xi

Acknowledgments   xiii

The Edwards Plateau   1

Topography   3
River Systems and Reservoirs   4
Climate   5
Vegetation   6
Conservation   8
Parks and Other Birding Areas   9
   Amistad National Recreation Area   11
   Balcones Canyonlands National Wildlife Refuge   11
   Brady Reservoir   12
   Canyon Lake   12
   Colorado Bend State Park   12
   Devils River State Natural Area   13
   Emma Long Metropolitan Park, City of Austin   13
   Enchanted Rock State Natural Area   14
   Garner State Park   14
   Government Canyon State Natural Area   15
   Guadalupe River State Park and
      Honey Creek State Natural Area   15
   Hill Country State Natural Area   16
   Inks Lake State Park   17
   Kickapoo Cavern State Park   17
   Lake Buchanan   18
   Lost Maples State Natural Area   18
   Park Chalk Bluff   19
   Pedernales Falls State Park   19
   South Llano River State Park   19

Edwards Plateau Birds 21

Taxonomy 23
Documenting Observations 23
Early History of Ornithological Investigations on the
    Edwards Plateau 24

Using This Book 32

Seasonal Definitions 33
Frequently Mentioned Locations 34

An Annotated List of Species 35

Species of Uncertain Occurrence on the Edwards Plateau 166
Species Expected to Occur on the Edwards Plateau 170
The Seasonal Distribution of Edwards Plateau Birds 173
Species of Special Interest 173

Selected References 211

Index 217

ILLUSTRATIONS AND TABLES

Drawings

1. Common Loon   36
2. Wood Duck   48
3. Bald Eagle   56
4. White-winged Dove   79
5. Barred Owl   85
6. Black-chinned Hummingbird   91
7. Golden-fronted Woodpecker   96
8. Ash-throated Flycatcher   103
9. Tufted (Black-crested) Titmouse   118
10. Cactus Wren   121
11. Northern Parula   134
12. White-throated Sparrow   153

Photographs

1. Henry P. Attwater   26
2. Howard G. Lacey ranch   27
3. Vernon Bailey   29
4. George Finlay Simmons   30

Color Photographs (following page 166)

1. Government Canyon State Natural Area
2. Devils River State Natural Area
3. Lost Maples State Natural Area
4. Kickapoo Cavern State Park
5. Honey Creek State Natural Area
6. West Nueces River
7. Green Heron
8. Black-bellied Whistling-Duck

9. Montezuma Quail
10. Greater Roadrunner
11. Eastern Screech-Owl
12. Common Poorwill
13. Black-chinned Hummingbird
14. Green Kingfisher
15. Vermilion Flycatcher
16. Scissor-tailed Flycatcher
17. Bell's Vireo
18. Black-capped Vireo
19. Western Scrub-Jay
20. Cave Swallow
21. Verdin
22. Cactus Wren
23. Bewick's Wren
24. Golden-cheeked Warbler—male
25. Golden-cheeked Warbler—female
26. Summer Tanager
27. Canyon Towhee
28. Harris's Sparrow
29. Pyrrhuloxia
30. Varied Bunting
31. Painted Bunting
32. Lesser Goldfinch

Maps

1. Subregions of the Edwards Plateau   2
2. Counties within the Edwards Plateau Physiographic Region   2
3. Average Annual Precipitation on the Edwards Plateau   5
4. Birding Locations on the Edwards Plateau   10

Tables

1. Partners in Flight: Priority Bird Species for the Edwards Plateau   9
2. Seasonal Distribution of Edwards Plateau Birds   175

FOREWORD

Since at least the days of the Republic of Texas (1836–1845), when the site of Austin was chosen as the new capital, Texans have revered their Hill Country and Central Mineral Region. German settlement in the mid-nineteenth century gave us a cultural legacy remaining today in New Braunfels, Fredericksburg, Boerne, Mason, and many other quaint communities nestled among the wooded hills and spring-fed valleys. The drier western plateau, then part of dreaded Comancheria, was entered only by brave souls indeed.

Modern Texans continue to regard the Edwards Plateau and its Hill Country as the historical and cultural heart of our state. Appropriately, it has in recent decades assumed a new role in step with our nation's rising interest in all things natural. Its legendary streams—Guadalupe, Comal, San Saba, Frio, Llano, Pedernales, Blanco, San Marcos, Devils, Medina, Sabinal, Nueces, whose very names speak to history—are treasured today by growing numbers of residents and ecotourists. Hummingbird feeders that attract such wonderfully improbable sights as Green Violet-ears number in the thousands along these stream valleys. Its life forms and their conservation now often take center stage in Texas biodiversity concerns.

The plateau is of international faunal fame. Blind catfishes and ghostly white salamanders live in an astonishing aquifer, often deep below Earth's surface. Without question though, the star attraction—birds—is the point of this book. For example, among the three highest profile endangered birds in Texas (Black-capped Vireo, Golden-cheeked Warbler, and Whooping Crane), the first two are specialists of the Edwards Plateau.

We naturalists who live on the Edwards Plateau or who visit it to enjoy the pleasures of its birdlife have, in this book, our first modern description of that fauna. The University of Texas Press has come to our aid for the third time in support of this need. They published Simmons's 1925 *Birds of the Austin Region* and Oberholser's 1974 *The Bird Life of Texas*. Both of these works now stand dog-eared on my shelves, and an updated and comprehensive Edwards Plateau focus has been needed for some time.

We are fortunate indeed that Mark Lockwood stepped forward to write this long-awaited book. Following teenage years of birding and earning a statewide reputation, young Lockwood finished bachelor's and master's degrees at Sul Ross State University. In 1991 he began a career with Texas Parks and Wildlife in the southwestern Edwards Plateau at Kickapoo Cavern State Park. It was here that his interest in the region matured, and he became a serious student of the plateau bird fauna. Today he continues his state career headquartered in Austin and has devoted much of his recent professional service to surveying the plateau distribution of Black-capped Vireo and Golden-cheeked Warbler. He has published many papers in both science and birding journals and is secretary of the Texas Bird Records Committee of the Texas Ornithological Society. I can imagine no finer background for the author of this book.

Count yourself fortunate that this book has arrived and that Lockwood is your guide. I recommend that you settle back for an enjoyable and highly informative read and then follow Lockwood's directions to a personal field study of Edwards Plateau bird life. And by all means, keep this book close at hand. This now is the modern baseline to which your discoveries will be compared.

TERRY MAXWELL

ACKNOWLEDGMENTS

This book is a reflection of the efforts of the many ornithologists and birders who have reported their findings on the Edwards Plateau. Over the past 40 years, much of that information was provided to the editors of what is now known as *North American Birds*. Without this free flow of information and the means with which to archive it, status and distribution works on a landscape scale would be a far more difficult undertaking. I would like to thank everyone who has taken the time to submit their sightings to their local birding group, the Texas Ornithological Society, or to *North American Birds*. Birders who contribute their sightings play an important role in documenting the ornithological history of Texas.

There is a group of people who have spent a considerable amount of time on the Edwards Plateau and who have shared detailed information about sightings from the region with me. I owe a debt of gratitude to John Arvin, Doug Booher, Kelly Bryan, Brush Freeman, Tony Gallucci, John Gee, Nick Jackson, John Karges, Greg Lasley, Terry Maxwell, Art and Hanna Richard, Willie Sekula, Chuck Sexton, Paul Sunby, and Sue Wiedenfeld. Sue Wiedenfeld also shared with me a database of Ernest and Kay Muller's observations. Don Connell provided one of the most significant sources of information about birds on the eastern plateau. He graciously allowed me to examine the banding records from the Driftwood Banding Station. This banding station has been in existence for almost 20 years, and Don's commitment to that effort is to be commended.

Reviewing the manuscript of this book was a daunting task. I would like to thank Brush Freeman, Greg Lasley, Terry Maxwell, Jim Peterson, David Riskind, Chuck Sexton, and Cliff Shackelford for their thoughtful comments. Their careful review greatly improved the final product. Dr. Stan Casto was instrumental in the development of the early history of ornithological investigation on the plateau section of the introduction. Stan provided me with details on many of these men as well as the photos that appear in that section of the book.

Kelly Bryan, Tim Cooper, and Greg Lasley graciously allowed me to use some of their photographs to illustrate this book. They are all talented photographers, and I am pleased to be able to include some of their work here. The pencil drawings that can be found scattered throughout the book are the work of Clemente Guzman III. Clemente is a graphics artist at Texas Parks and Wildlife, and it has been my pleasure to work with him on several projects.

Over a five-year period, I gathered data for the species accounts included in this book. Some of those data came from the specimens housed at museums and universities. I would like to thank the museum curators and collection managers of the following institutions who kindly shared information about their Texas holdings with me:

American Museum of Natural History
Burke Museum, University of Washington
Centennial Museum, University of Texas at El Paso
Chicago Academy of Sciences
Cornell University
Dallas Museum of Natural History
Denver Museum of Natural History
Field Museum of Natural History
Florida Museum of Natural History
Los Angeles County Museum of Natural History
Museum of Southwestern Biology, University of New Mexico
Museum of Vertebrate Zoology, University of California
National Museum of Scotland
Oklahoma Museum of Natural History
Peabody Museum of Natural History, Yale University
Philadelphia Academy of Natural Sciences
Royal Ontario Museum
Sam Houston State University
Slater Museum of Natural History, University of Puget Sound
Strecker Museum, Baylor University
Sul Ross State University
Texas A&M University—Corpus Christi
Texas Cooperative Wildlife Collection, Texas A&M University
The Museum, Texas Tech University
United States National Museum
University of Connecticut
University of Kansas Natural History Museum

University of Michigan Museum of Zoology
University of Texas at Austin
West Texas A&M University
Western Foundation of Vertebrate Zoology

I would also like to thank David Riskind. David is an ecologist with whom I have worked for most of my career at Texas Parks and Wildlife. Although not a birder, he has changed my perspective on birding and has introduced me to the bigger picture of landscape ecology and conservation.

My family enjoyed the outdoors, although none of them had any particular interest in birds. I am forever grateful for the patience and support that my parents, Robert and Sharon Lockwood, and grandparents, W. O. and Marcia Lockwood and M. T. and Verna Darden, gave me as I began exploring the natural world. Their willingness to take me to see a bird or to an out-of-the-way place, propelled me along the path that I have chosen. I hope that I can live up to the example that they have provided.

Finally, I want to give special thanks to Cindy, my wife. Her patience, encouragement, and support have helped me accomplish many goals in life, including writing this book.

BIRDS *of the* TEXAS HILL COUNTRY

THE EDWARDS PLATEAU

The Edwards Plateau, perhaps better known as the Texas Hill Country, has scenic vistas and clear streams and is an ecologically and geologically distinctive region of the state. This extensive plateau of central and west-central Texas covers over 36,000 square miles, or about 17 percent of the state. This region is larger than the entire state of Louisiana. Among birders, the Hill Country is best known for two rare songbirds, the Golden-cheeked Warbler and Black-capped Vireo, but they are just part of the varied avifauna to be found there.

The delineation of the Edwards Plateau has been determined differently by researchers over the years. For the purposes of this book, I have chosen to follow the boundaries determined by the Natural Regions of Texas developed by the Lyndon B. Johnson School of Public Affairs of the University of Texas at Austin (1978). This group of scientists and conservationists divided the Edwards Plateau into three subregions: the Live Oak–Mesquite Savannas of the northern and western plateau, the Lampasas Cut Plains, and the Balcones Canyonlands. Each of the subregions is distinctive because of its topography and ecology. The Llano Uplift is often considered a subregion of the plateau, even though geologically it is quite different. Despite the differences in substrate, the vegetation and bird life are quite similar to the surrounding Edwards Plateau. For the purposes of this book, it will be included as a subregion (map 1). The LBJ School treatment did not include the Stockton Plateau as a subregion, and so it is not included as such here. Although geologically very similar, the Stockton Plateau is more arid, and the avifauna is strongly influenced by the Chihuahuan Desert.

The coverage area for this book includes all or part of 26 counties and is largely circumscribed by the LBJ School treatment (map 2). The Lampasas Cut Plains and the extreme northwestern portion of the Live Oak–Mesquite Savannas, which includes portions of the Concho Valley, are not included in the coverage area of this book. It is important to note that only the area of each county within the boundaries of the plateau, as described above, is considered.

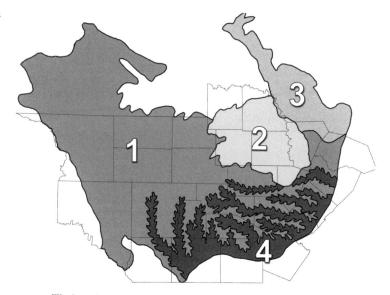

MAP 1. *The boundaries of the Edwards Plateau used in this treatment follow those defined by the Natural Regions of Texas developed by the Lyndon B. Johnson School of Public Affairs (1978). The plateau is divided into four subregions: (1) Live Oak–Mesquite Savannas, (2) Llano Uplift, (3) Lampasas Cut Plains, and (4) Balcones Canyonlands.*

MAP 2. *The area of the Edwards Plateau covered in this book includes all or part of 26 counties in central and west-central Texas designated here.*

The Edwards Plateau is the southernmost extension of the Great Plains and is defined by its geology. The plateau is a formation of Cretaceous limestone that slopes from northwest to southeast and covers about 27.9 million acres. The Balcones Escarpment forms the southern and eastern boundary of the plateau. The western boundary is marked by the Pecos River, which separates the geologically similar Edwards and Stockton Plateaus. To the north, the plateau is bound by the Rolling Plains. Although the two regions are ecologically similar, there is a distinct geological change, which defines the boundary. The Rolling Plains form a transitional zone between the Edwards Plateau and the High Plains to the north.

Ecologically, the Edwards Plateau is generally treated as a distinct biotic province (Blair 1950). Unique combinations of vegetation types, ecology, flora, fauna, and climate define biotic provinces. Although the Edwards Plateau fulfills many of these criteria, particularly in the flora, the fauna is more of a mixture of elements from the surrounding provinces. For this reason, there are areas of the plateau where birds normally associated with other physiographic regions of Texas can be found. For example, on the southwestern plateau, birds from the South Texas Plains and the Trans-Pecos come together along with the birds that range from the plateau northward through the Rolling Plains. Such "mixes" form a unique, and somewhat unexpected, assemblage of species.

TOPOGRAPHY

Elevations generally increase from the southeast to the northwest and range from 2,348 feet at Ozona on the western plateau to 1,710 at Junction on the central plateau to 550 feet at Austin to the east. The landscape of the plateau is defined by the erosive power of water. Several rivers cross the Edwards Plateau and generally have a southerly or southeasterly flow to the escarpment and on to the Gulf of Mexico.

The Balcones Canyonlands border the escarpment on the southern and eastern portions of the plateau and are the most rugged. This is the true Hill Country, where fast-moving streams in steep-sided canyons are not uncommon. Broad, gently rolling hills with shallow river valleys and relatively few steep slopes characterize the central plateau. Limestone formations and rocky slopes are still evident. The terrain of the northwestern plateau, such as in Crockett County, becomes even more flat and unbroken.

Along the northern boundary of the plateau, the topography is very similar to the Rolling Plains. The Permian and Pennsylvanian deposits of the Rolling Plains are the primary factors that separate it from the plateau. Despite its name, the Llano Uplift is a basin compared to the surrounding Edwards Plateau, although it originated as an uplift (Riskind and Diamond 1988). Granite outcrops can be found on the uplands throughout the region. Some of these outcrops are very large, towering as much as 450 feet above the surrounding landscape. The granitic substrate of the Llano Uplift clearly separates it from the surrounding limestones of the rest of the plateau.

RIVER SYSTEMS AND RESERVOIRS

Several major rivers and innumerable small streams and creeks cross the Edwards Plateau. Some of the major rivers include, from west to east, the Devils, Nueces, Frio, Medina, Guadalupe, Pedernales, Llano, and Colorado Rivers. These rivers and their tributaries have sculpted the Texas Hill Country into what we see today through the erosion of the surrounding limestone. Erosion continues at an even more accelerated rate today as disturbance of the soil and changes in the vegetative cover of the plateau have led to increased water runoff and soil erosion. In those regions where the healthy vegetation communities—either grassland or forest—exist, the streams and small rivers are still clear.

Reservoirs have been constructed on the Colorado, Guadalupe, and Medina Rivers and the Rio Grande. Most of these have been built to provide water to nearby urban areas. The reservoirs on the Colorado River form what is known as the Highland Lakes chain and include Lake Buchanan, Inks Lake, Lake Lyndon B. Johnson, Lake Marble Falls, and Lake Travis. The Pedernales River also flows into Lake Travis. Canyon Lake is the only reservoir on the Guadalupe River as is Medina Lake on the Medina River. Although there are many water impoundments on the Rio Grande, only part of Lake Amistad in Val Verde County is on the Edwards Plateau. Two other small reservoirs can be found on the plateau, Brady Reservoir and Lake Georgetown. Brady Reservoir is on Brady Creek, a tributary of the San Saba River, which is in turn a tributary of the Colorado River. Lake Georgetown is on the San Gabriel River.

CLIMATE

The Edwards Plateau becomes more arid from east to west. The western plateau is semiarid with an average annual rainfall in Crockett County of about 18 inches. This increases to just over 33 inches in Hays County on the southeastern plateau (map 3). There are two peaks of rainfall during the year, April through June and September through October. The increase in precipitation is more obvious along the eastern edge of the plateau. For the far western portions of the plateau, the winter season, November through March, is particularly dry with average precipitation of less than five inches in Ozona for that period.

The hottest region of the Edwards Plateau is in southern Val Verde

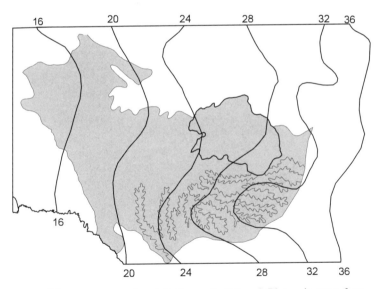

MAP 3. *The average annual precipitation on the Edwards Plateau increases from west to east, ranging from 18 inches in western Crockett County to just over 33 inches on the southeastern plateau.*

County at Del Rio. The average high temperature there is 80.8° with July usually being the hottest month with an average high temperature of 96.1°. To the north in Brady, the average high temperature is 77.4° with July usually being the hottest month with an average high temperature of 95.2°. The coldest month for both locations is January with the average low temperature being 38.5° in Del Rio and 30.4° in Brady.

VEGETATION

The vegetation of the Edwards Plateau has many unique aspects. Many eastern species reach their western limits on the floodplains of the many rivers that cross the plateau. There are also isolated populations of plants that were once widespread during the more mesic Pleistocene 15,000 years ago. It is also a center of endemism—a region where many species and subspecies of plants have evolved.

The Balcones Canyonlands are dominated primarily by woodlands and forests with grasslands restricted to broad divides between drainages (Riskind and Diamond 1988). Protected canyons and mesic south- and east-facing slopes support diverse Ashe Juniper (*Juniperus ashei*)- oak forests. This habitat is found only on the Edwards Plateau and surrounding areas with similar geology in north-central Texas and in northern Coahuila, Mexico. Ashe Juniper–oak woodlands are generally found on shallow soiled, steep slopes in the Balcones Canyonlands and occasionally on upland regions in other areas of the plateau. A mature closed-canopy, short-stature forest characterizes this habitat type. These forests typically have a canopy 15 to 25 feet above the forest floor. The dominant oak species in these woodlands differs depending on the location. Lacey Oaks (*Quercus laceyi*) are common on the southwestern plateau, whereas Texas Red Oak (*Q. buckleyi*) is more common in the east. Other trees often found in these forests include Plateau Live Oak (*Q. fusiformis*), Escarpment Black Cherry (*Prunus serotina*), Texas Ash (*Fraxinus texensis*), Cedar Elm (*Ulmus crassifolia*), and Texas Sugarberry (*Celtis laevigata*). These woodlands vary from being closed canopy, 100 percent canopy cover, to having canopy cover as low as 35 to 40 percent. Where the forest is closed canopy, there typically is little or no understory.

Another important component of the vegetation of the Edwards Plateau is gallery or riparian woodlands. Riparian woodlands are found following streams and rivers and offer the most diverse habitat on the plateau. These woodlands are often taller in stature than surrounding oak-juniper forests. It is not uncommon for trees in these woodlands to be 50 to 70 feet tall. Some of the trees frequently found in these woodlands include Sycamore (*Platanus occidentalis*), Bald Cypress (*Taxodium distichum*), Pecan (*Carya illinoinensis*), and Black Willow (*Salix nigra*). Not all of these forests are closed canopy, which allows for the development of some understory species. Many eastern species of plants reach their western limits in these gallery forests.

Two interesting aspects of the vegetation of the Balcones Canyonlands are relictual populations of Bigtooth Maple (*Acer grandidentatum*) and Mexican Pinyon (*Pinus remota*). The maples are found in the area surrounding western Bandera and eastern Real Counties. Lost Maples State Natural Area gets its name from the population of maples found there. On the plateau as treated herein, the pinyons range from Real County westward to eastern Val Verde County.

Much of the northern and western plateau is characterized by semi-open grasslands and shrublands on the uplands with riparian corridors along the drainages. Canopy cover is more open in the uplands, forming a savanna-like appearance with widely scattered trees. This change in habitat is due to several edaphic factors. One of the most important is the lower available moisture away from the rivers and protected canyons. Upland areas are also more prone to such natural disturbances as wildfires. Plateau Live Oak and Ashe Juniper are the common trees in the east with Honey Mesquite (*Prosopis glandulosa*) and Red-berry Juniper (*Juniperus pinchotii*) becoming the dominant trees in the west. A wide variety of grasses can be found in good-condition grasslands with Curly Mesquite (*Hilaria belangeri*) and other mid- and short grasses such as Side-oats Grama (*Bouteloua curtipendula*) and Little Bluestem (*Schizachyrium scoparium*) being common. Woody plants forming shrublands have invaded many of these areas.

A common sight on the Edwards Plateau today is the existence of extensive shrublands and thickets of second-growth juniper. Shrublands are landscapes in which low growing woody plants dominate the vegetation communities. These shrublands are often the result of disturbance, either man-made or natural. Examples of natural disturbances include tornadoes, flash flooding, and wildfires. Shrublands often develop when livestock are removed after years of overgrazing. The suppression of fire on the plateau over the past 100 years has resulted in the development of shrublands in areas that were once grasslands.

The vegetation of the Edwards Plateau has been heavily modified since Europeans began colonizing the area. The primary industry of the region is ranching with some traditional farming restricted to floodplains and other areas with deeper soils. Over the past 150 years, considerable changes have taken place. Forested land has been cleared to form open pastures for grazing, and invasive woody plants have colonized other more open habitats in other areas.

CONSERVATION

Threats to the avian habitats on the Edwards Plateau are similar to those found in woodland and forest habitats throughout the United States. Fragmentation of old-growth forests is one of the major threats in the region. Urbanization has also impacted habitats on the Edwards Plateau. Although primarily a problem around Austin, Kerrville, and San Antonio, many of the smaller communities on the plateau are expanding and impacting native habitats as well. The construction of reservoirs along the Colorado and Guadalupe Rivers has also resulted in the loss of hundreds of acres of bottomland hardwoods.

Riparian woodlands have been heavily impacted by agricultural activities within the floodplains of the many rivers and streams found on the Edwards Plateau. Cattle, sheep, and goat production is the primary focus of ranching activity on the plateau. The impacts to bird populations by agricultural activities depend greatly on the quality of stewardship shown by the individual landowner. Those landowners that are able to use short-duration, rotational grazing and other management techniques to protect the natural plant communities on their land ensure that habitat degradation is minimized. In the past 150 years, however, most of the habitat on the Edwards Plateau has been modified to some extent.

Texas Partners in Flight has developed a list of species of concern for each physiographic area of Texas. Seven variables are considered in order to evaluate the population stability for a particular species. These priority variables are designed to reflect the conservation needs of a species both on a global and state level. The global priority variables for each species are breeding distribution, nonbreeding distribution, and relative abundance. Local variables include threats to the breeding population, threats during the nonbreeding seasons, statewide population trends,

TABLE 1

Partners in Flight: Priority Bird Species for the Edwards Plateau

Included here are breeding species and a short list of peripheral species with high global priority ranking. For each category, species are listed by their priority ranking (highest priority first).

Highest overall priority
- Golden-cheeked Warbler
- Black-capped Vireo
- Bell's Vireo

High overall priority
- Painted Bunting
- Montezuma Quail
- Black-chinned Hummingbird
- Rufous-crowned Sparrow
- Cave Swallow
- Gray Vireo
- Canyon Towhee
- Cassin's Sparrow
- Orchard Oriole
- Northern Bobwhite
- Yellow-billed Cuckoo
- Elf Owl
- Louisiana Waterthrush

Physiographic area priority species
- Wild Turkey
- Ladder-backed Woodpecker
- Bewick's Wren
- Lark Sparrow
- Vermilion Flycatcher
- Field Sparrow
- Lesser Goldfinch

Additional species with global priority
- Scissor-tailed Flycatcher
- Prothonotary Warbler
- Kentucky Warbler
- Chuck-will's-widow
- Red-headed Woodpecker
- Curve-billed Thrasher

and conservation activities. For a given species, each of these seven variables is assigned a number between one and five based on specific criteria. For the Edwards Plateau physiographic region, 29 species of concern have been identified (table 1).

PARKS AND OTHER BIRDING AREAS

Most birders visiting the Edwards Plateau are in search of two endangered songbirds, the Golden-cheeked Warbler and Black-capped Vireo.

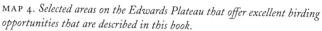

MAP 4. *Selected areas on the Edwards Plateau that offer excellent birding opportunities that are described in this book.*

1. *Lake Amistad National Recreation Area*
2. *Devils River State Natural Area*
3. *Kickapoo Cavern State Park*
4. *Garner State Park*
5. *Lost Maples State Natural Area*
6. *South Llano River State Park*
7. *Brady Lake*
8. *Enchanted Rock State Natural Area*
9. *Hill Country State Natural Area*
10. *Guadalupe River State Park and Honey Creek State Natural Area*
11. *Canyon Lake*
12. *Pedernales Falls State Park*
13. *Inks Lake State Park*
14. *Lake Buchanan*
15. *Colorado Bend State Park*
16. *Park Chalk Bluff*
17. *Balcones Canyonlands National Wildlife Refuge*
18. *Government Canyon State Natural Area*
19. *Emma Long Metropolitan Park, City of Austin*

Even though most of the plateau is privately owned, there are many publicly accessible places where these species and others can be observed. In fact, most of the regularly occurring birds listed in this book can be found in the many state and private parks in the region.

Each of the parks or recreational areas listed here has something unique to offer the visiting birder (map 4). This listing is intended to provide a brief description of the park, lake, or recreational area. More detailed descriptions and contact information for these and other sites on the Edwards Plateau can be found in the bird-finding guides of the region (Kutac 1998, Lockwood et al. 1999, Wauer and Elwonger 1998, Texas Parks and Wildlife 2000).

Amistad National Recreation Area

COUNTY: **Val Verde**
ACREAGE: **57,000**
CHECKLIST: **Sorola (1999)**

Only the eastern half of this large reservoir is within the Edwards Plateau physiographic region. The vegetation surrounding the lake is primarily mixed desert scrub. In the arroyos and drainages leading into the lake, the vegetation is denser and taller, providing better avian habitat. There are a few areas around the lake where small patches of willows and other riparian species have developed, but these are rare. Most of the recreation area is accessible only by boat. As with any large body of water in an arid region, waterbirds are well represented. On some of the many islands in the lake, small nesting colonies of Snowy Plover, Laughing Gull, and Least Tern are of particular interest.

Balcones Canyonlands National Wildlife Refuge

COUNTIES: **Burnet, Travis, and Williamson**
ACREAGE: **10,000+**
CHECKLIST: **USFWS in progress**

Balcones Canyonlands National Wildlife Refuge is located in portions of Burnet, Travis, and Williamson Counties. The refuge contains extensive Ashe Juniper–oak woodlands and has a high diversity of habitats, from juniper-oak woodlands to shin oak communities to open grasslands, a diversity that makes it an extremely important refugium on the plateau. Most of the resident species expected on the eastern plateau are present on the refuge. The grasslands provide quality habitat for otherwise rare species on the plateau, such as Sedge Wren and Le Conte's Sparrow. The refuge is home to sizable populations of Black-capped Vireos and Golden-cheeked Warblers. A viewing stand provides the best opportunities to see Black-capped Vireos in the Austin area. The refuge is in the process of developing visitor services and opening areas for public access. For current information, contact the refuge office in Austin.

Brady Reservoir

COUNTY: McCulloch
ACREAGE: unknown
CHECKLIST: n/a

Birders rarely visit this site. It is a small, isolated reservoir and undoubtedly provides habitat to many species of waterbirds. There are records of species typical of the Highland Lakes, such as Common Loon, Horned Grebe, and Red-breasted Merganser. Closer scrutiny of this lake would likely produce some interesting records and many county firsts.

Canyon Lake

COUNTY: Comal
ACREAGE: 8,240
CHECKLIST: n/a

There are several parks surrounding Canyon Lake that afford access to the lake. A few of these parks contain Ashe Juniper–oak woodlands. The park most frequently visited by birders is Canyon Park on the north shore. Canyon Park is on a peninsula, and the coves on both sides are excellent for loons, ducks (Greater Scaup in particular), gulls, and other waterbirds. There are some woodlands within the park, but it does not provide habitat for Golden-cheeked Warblers or Black-capped Vireos.

Colorado Bend State Park

COUNTY: San Saba
ACREAGE: 5,328
CHECKLIST: Kutac (1997)

Colorado Bend State Park is located on the Colorado River above Lake Buchanan. Prior to state acquisition, there was an aggressive campaign to remove Ashe Juniper from upland areas. Where the juniper was removed, these dry uplands support highly disturbed grasslands with scattered oak mottes. The remainder of the uplands is dominated by dense juniper-oak woodland with a high percentage of Ashe Juniper. Shallow, dry canyons in the cleared portions of the uplands contain mixed shrublands dominated by Texas Persimmon and Agarita. The more mesic slopes and wet canyons contain mixed evergreen-deciduous forests dominated by Plateau Live Oak, Texas Red Oak, and Cedar Elm with a few Sycamores and Pecans along the watercourses. The terraces along the river currently support a highly disturbed gallery forest.

Golden-cheeked Warblers can be found in the gallery forests and wet canyons in the park. The uplands contain typical Edwards Plateau birds such as Common Poorwill, Ash-throated Flycatcher, Western Scrub-Jay, Bewick's Wren, and Field Sparrow. The gallery forest along the river offers an interesting contrast, with eastern woodland species such as Chuck-will's-widow, Great Crested Flycatcher, and White-eyed, Yellow-throated, and Red-eyed Vireos.

Devils River State Natural Area

COUNTY: **Val Verde**
ACREAGE: **19,988**
CHECKLIST: **Bryan (1999)**

Devils River State Natural Area is near the westernmost boundary of the Edwards Plateau. Open shrublands and semidesert grasslands dominate this arid region. Stands of Plateau Live Oak and Pecan occur frequently on alluvial deposits immediately adjacent to the river.

The Chihuahuan Desert has a strong influence on the park's avifauna. Zone-tailed Hawk, Western Screech-Owl, Elf Owl, Gray Vireo, Black-tailed Gnatcatcher, Canyon Towhee, Black-throated Sparrow, Varied Bunting, and Scott's Oriole can be found at this park. Species more often associated with South Texas, including Common Ground-Dove, Brown-crested Flycatcher, Long-billed Thrasher, Olive Sparrow, and Hooded Oriole, are also present.

Emma Long Metropolitan Park, City of Austin

COUNTY: **Travis**
ACREAGE: **1,000**
CHECKLIST: **n/a**

Emma Long Metropolitan Park, better known as simply City Park, is located in northwestern Austin along Lake Travis. City Park is well-known as an easily accessible location for Golden-cheeked Warblers in the Austin area. Other typical Hill Country species are also evident in the park. One of the best birding locations is along Turkey Creek Trail. The lakefront area of the park is often crowded.

Enchanted Rock State Natural Area

COUNTIES: Llano and Gillespie
ACREAGE: 1,643
CHECKLIST: Mueller and Mueller (1999)

Enchanted Rock State Natural Area surrounds a large granite outcrop on the Llano Uplift. The oak-hickory woodlands that develop on the granitic soils are similar to those found in the Cross Timbers region of eastern Texas. Texas Red Oaks and Ashe Juniper are absent here but are common on nearby limestone soils. The park habitats include oak-hickory woodlands and savannas and open Honey Mesquite–Cedar Elm woodlands. Along Sandy Creek, there is a gallery woodland of oak, elm, hickory, and White Buckeye (*Aesculus arguta*).

The bird life here is fairly typical of the Edwards Plateau. Resident birds include Northern Cardinal, Eastern Bluebird, Carolina and Bewick's Wrens, Canyon Towhee, Golden-fronted and Ladder-backed Woodpeckers, Carolina Chickadee, and Tufted Titmouse.

Garner State Park

COUNTY: Uvalde
ACREAGE: 1,419
CHECKLIST: Mueller and Mueller (1998)

Garner State Park is located in northern Uvalde County on the Frio River. Most of the park is within the floodplain and terraces of the Frio. This area has been heavily modified but contains some remnant of the Bald Cypress–Sycamore community that once bordered the river. Some Pecan–Texas Sugarberry woodlands remain on the gently rolling outwash plains of the northern half of the park, and several old fields are covered with grass. There are areas of mixed shrublands, particularly along the northern border of the park. Ashe Juniper–oak wood-lands dominate the limestone hills in the southwestern part of the park. The small mesic canyons and north- and east-facing slopes have well-developed woodlands with extensive stands of Lacey Oak, Texas Red Oak, and other deciduous hardwoods. South- and west-facing slopes support shrublands with the dominant plants being Guajillo and Texas Persimmon.

A small population of Golden-cheeked Warblers can be found in the limestone hills, and Yellow-throated Warblers frequent the Bald Cy-press that line the Frio River.

Government Canyon State Natural Area

COUNTY: **Bexar**
ACREAGE: **7,043**
CHECKLIST: **n/a**

Government Canyon State Natural Area is currently not open to the public, pending development. The park, which is expected to open in 2002, straddles the Balcones Escarpment in northwestern Bexar County with most of the park lying north of the fault line. North of the escarpment, the vegetation is largely Ashe Juniper–oak woodlands. A small population of Golden-cheeked Warblers is present as are most of the other expected Hill Country birds. The area below the escarp-ment was formerly live oak–mesquite savanna, but is heavily invaded with shrubby plants. Currently a large-scale restoration project is under way to return this area to a more natural state. Common Ground-Dove is surprisingly abundant at this park.

Guadalupe River State Park and Honey Creek State Natural Area

COUNTIES: **Kendall and Comal**
ACREAGE: **4,231**
CHECKLIST: **Wiedenfeld (2001)**

The uplands at Guadalupe River State Park are gently rolling hills and support oak woodlands or savannas. Plateau Live Oak and Ashe Juniper dominate these woodlands. Because of the openness of the woodlands, there is a well-developed understory of Texas Persimmon, Agarita, and other shrubs. Along the Guadalupe River is a fairly diverse woodland with a combination of Ashe Juniper and oaks and a mix of riparian species.

Much of Honey Creek State Natural Area was at one time cleared of juniper. The most interesting area is the main Honey Creek drainage, which contains an extensive stand of Bald Cypress with an understory of Dwarf Palmetto (*Sabal minor*). The remaining uplands away from the immediate vicinity of Honey Creek are dominated by dense thickets of second-growth Ashe Juniper and open old fields.

Honey Creek is open only to tours arranged through Guadalupe River State Park. The avifauna of the state park is unremarkable, with common Edwards Plateau species; however, a few nesting pairs of Northern Parula and Yellow-throated Warblers are found along the river. The woodlands along the river can also be an excellent migrant trap. There is a small population of Golden-cheeked Warblers along Honey Creek.

Hill Country State Natural Area

COUNTIES: **Bandera and Medina**
ACREAGE: **5,370**
CHECKLIST: **Lockwood (1995)**

Hill Country State Natural Area can be divided into two sections. High ridges and deep canyons dominate the northern half of the park. The southern half is predominately rolling hills with a few shallow canyons in the extreme southern end of the park. The mesic canyons in the northwestern section are only accessible by foot and require a long hike. Most of these canyons have been cut over for cedar, leaving the best woodland habitats in small, steep side canyons. These protected side canyons have small patches of deciduous hardwood forest. These woodlands are most accessible in the Twin Peaks area near the northern trailhead. The remainder of the park is very savanna-like with open expanses dotted with oak mottes. There are dense shrublands on some of the low hills. West Verde Creek runs through the southern portion of the park, where there are some remnants of the riparian woodland that once followed its banks.

Both Black-capped Vireos and Golden-cheeked Warblers are summer residents in this park. Common Ground-Dove, Vermilion Flycatcher, Canyon Towhee, and Scott's Oriole are common summer residents as well.

Inks Lake State Park

COUNTY: **Burnet**
ACREAGE: **1,201**
CHECKLIST: **Kramer (1994)**

Inks Lake State Park is located below Buchanan Dam on the east side of Inks Lake. The shallow soils and rocky outcrops of the uplands in the park support Plateau Live Oak mottes and a few small patches of Ashe Juniper–oak woodland. The creek bottoms and floodplain along the lake support a few small riparian woodlands dominated by Pecan and Texas Sugarberry.

The park is home to typical Edwards Plateau species such as Western Scrub-Jay, Bewick's Wren, and Rufous-crowned Sparrow. Common Loons, Horned Grebes, and a variety of ducks can be found in winter on Inks Lake.

Kickapoo Cavern State Park

COUNTY: **Kinney**
ACREAGE: **6,368**
CHECKLIST: **Bryan and Lockwood (1993)**

The landscape at Kickapoo Cavern is predominately steep limestone hills with extensive canyons. The southwestern plateau is fairly arid, and open shrublands dominate upland areas. The canyons are also dominated by woody shrubs, but the structure of the vegetation is somewhat different, being denser and with taller plants. Ashe Juniper is common as are Plateau Live Oak mottes. There is no surface water in the park except following heavy rains.

Kickapoo Cavern is best known for the large population of Black-capped Vireos found there. The avifauna is a unique combination of birds from the South Texas Plains, the Trans-Pecos, and the Edwards Plateau. Breeding birds include Bell's and Gray Vireos, Long-billed Thrasher, Varied Bunting, and Hooded and Scott's Orioles.

Lake Buchanan

COUNTIES: **Llano and Burnet**
ACREAGE: **23,000+**
CHECKLIST: **Highland Lakes Birding and Wildflower Club (1999)**

Lake Buchanan is probably the best reservoir for water birding on the plateau. The most advantageous time to visit is during migration or in the winter. It is the winter home of several Bald Eagles as well as Common Loons, Horned Grebes, Double-crested Cormorants, Red-breasted Mergansers, and Bonaparte's, Ring-billed, and Herring Gulls. Rare gulls have certainly made an appearance here, but there are very few records. The surrounding terrain is dominated by limestone hills and covered with Ashe Juniper–oak woodlands, but little access to that habitat is available in the immediate vicinity of the lake.

Lost Maples State Natural Area

COUNTY: **Bandera**
ACREAGE: **2,174**
CHECKLIST: **Heidemann (1996)**

Lost Maples is situated in an area of great biological diversity and species richness. The park is characterized by deeply incised, moist canyons and a well-known population of Bigtooth Maples. The park has three major habitat types: grasslands and shrublands, mixed evergreen and deciduous woodlands, and riparian woodlands. Diverse oak-juniper woodlands cover most of the slopes within the park; only a few arid west-facing slopes are dominated by shrublands. The ridge tops between the deep canyons are where the few grasslands on the park can be found. The most important and interesting habitat is the riparian woodlands along the canyon bottoms. The woodlands are incredibly diverse botanically and offer the best birding in the park.

Lost Maples is also well known for the very large population of Golden-cheeked Warblers found there. In addition, there is a small population of Black-capped Vireos. Many eastern species are common in the park, including Great Crested Flycatcher, Yellow-throated and Red-eyed Vireos, and Indigo Bunting. Green Kingfishers are year-round residents.

Park Chalk Bluff

COUNTY: Uvalde
ACREAGE: 500
CHECKLIST: n/a

A private park along the Nueces River opposite the large exposed cliff face known as Chalk Bluff. Some riparian woodland exists, but most was destroyed in a fall 1996 flood. The remainder of the park is composed of a Plateau Live Oak woodland and some mixed shrublands. Many species associated with the South Texas Plains are found here, including Ringed Kingfisher, Brown-crested Flycatcher, Long-billed Thrasher, and Olive Sparrow.

Pedernales Falls State Park

COUNTY: Blanco
ACREAGE: 5,211
CHECKLIST: Booher (1996)

A well-developed riparian forest can be found on the terraces above the Bald Cypress–lined Pedernales River. This gallery forest gives way to diverse hardwood forests in mesic canyons that lead away from the river. The uplands of the park are dominated by juniper breaks, open savannas with oak mottes, and scattered Honey Mesquite and Cedar Elm woodlands.

There is a fairly large population of Golden-cheeked Warblers present in the woodlands along the river and main drainages as well as in a small upland oak-juniper woodland in the northwestern corner of the park. Overall, the bird life is similar to that of Colorado Bend State Park. Species characteristic of arid western habitats such as Western Scrub-Jay, Ash-throated Flycatcher, and Rufous-crowned Sparrow can be found in the uplands, and Great Crested Flycatcher, Eastern Phoebe, and Red-eyed Vireo are present in the mesic canyons.

South Llano River State Park

COUNTY: Kimble
ACREAGE: 2,656
CHECKLIST: Jackson (1991)

The bottomlands of the South Llano River support a Pecan forest as well as a narrow riparian woodland that also includes sycamores, oaks, and elms. The canyon leading away from the floodplain has deciduous woodlands dominated by hackberry and four oaks: Plateau Live Oak, Texas Red Oak, Lacey Oak, and Chinquapin Oak (*Quercus muehlenbergii*). The drier canyon slopes are covered in an open Ashe Juniper–oak woodland.

Green Kingfishers frequent the clear river, while birds typical of the Edwards Plateau can be found in the wooded uplands. Wild Turkeys roost in the Pecan bottomlands along the Llano River during the winter. A small population of Black-capped Vireos is present on the adjoining Walter Buck Wildlife Management Area.

EDWARDS PLATEAU BIRDS

The geographic location of the Edwards Plateau is one of the chief reasons why so many species of birds can be found there. The central location of the plateau on the continent means that migratory birds from both eastern and western North America pass through the region. The river valleys that cross the plateau act as migration corridors for many of these species. The southern latitude of the plateau also adds to the diversity of birds found there. Many migratory birds from the northern parts of the continent spend the winter in the moderate climate of central Texas.

As has been previously mentioned, the avifauna of the Edwards Plateau is an assemblage of species from the surrounding physiographic regions of the state with strong influences from both the west and east. There is also a sprinkling of birds that are closely tied to the unique aspects of the plateau's vegetation. The net result of these influences is that the avifauna varies considerably over the plateau, even within similar habitat types. Despite the abundance of water on the plateau, there is very little habitat for shorebirds, and the presence of man-made reservoirs provides the only habitat available for many waterbirds. A total of 420 species have been satisfactorily reported from the Edwards Plateau, more than half of which are passerines. Overall, the avifauna of the region is poorly documented. Several species included in this book are based on observations of experienced birders with minimal documentation to support the sightings. Most of these species are included in a small "status uncertain" section after the species accounts; however, a few species that have been reported numerous times are therefore included as a regularly occurring species.

The avifauna of the western plateau has many influences from the arid habitats found in the Trans-Pecos and north-central Mexico. Several widespread species, such as Cactus Wren, Black-throated Sparrow, and Pyrrhuloxia are often thought of as desert species. Several species that are primarily associated with the southwestern United States reach the easternmost edge of their distribution on the western plateau. Chief among these are Zone-tailed Hawk, Gray Vireo, Varied Bunting, and Scott's Oriole.

The avifauna of the southwestern plateau features a unique combination of species from the Trans-Pecos, Edwards Plateau, and South Texas Plains. In addition to the birds mentioned above, South Texas species such as Long-billed Thrasher, Olive Sparrow, and Hooded Oriole can be found. Typical plateau birds found here include Bell's, White-eyed, and Black-capped Vireos, Western Scrub-Jay, Common Raven, and Field Sparrow.

The rivers on the Edwards Plateau play an important role in the biogeography of the region. These rivers, through the deposition of alluvium in floodplains and terraces along their courses, also provide the conditions needed for the development of riparian forests along their banks. These riparian corridors provide habitat to many species that would otherwise not be found on the plateau. Many Carolinian species normally associated with hardwood forests farther east, such as Barred Owl, Acadian Flycatcher, Red-eyed Vireo, and Northern Parula, can be found along the riparian corridors of these rivers. It is interesting to note that some of these birds are restricted to certain river systems because of the relative abundance of certain trees. For example, Yellow-throated Warblers are found only along the Frio and Guadalupe River systems where Bald Cypress is common.

Several species that are normally associated with South Texas encroach on the plateau along the floodplains of the rivers that drain the western plateau, such as the Nueces and Sabinal Rivers. Some of these birds are also present locally in upland areas along the southwestern fringe of the plateau. Long-billed Thrasher and Olive Sparrow are probably the two best examples. Perhaps the most common bird that is usually associated with South Texas is the Green Kingfisher, which is found along many of the river systems of the plateau.

Riparian corridors are, of course, adjacent to more arid upland habitats. As a result, there are several instances where birds from the east and west come into close contact. An example of this is Carolina and Bewick's Wrens. The Carolina Wrens are almost exclusively found in the more mesic riparian corridors, while the Bewick's Wrens favor the drier uplands. In many areas, these two species overlap. Another classic example can be found with the eastern Great Crested Flycatcher and the western Ash-throated Flycatcher.

TAXONOMY

This annotated list of birds that have been documented on the Edwards Plateau follows the classification and nomenclature of the American Ornithologists' Union's *Check-list of North American Birds*, 7th edition (1998), including changes in the forty-second supplement (A.O.U. 2000). During the last 20 years, the study of the systematic status and taxonomic relationships of birds in North America has received more attention than ever before. The development and use of molecular techniques, such as DNA hybridization, has brought a new twist to the study of taxonomic relationships. Some of these molecular studies have supported traditional taxonomic views, while others have resulted in changes.

With the seventh edition of the A.O.U. checklist (1998), the concept of Groups within a species was introduced. Groups are geographic assemblages of subspecies in a polytypic species. In other words, they are groupings of subspecies from a specified geographic area that are distinct from other subspecies within the species. In some cases, these Groups may have been recognized as species in the past or, in a few cases, may represent potential species-level changes that have been proposed by recent studies. The recognition of Groups is meant to bring attention to taxonomic questions. Where Groups are recognized within species that occur on the Edwards Plateau, such as the Yellow-rumped Warbler, they will be noted.

DOCUMENTING OBSERVATIONS

In the past, ornithologists expended much of their energy in gathering distributional information about birds, a task largely accomplished through the collection of specimens. Today, basic status and distribution information is primarily gathered by birders. It is important to understand that observations do not carry the same validity as specimens, so as birders we must use other means to document our sightings. A carefully written description accompanied by a photograph or sound recording is the best way to thoroughly document a sighting. While it may not always be possible to get a photograph or recording, written descriptions can always be prepared.

Birders have not always recognized the need for such documentation, but that has changed over the past 15 to 20 years. In Texas this awakening began in 1988, when the Texas Bird Records Committee (TBRC) developed a list of birds for which it requested documentation. This list consisted of species that have occurred less than four times per year over a 10-year average. The TBRC is a standing committee of the Texas Ornithological Society (TOS). The TBRC maintains the official list of bird species for Texas and publishes annual reports of its activities in the *Bulletin of the Texas Ornithological Society* and an annotated statewide checklist, *The TOS Checklist of Texas Birds* (1995).

The sightings that pass the scrutiny of the TBRC are referred to as records, as opposed to undocumented sightings, reports, or observations. Only a small number of the species that occur in Texas are reviewed; these species are commonly referred to as *Review Species.* The TBRC maintains files on each record that are housed at the Texas Cooperative Wildlife Collection (TCWC) at Texas A&M University. Photographs accompanying these records are deposited into the Texas Photo Record File (TPRF), also housed at the TCWC. Photographic documentation of many non-TBRC review species is also included in the TPRF. Similarly, audio recordings are housed at the Texas Bird Sounds Lab (TBSL) at Sam Houston State University.

EARLY HISTORY OF ORNITHOLOGICAL INVESTIGATIONS ON THE EDWARDS PLATEAU

Although the Spanish explorers of the seventeenth and eighteenth centuries recorded casual observations of the bird life of the Texas Hill Country, it was not until the 1870s that trained observers studied the avifauna. Beginning in the late 1870s, ornithologists and other people interested in Texas birds, began to visit the Edwards Plateau. One of the first ornithologists was Nathan Clifford Brown from Portland, Maine. Brown's observations were centered around Boerne, where he remained between December 1879 and April 1880 as well as from late January to early April 1883. Brown summarized his work in two papers (Brown 1882b, 1884) that provided the first account of the avifauna of the region. He compiled a list of over 100 species, which included range expansions of many species. Brown was the first to notice the mixture of eastern and western species that winter on the plateau. He reported several first records for the region, including Mountain Plover, Western Bluebird, and Fox, Harris's, and White-throated Sparrows. Brown (1882a) also described the subspecies of Rufous-crowned Sparrow (*Aimophila ruficeps eremoeca*) that occurs on the plateau. He also documented the occurrence of Eskimo Curlew on the plateau.

By the mid-1880s, observers were present in San Antonio, Kerrville, and San Angelo. William Lloyd was an Irishman who moved to San Antonio in 1876, but it was not until he moved to the Concho Valley in 1880 that he became interested in natural history (Maxwell 1979). Under the tutelage of John Loomis, Lloyd learned to preserve bird specimens and began studying the birds of Tom Green and Concho Counties. Although he didn't spend much time in the area covered by this book, his work (Lloyd 1887) is an important contribution to understanding the avifauna of west Texas. He provided a benchmark from which others could compare their work and from which to develop a better understanding of the avifauna of the region. His notes on the relative abundance of the avifauna of upland habitats, as well as migrants, are particularly applicable to the avifauna of the live oak–mesquite savannas of the northwestern plateau. Lloyd spent almost seven years observing and studying the birds of the Concho Valley and provided one of the first comprehensive studies of birds from western Texas.

Henry Philemon Attwater was a student of natural history by the time he arrived in San Antonio in 1884. Attwater began studying birds, particularly their nesting habits, and published major papers in 1887 and 1892. It is clear that most of his observations are from areas to the south and east of the Balcones Escarpment. Although very few observations are directly attributable to the plateau, the detailed species accounts do provide some of the first information available from the region. Attwater reported 242 species from the San Antonio region. His papers, when compared to those of Brown and Lloyd, laid a foundation from which future ornithologists could gauge their observations. One of the interesting aspects of Attwater's 1892 paper was his concern for the continued abundance of the Golden-cheeked Warbler: he predicted that it would become a rare bird.

Henry Attwater was also one of the Texas contributors to the A.O.U.-sponsored Mississippi Valley Migration Study. Fifteen individuals from 13 observation stations contributed to the Migration Study during 1884 and 1885. Three of them were located on the plateau, including Fritz Grasso at Sisterdale (Kendall County), Ira B. Henry at Mason,

PHOTO 1. *Henry P. Attwater, from the Deane Ruthven Collection, Library of Congress*

and Thomas W. Scott in Del Rio. There were also three observers in San Antonio: Attwater, Gustave Jermy, and Matthias Newell. Although their observations have relevance to the avifauna of the Edwards Plateau, they were not stationed on the plateau. Just to the north, William Lloyd contributed observations from Paint Rock and San Angelo. When the study was published in 1888, only observations by Attwater,

PHOTO 2. *Howard G. Lacey ranch, photographed by Arthur Howell in 1906, from the National Archives, Library of Congress*

Henry, and Lloyd were included (Casto 1992). In addition to contributing to the Migration Study, Ira Henry is credited with "rediscovering" Lesser Goldfinches in Texas after a reported 40-year absence (Cooke 1885).

Howard George Lacey made the greatest contribution to the early investigations of the birds on the Edwards Plateau. Lacey was born in England on 15 April 1856 and in 1882 moved to Kerr County, where he began ranching on Turtle Creek, about seven miles southwest of Kerrville. His interest in natural history quickly brought him a nationwide reputation as a careful observer and an enthusiastic collector. He worked closely with the United States Museum of Natural History, providing collections of insects, plants, mammals, and birds to the museum. Among his collections were several undescribed species and subspecies. The Lacey Oak (*Quercus laceyi*) and three subspecies of mice are named in his honor. Lacey's interest in natural history was well known within the Kerrville community, and as a result he was kept abreast of unusual sightings.

The Lacey Ranch soon became the hub of ornithological and other biological investigations in Kerr County and the surrounding area. Many of the well-known ornithologists of the time made stops at the Lacey Ranch, including Frank Armstrong, Henry Attwater, and Arthur Howell. Lacey published an annotated checklist of the birds of Kerr County in 1911 and an addendum in 1912. These papers documented range extensions of many species as well as several first records for the plateau, including Neotropic Cormorant, Black-bellied Whistling-Duck, Couch's Kingbird, and Black-headed Grosbeak. Lacey collected the type specimen of the endemic subspecies of Western Scrub-Jay (*Aphelocoma californica texana*) from the plateau. He also reported the first Evening Grosbeak for Texas. Lacey continued his investigations until failing health caused him to sell his ranch and return to England in 1919. He visited Kerrville only once more before his death in 1929. Unlike most of the ornithologists that visited the plateau in the late 1800s and early 1900s, Howard Lacey was a resident. He spent almost 40 years studying the natural history of Kerr County and its avifauna in particular. This intense interest undoubtedly gave him an excellent understanding of the dynamics of the avifauna of the central Edwards Plateau. Much of what was included in Oberholser's *The Bird Life of Texas* from Kerr County can be directly attributed to Howard Lacey.

Lacey's publications attracted the attention of Austin Paul Smith. Smith was a very active ornithologist in Texas in the early 1900s. Most of his work in Texas was in the Lower Rio Grande Valley, although he did occasionally venture to other areas of the state. He made one extended trip to Kerr County, remaining at Ingram from November 1914 to July 1915. Within a 10-mile radius of Ingram, he observed approximately 150 forms, species, and subspecies. Smith's paper, published in 1916, is a valuable supplement to Lacey's work. It includes additional information for 50 species and first county records for MacGillivray's Warbler and Eastern Towhee.

In about 1890, the Biological Survey of Texas was begun under the leadership of Vernon Bailey. Bailey, a mammalogist, was joined by ornithologists William Lloyd, Harry Oberholser, and Arthur Howell, as well as other men known for their collecting abilities and field expertise in ornithology. Over the next 15 years, these naturalists made numerous visits to the plateau. They compiled notes on the birds observed along major travel routes and around population centers such as Kerrville, Junction, Rocksprings, Mason, and Boerne. During the early years of the survey, the field agents traveled by railroad and later by car. Many

PHOTO 3. *Vernon Bailey, from the Deane Ruthven Collection, Library of Congress*

PHOTO 4. *George Finlay Simmons, from the Deane Ruthven Collection, Library of Congress*

of their observations were made near towns or within short walking or riding distances. Bailey published the final report in 1905, although data collection continued for almost 40 years. Oberholser was assigned to write the section on birds, but his manuscript became too large and was not included. The data collected between 1890 and 1905, as well as those collected during the remainder of the survey, became the foundation on which *The Bird Life of Texas* (Oberholser 1974) was built. The observations and collections made by the Biological Survey are some of the best documentation of the status and distribution of the avifauna of the Edwards Plateau. These data provide a basis from which to gauge changes in distribution and abundance over the past 100 years.

Another ornithologist in the region was George Finlay Simmons. Simmons lived in Austin for short periods between 1899 and 1919. He began studying birds in 1910 and published on several topics between 1913 and 1915. Simmons began studying the bird life of the Austin area in earnest in 1915. He moved back to Austin in 1919 and remained there, becoming a faculty member at the University of Texas. Between 1919 and 1923, Simmons devoted much of his time to field work. Simmons led a group of active observers, and their collective experience forms the foundation of *Birds of the Austin Region,* which was published in 1925. This valuable reference contains lengthy species accounts, including dates and locations of hundreds of observations. *Birds of the Austin Region* includes data collected over decades and was the most comprehensive regional study of Texas birds of its time. It provides an important base of information for comparing changes in the avifauna of central Texas.

USING THIS BOOK

The annotated list of species includes, to the best of my knowledge, every bird reliably reported on the Edwards Plateau through 2000. The information concerning the status and distribution of these birds was derived from many sources. One of the most important sources of information used in this book was the quarterly "Texas Region" column published in *North American Birds*. Although most of the sightings contained in the "Texas Region" reports are undocumented, this publication is the best source of information on regionally important sightings in Texas. Many records are listed as documented within the species accounts. For these records, there is either a photograph deposited in the Texas Photo Record File, an accepted record by the TBRC, or a written description of the bird in question. Some of the written descriptions are from submission to *North American Birds,* and others are from private field notes. Undoubtedly many other documented records of rare birds from the Edwards Plateau have not come to my attention. I encourage observers to submit photographs and written descriptions to the *North American Birds* editors and to the Texas Photo Record File.

In each of the species accounts, I have tried to include four components: relative abundance, distribution, habitat preference, and timing of occurrence. For permanent, summer, and winter residents, this is fairly straightforward. But for migrants, particularly irregular or very uncommon ones, this can be a very difficult task. For some groups of birds, such as shorebirds or waterfowl, habitat preferences are not always listed. These species are not found in habitats different from anywhere else within their ranges. Following the species accounts is a list of species that have been reported from the plateau, but whose status is uncertain. This includes undocumented *Review Species* and a few other birds that have been reported by experienced observers, but for which no documentation exists. These are generally peripheral species that could reasonably be expected to occur again and should be documented if discovered. A short list of species that I expect to be found on the Edwards

Plateau in the future is also included. For quick reference, consult the checklist found after the species accounts. This checklist will give an overview of relative abundance.

Attempting to define the relative abundance of a particular species is often difficult. Habitat specialists may be very common locally but, at the same time, rare regionally. Long-term population trends and fluctuations may not be readily apparent, thus making judgments about abundance even more difficult. For this reason, I have adopted a fairly general abundance scale. This scale is intended to give a general sense of what might be expected:

abundant—normally present in proper habitat, often in large numbers. Should be easily found on a given day.

common—normally present in proper habitat, should be found on a given day

uncommon—normally present in proper habitat in small numbers, can be missed on a given day

occasional—irregularly present in proper habitat and season, cannot be expected on a given day

rare—not expected, annual, although occurring only a few times per year

very rare—not expected, occurs regularly, although not on an annual basis

casual—occurs very irregularly, but reasonably expected to occur again

accidental—average of one or two records every 10 years

irregular—present during most years, sometimes numerous, but absent during some years

local—not generally distributed throughout the given range. Found only in small areas within the larger region, often habitat specialists.

SEASONAL DEFINITIONS

spring = March–May
summer = June–mid-August
fall = mid-August–mid-November
winter = mid-November–February

FREQUENTLY MENTIONED LOCATIONS

Boerne—located approximately 25 miles northwest of San Antonio along IH 10 in Kendall County.

Burnet—northwest of Austin in Burnet County, 12 miles east of Lake Buchanan Dam

Canyon Lake—approximately 15 miles northeast of New Braunfels, Comal County

central plateau—roughly including an area west of a line from Hondo north through Kerrville and east of a line corresponding with the Uvalde-Kinney County line

Colorado Bend State Park—on the Colorado River above Lake Buchanan in San Saba and Lampasas Counties

Concan—northern Uvalde County along the Frio River, south of Garner State Park

Devils River State Natural Area—central Val Verde County along the Devils River

Driftwood Banding Station—located southeast of Austin and south of Dripping Springs in Hays County

eastern plateau—roughly including an area east of a line from Hondo north through Kerrville

Eldorado—county seat of Schleicher County

Ingram—west of Kerrville on Texas Highway 27 along the Guadalupe River in Kerr County

Junction—county seat of Kimble County

Kerrville—county seat of Kerr County

Kickapoo Cavern State Park—located 22 miles north of Brackettville in northern Kinney and southern Edwards Counties

Lake Amistad—on the Rio Grande northeast of Del Rio

Lake Buchanan—on the Colorado River northeast of Austin

Lost Maples State Natural Area—southwest of Kerrville in western Bandera County near Vanderpool

Ozona—county seat of Crockett County

western plateau—roughly including an area west of a line corresponding with the Uvalde-Kinney County line

AN ANNOTATED LIST OF SPECIES

FAMILY GAVIIDAE: Loons

Red-throated Loon (*Gavia stellata*)

Accidental. There is one record of this species from the Edwards Plateau: two individuals were present at Canyon Lake from 8 to 30 December 1996 (TBRC 1996-182). Despite there being only one record for the region, this species should be expected to occur again. Red-throated Loons have been found almost annually during the 1990s on reservoirs in north-central Texas. Within the last 10 years, there have been 11 documented records involving 18 individuals from that region of the state. All of those records fall between 7 November and 23 March. *Review Species*

Pacific Loon (*Gavia pacifica*)

Accidental. There are three documented records for the region. Two of these records are from Canyon Lake, where a single bird was present from 27 to 29 January 1987 (TBRC 1988-4) and two were present from 1 to 23 January 1997. The third record was a bird at Lake Amistad on 12 January 2000. As with the previous species, Pacific Loons should be expected to occur within the region again. When removed from the TBRC review list in 1996, there were more than 60 accepted records from Texas. The peak time of occurrence in Texas has been between mid-November and late March; however, birds have lingered well into May on several occasions.

Common Loon (*Gavia immer*)

Uncommon migrant and winter resident on large reservoirs, including Lake Amistad. Common Loons appear to be more common on Lake Buchanan and Canyon Lake than other locations on the eastern plateau and are occasionally found on smaller bodies of water. Fall migrants typically arrive in late October, but have been noted as early as mid-

DRAWING 1. *Common Loon*

September. Winter residents normally begin to depart in early March, but have been known to linger to early May. Although Common Loons are normally seen in basic plumage during their winter stay, by mid- to late March some of those that remain molt into breeding plumage.

FAMILY PODICIPEDIDAE: Grebes

Least Grebe (*Tachybaptus dominicus*)

Rare postbreeding wanderer to the eastern plateau and southern Val Verde County. Individuals have been reported beginning in mid-August, but the peak of occurrence appears to be between mid-November and early January. Least Grebes very rarely remain through the winter. This species has been considered a rare winter resident in the Del Rio area, but this does not appear to be supported by the available reports. Least Grebes are sensitive to cold weather, which might preclude them from overwintering during most years. This species occurs more regularly from eastern Travis County southward along the edge of the plateau and has bred irregularly in southern Bexar County. There are also two summer records for the plateau: a single adult at Junction on 30 May 1988 and another near Uvalde on 8 June 1960.

Pied-billed Grebe (*Podilymbus podiceps*)

A common migrant and winter resident throughout the region. Fall migrants begin arriving in mid-September with most wintering individuals and spring migrants departing by late April. Pied-billed Grebes are generally rare to locally uncommon during the remainder of the year. Nesting activity has been rarely noted on the plateau. Breeding has been frequently documented in eastern Travis County southward along the edge of the plateau to southern Bexar County. Pied-billed Grebes can be found on almost any body of water, although they are rarely seen on rivers with a consistent current.

Horned Grebe (*Podiceps auritus*)

Uncommon winter resident from late October to mid-March, rarely lingering to late March. Most frequently found on the larger reservoirs of the region, such as Canyon Lake, Lake Amistad, and Lake Buchanan. Although present every winter, rarely are large numbers of this species reported. On reservoirs in north-central Texas, up to 200 individuals have been counted at a single location. On the plateau, it is more likely to encounter a maximum of 15 to 20 individuals.

Red-necked Grebe (*Podiceps grisegena*)

Accidental. There is one record of this species from the plateau. An adult Red-necked Grebe was present on Lake Austin, Travis County, from 18 December 2000 to 14 January 2001 (TBRC 2000-142). This individual represented only the sixteenth documented record for the state. Almost all of the records for this species from Texas over the past decade have come from the northeastern quarter of the state. *Review Species*

Eared Grebe (*Podiceps nigricollis*)

Migrant and winter resident throughout the region. Uncommon from mid-September to late October, becoming common through March, when most of the wintering birds depart. Spring migrants and lingering winter residents can normally be found until early May. Most birds observed from late March through April have molted into breeding plumage.

Western Grebe (*Aechmophorus occidentalis*)

Rare midwinter visitor from late November through early February and very rare spring migrant. Western Grebes are primarily found on large bodies of water. This species has been recorded most frequently on Lake Buchanan and Lake Amistad. They appear to be increasing in abundance in the Trans-Pecos, where it is now a common migrant and winter resident. A similar increase in abundance has been noted on the reservoirs in the San Angelo area, although the number of individuals present is still much lower. For these reasons, Western Grebes should be expected to occur more frequently at Lake Amistad. In the central Trans-Pecos, they typically arrive in mid-September and remain until early May. In recent years, a few have remained through the summer.

FAMILY SULIDAE: Boobies and Gannets

Blue-footed Booby (*Sula nebouxii*)

Accidental. One of the two records for this species from Texas is from the Edwards Plateau. An immature plumaged bird was discovered on Lake Lyndon B. Johnson at Granite Shoals, Burnet County, on 2 June 1993. The bird faithfully roosted on a diving board for over a year until 6 October 1994. This Blue-footed Booby may have been seen by more people that any other single bird in Texas. Over 5,000 people signed a register at the bird's favorite roost. By the time the bird departed, it had molted into adult plumage. Amazingly, the bird was rediscovered on another Colorado River reservoir 90 miles away. It stayed at Lake Bastrop, Bastrop County, from 10 December 1994 to 12 April 1995. *Review Species*

FAMILY PELECANIDAE: Pelicans

American White Pelican (*Pelecanus erythrorhynchos*)

Occasional to uncommon migrant over the entire plateau. Most often observed overhead in migrating flocks, sometimes comprised of over 100 individuals. Spring migration occurs between late February and late May. Fall migrants are seen between mid-September and mid-November. Small numbers often overwinter on some of the larger reservoirs in the region, where a few wintering birds are normally at Lake

Buchanan and Lake Amistad. This species is much less frequently reported in the western half of the region, but this is probably a function
of fewer observers and a general lack of stop-over habitat. American
White Pelicans are common migrants and winter residents on reservoirs
in Tom Green County just to the north of the region.

Brown Pelican (*Pelecanus occidentalis*)

Casual visitor with records from all seasons. The coastal Texas population of this Endangered Species has enjoyed a steady increase over the
past 15 years, which may account for the increase in plateau sightings
over the past decade. The first documented record for the plateau was
an immature bird that spent the night of 16 August 1990 on a telephone
pole in a residential area at Helotes, Bexar County, far from any body of
water. Since then there have been seven additional records from scattered locations across the region. Four of those are from May, and single
records are from March, July, and December. Almost all of the records
are of immature birds, and all but two involved single individuals. A
single bird was present on Lake Travis, Travis County, from 4 to 27 May
1991, when a second bird joined it. Two birds were also discovered on
Lake Amistad on 27 December 1998.

FAMILY PHALACROCORACIDAE: Cormorants

Neotropic Cormorant (*Phalacrocorax brasilianus*)

Occasional, but increasing summer resident on the larger reservoirs
of the eastern plateau. Spring migrants appear in early March. Fall
migrants depart in early September with some lingering until early
November. Neotropic Cormorants are most frequently reported during
April, May, and September, but this is more likely a function of increased observers during those months rather than an actual increase in
abundance. This species may be overlooked in winter when large numbers of Double-crested Cormorants are present. Neotropic Cormorants
are uncommon permanent residents in southern Val Verde County and
appear to be steadily increasing in this region of the plateau.

Double-crested Cormorant (*Phalacrocorax auritus*)

Common to locally abundant winter resident along rivers and reservoirs throughout the plateau. Fall migrants begin appearing in mid-
September, but the majority of the wintering birds do not arrive until

late October. Most depart by the end of April, with a few remaining until late May. Double-crested Cormorants occasionally linger throughout the summer, but there is no evidence of nesting on the plateau.

FAMILY ANHINGIDAE: Anhingas

Anhinga (*Anhinga anhinga*)

Casual spring and late summer visitor. Only a handful of recent records exists for this species from the plateau. There is no discernible pattern to the records, which are from all seasons. Records are from the eastern plateau or Lake Amistad, including one on the Devil's River north of the reservoir. Anhingas are likely to be observed most frequently as spring migrants or postbreeding wanderers in late summer. This species was apparently a rare summer resident over the eastern Edwards Plateau in the early 1900s. Lacey (1911) reported that they sometimes bred along the Guadalupe River, and Simmons (1925) listed it as a breeding bird along the Colorado River and Barton Creek.

FAMILY ARDEIDAE: Herons and Egrets

American Bittern (*Botaurus lentiginosus*)

Rare migrant and very rare winter visitor throughout the region. Migrants have been reported from early April to early May and late September through October. There are only a few winter records of this species, including two specimens collected near Ingram, Kerr County, on 21 February 1915. American Bitterns are most frequently encountered in marshy habitats, particularly where cattails are present.

Least Bittern (*Ixobrychus exilis*)

Very rare migrant and summer resident throughout the region. Most of the records from the plateau appear to pertain to migrating birds. The majority of reports are from May and September. Least Bittern is a very local summer resident throughout the region. Cattail marshes are used most frequently for nesting. This habitat appears to be very localized on the plateau, although more extensive marshes may exist on private lands. Least Bitterns may have been a more common breeding species in the late 1800s and early 1900s than they are now. Lloyd and Lacey noted this species at three locations along the Rio Grande and Devils River between 1890 and 1910. They were also found at scattered locations in northern Bexar and Comal Counties in the 1930s. There are no recent nesting records from the plateau, although this species is probably still a local breeder.

Great Blue Heron (*Ardea herodias*)

Common permanent resident throughout the plateau. Despite the widespread occurrence of this species on the plateau, it is a very local nester in the region. Nesting locations are frequently along drainages in small canyons away from human disturbance. Great Blue Herons frequently form small nesting colonies or heronries, but isolated pairs can also be found. Great Blues are most visible after the breeding season has concluded, when they can be found on almost any river, pond, or lake on the plateau.

Great Egret (*Ardea alba*)

Occasional spring migrant, uncommon fall migrant, and postnuptial visitor to the plateau. Great Egret is also an occasional to locally uncommon winter visitor. Spring migrants can be found between late March through May. Postbreeding dispersal typically begins in mid-July, although individuals have been noted as early as 5 July. Fall migrants can be found in the region through October. There are a few summer reports for this species, but these birds are probably nonbreeding individuals that have lingered into June.

Snowy Egret (*Egretta thula*)

Occasional migrant and postnuptial visitor on the plateau. Spring migration occurs between late March and late May, although the peak is between late April and mid-May. Fall migrants are found from late July through mid-October with a peak during September. Snowy Egret is also a rare winter visitor to the region. Most of the winter records are from December and early January and may be lingering migrants rather than winter residents.

Little Blue Heron (*Egretta caerulea*)

Occasional postbreeding wanderer and rare spring migrant on the plateau. Peak occurrence is from early August through September. Spring migrants have been found on the plateau between late March and mid-May. Almost all of the records from the plateau are of single immature birds. Little Blue Heron is an uncommon breeding bird to the east of the plateau from Bell County south to Bexar County. They can be very common during August and September. Considering the influx of postbreeding birds to this area, this species should be reported from the plateau more frequently.

Tricolored Heron (*Egretta tricolor*)

Occasional postbreeding wanderer and rare spring migrant on the plateau. Peak occurrence on the plateau is from mid-July to late September. This species is rarely recorded during the early summer and is very rare in winter in the region. The majority of the birds recorded on the plateau are in juvenile plumage. Most observations are of single birds, but multiple individuals are occasionally reported with a high of seven at Boerne on 2 September 1982. Tricolored Herons are regular visitors in larger numbers to the lakes and ponds just to the south and east of the escarpment. As with the Little Blue Heron, this species should be found along the southeastern edge of the plateau with greater regularity.

Cattle Egret (*Bubulcus ibis*)

Common migrant throughout the plateau, occasionally seen in flocks of over 100 individuals. Spring migrants have been noted between early March and mid-May. Fall migrants are seen from late August through October. No evidence of breeding has been found for this species on the plateau, but it is likely only a matter of time before small heronries become established on the eastern plateau. This species has rarely been found during the early summer and has been reported only twice during the winter for the region.

Green Heron (*Butorides virescens*)

Common migrant and a rare winter resident on the plateau. Green Heron is also a locally uncommon to rare breeder in the region. Spring migrants pass through the region from late March to late May. Fall migrants can be found between early September and late October. Typically, Green Herons nest singly or in loose colonies; on the plateau, however, colonies are rare. This species is considered a fairly common nester in the Concho Valley and may occur more frequently as a breeder than is currently believed. Green Herons frequent areas of slow-moving water along streams and rivers as well as man-made bodies of water.

Black-crowned Night-Heron (*Nycticorax nycticorax*)

Rare migrant and irregular winter visitor to the entire plateau. Black-crowned is the rarer of the two night-herons. Even though there are few records, the peak migration periods appear to be mid-March through April and mid-September through October. Birds found during early winter and even up to early January may be lingering migrants rather than true wintering birds. Black-crowneds are most frequently found at tree-lined stock ponds. The crepuscular and nocturnal nature of this species makes accurately assessing its abundance difficult.

Yellow-crowned Night-Heron (*Nyctanassa violacea*)

Uncommon and local breeder on the eastern plateau and possibly throughout the region. Yellow-crowned Night-Herons arrive in mid-April and depart by mid-October. On rare occasions, a few linger into early winter. They normally nest in loose single-species colonies, but single nests are not uncommon. They primarily nest in trees overhanging or very near water. They breed along rivers and streams, such as along the Colorado River and its tributaries in Travis County. This species is rarely encountered on the central and western plateau. As with Black-crowned Night-Herons, the habits of this species make its status difficult to ascertain.

FAMILY THRESKIORNITHIDAE: Ibises and Spoonbills

White Ibis (*Eudocimus albus*)

Accidental. There are four records of this species from the region: two each from spring and fall. The fall records are both from near Kerrville, with a single bird on 26 August 1982 and two birds from 13 August to 11 September 1986. The spring records include a single individual at Inks Lake National Fish Hatchery 19–21 May 1996 and five subadult birds seen flying along the Guadalupe River at Kerrville on 22 April 2000. White Ibis is a regular, but uncommon postbreeding visitor to the wetlands just to the east of the escarpment near Austin and San Antonio. They should be looked for between mid-August and mid-October. The paucity of records is probably due to limited available habitat and a lack of observers during the proper season.

White-faced Ibis (*Plegadis chihi*)

Occasional spring migrant and uncommon fall migrant throughout the region. Spring migrants typically occur between mid-April and late May. Fall migrants begin arriving in mid-July with a peak between early August and early October. Late migrants occasionally linger to early January, mostly in southern Val Verde County, where this species has been frequently recorded on the Del Rio Christmas Bird Count in recent years.

Roseate Spoonbill (*Ajaia ajaja*)

Accidental. This species has been reported five times from the Edwards Plateau: twice in the summer and three times in the fall. The summer records consist of two birds in Mason County from 13 July to 2 August 1988 and a single bird near Hunt, Kerr County, on 16 June 1993. The fall records are single individuals at Ozona, Crockett County, on 7 September 1976; Gillespie County on 21 September 1989; and Lake Amistad on 18 September 1999. Like the White Ibis, spoonbills are regular postbreeding visitors to the east of the escarpment and should be looked for between early August and mid-October.

FAMILY CICONIIDAE: Storks

Wood Stork (*Mycteria americana*)

Rare postbreeding wanderer to the eastern Edwards Plateau; very rare farther west. These birds have been recorded between early July and late September in the region. Wood Storks have been most frequently encountered in the counties along the extreme eastern and southeastern edges of the region. Wood Storks are regular visitors to southeastern Bexar County northward through western Bastrop County during this period. They are also found almost annually in a single location in Concho County. Wood Storks are not known to breed in Texas, and the origin of the postbreeding wanderers in Texas is unknown. The closest breeding locations are Georgia and Florida to the east and Tabasco, Mexico, to the south.

FAMILY CATHARTIDAE: New World Vultures

Black Vulture (*Coragyps atratus*)

Common permanent resident over much of the plateau. Black Vultures are most common along the eastern plateau, becoming less common westward. Although seasonal movements of Black Vultures may be less noticeable than those of Turkey Vultures, migrating flocks can be expected from early March to mid-April and again in mid-September through November.

DRAWING 2. *Wood Duck*

...ate the possibility of a hybrid Eurasian × American Wigeon and was ...ot accepted by the TBRC. Hybrid Eurasian × American Wigeons have ...een documented in Texas on several occasions. Close photographs and ...detailed description of the head, breast, and flanks are needed to docu-...ent the occurrence of Eurasian Wigeon.

American Wigeon (*Anas americana*)

...ommon to abundant winter resident throughout the region. Ameri-...an Wigeons begin to arrive in early September but are uncommon until ...rly October. Wintering birds remain through March with a few indi-...duals lingering into late April. As with other puddle ducks, American ...igeons are found in a variety of habitats, including large reservoirs,

---

Turkey Vulture (*Cathartes aura*)

Abundant spring migrant and summer resident throughout the region. Over all but the eastern edge of the plateau, Turkey Vultures become less common in late fall and are rare in winter. In the eastern third of the region, they remain common during the fall and winter months. Spring migrants begin arriving on the plateau in late February to early March. Movements of Turkey Vultures in the fall are noted from mid-September through early November.

FAMILY ANATIDAE: Ducks, Geese, and Swans

Black-bellied Whistling-Duck (*Dendrocygna autumnalis*)

Common permanent resident on the southern and central Edwards Plateau. For the remainder of the region, they are rare but are increasing as a summer visitor and occasional breeder. Black-bellied Whistling-Duck was first recorded on the plateau in the fall of 1906 and was subsequently considered to be accidental. In the late 1950s, this species began to be reported with increasing frequency along the southern edge of the plateau. But it wasn't until the mid-1980s that they began to become established as a permanent resident. It is not uncommon to see large concentrations during the fall and winter. The high count of 105 on the 1997 Boerne Christmas Bird Count illustrates this point.

Greater White-fronted Goose (*Anser albifrons*)

Rare spring and occasional fall migrant for the entire plateau. This species is probably overlooked during migration. As with other geese, the White-fronted Goose is normally seen flying overhead and is rarely seen on the ground. Spring migrants pass over the area from March through mid-April. Autumn migrants begin to appear in mid-September, but the peak of migration is from mid-October to mid-November. There is a large wintering population of White-fronted Geese in agricultural areas in eastern Uvalde and western Medina Counties. Texas Parks and Wildlife surveys estimate this population is over 20,000 birds. Obviously, all of these birds pass over the plateau during migration, and it is likely that some occasionally wander onto the plateau during the winter.

Snow Goose (*Chen caerulescens*)

Rare spring and fall migrant for the entire plateau. This species is most often seen flying overhead and is rarely seen on the ground. Spring migrants can be found between late February through mid-April. Fall migrants appear from late September to early November. There are a few Snow Geese, probably fewer than 2,000, with the wintering population of Greater White-fronted Geese in eastern Uvalde and western Medina Counties, and they may occasionally be seen on the plateau.

Ross's Goose (*Chen rossii*)

Casual winter visitor throughout the region. There are six winter sightings of this species from the region. Five of these sightings involved birds that were seen only once. Single individuals were present along the Devils River on 6 February 1965 and at Lake Buchanan on 19 December 1984. Two birds were noted at Balcones Canyonlands National Wildlife Refuge on 18 November 1999, Lost Maples State Natural Area (seen overhead with Snow Geese) on 24 November 1999, and Lake Amistad on 27 December 1999. The only record of a Ross's Goose overwintering on the plateau was one present in Mason County during the winter of 1996–1997. Ross's Geese undoubtedly occur as rare migrants over the eastern plateau. The population wintering on the upper Texas coast was estimated to be more than 10,000 in 1998. Some of these birds are likely to wander over the eastern plateau during migration. Snow Goose flocks should be examined carefully.

Canada Goose (*Branta canadensis*)

Rare migrant and winter visitor for the entire plateau. Most often seen flying overhead; rarely seen on the ground. Spring migrants can be found between late February through mid-April. Fall migrants appear from late September to early November. Canada Geese winter locally on rare occasions on the plateau. Often these records involve single individuals. There are small numbers of Canada Geese, probably fewer than 500, that can be found associating with the wintering flocks of Snow and White-fronted Geese in eastern Uvalde and western Medina Counties. The small-sized northern populations have been treated as a different species by some authors. Recent research appears to support that treatment.

Tundra Swan (*Cygnus columbianus*)

Very rare winter visitor to the plateau. There are nine repo species from the region, including one specimen from Kimb All of the records fall between 16 November and 25 March these reports involved more than one individual with a hig three present in northwestern Hays County on 18 January i encountered on the plateau must be carefully examined. **Mute Swans** (*Cygnus olor*) are breeding in urban settings in and Kerrville areas and possibly elsewhere. These birds can b dering, at least locally, over the plateau. Although the p these birds appears to be growing, at present there are too f als to establish a viable breeding population. These birds ori domesticated stock and are not considered an establishe species.

Wood Duck (*Aix sponsa*)

Wood Ducks are uncommon and somewhat local perman throughout the region. During most of the year, they ar calm streams and rivers with well-developed riparian woo ing the fall and winter, Wood Ducks are found in a wi habitats, including larger bodies of water and city park during the early spring, they can be found in small group individuals or less. Wintering flocks of more than 50 in been reported.

Gadwall (*Anas strepera*)

One of the most common wintering ducks in the regio rive in early October and remain until early May. The variety of habitats, from large reservoirs to stock pond lakes. Typically found in small groups, this sociable du ates with other puddle ducks. Although they seem to ea people in city parks, Gadwall in remote settings are oft readily.

Eurasian Wigeon (*Anas penelope*)

Accidental. A drake of this species, shot by a hunter January 1998 (TBRC 1998-92), represents the only do for the region. However, a drake Eurasian Wigeon w Lake Amistad from 2 to 5 February 1996. The descrip stock ponds, and city park lakes. This species is one of the most common wintering ducks in the region.

American Black Duck (*Anas rubripes*)

Accidental. There is one documented record of this species from the plateau. An American Black Duck was banded in New York on 12 August 1974 and was recovered at Lake Buchanan, Burnet County, on 7 January 1976. This species has been reported on the plateau on at least three other occasions. These reports are from December and January, and two are associated with Christmas Bird Counts. No details accompany these reports. Close photographs with detailed descriptions, including the internal patterns of breast feathers, are required to separate American Black Duck from the very similar Mottled Duck. *Review Species*

Mallard (*Anas platyrhynchos*)

Uncommon winter resident throughout the region, becoming occasional to rare and local during the summer. Wintering birds generally begin to arrive in mid-August and remain through March. Isolated nesting records are known, primarily from the northwestern quarter of the plateau. As opposed to many areas of the Mallard's winter range, they are not normally found in large congregations on the plateau.

Mottled Duck (*Anas fulvigula*)

The status of Mottled Duck on the plateau is not clear. This species is apparently a very rare winter visitor to the reservoirs in the eastern third of the plateau, with reports in December, January, and February. They have also been reported in winter and spring from southern Val Verde County. In addition, there is a breeding record from Lake Buchanan, where two adults with five ducklings were found on 25 May 1991. Mottled Ducks arrive on water impoundments in the Austin and San Antonio areas in July almost annually and have remained through the winter.

Blue-winged Teal (*Anas discors*)

Common migrant over the entire plateau and a rare and sporadic summer resident in the northwestern plateau east to the Llano Uplift. Spring migrants are common from late March to mid-May, becoming uncommon for the remainder of May. Blue-winged Teal are usually the first ducks to arrive on the plateau in the fall, with migrants arriving in early August. This species is common through mid-October with a few individuals lingering into December. There are very few breeding records for the plateau, but Blue-wingeds are regular nesters in the Concho Valley just to the north.

Cinnamon Teal (*Anas cyanoptera*)

Occasional migrant and winter resident throughout the region. Fall migrants begin arriving in early October and wintering individuals and spring migrants remain until late April. Cinnamon Teal do not appear to be more common as migrants than as winter residents. They are often found in more secluded locales than the closely related Blue-winged Teal. Cinnamon Teal are not normally found associating with other puddle ducks.

Northern Shoveler (*Anas clypeata*)

Common to locally abundant migrant and winter resident on the plateau. Shovelers are present on the plateau from early September through mid-May. Large concentrations can sometimes be seen in protected coves on large reservoirs. Northern Shoveler is another of the most common wintering puddle ducks in the region. They have an affinity for sewage treatment facilities with open water. The nutrient rich water is a perfect medium for the tiny diatoms and copepods on which they feed.

Northern Pintail (*Anas acuta*)

Uncommon migrant and winter resident throughout the region. Pintail begin arriving in early September, but are often hard to find until later that month. They are present through March and occasionally linger through April. Northern Pintail are found in very large concentrations on playas in the southern Panhandle and South Plains, but large flocks are rarely encountered on the Edwards Plateau.

Green-winged Teal (*Anas crecca*)

Common migrant and winter resident throughout the region. Fall migrants begin arriving in mid-August and are uncommon until late October when the majority of the wintering population arrives. Green-winged Teal remain common through early April with some lingering until late in the month. The number of birds present in the early fall may be greater than records indicate, as basic plumaged birds are overlooked among the more common Blue-winged Teal.

Canvasback (*Aythya valisineria*)

Uncommon winter resident over the entire plateau. Wintering birds typically arrive in mid- to late October and depart by the end of March, rarely lingering through April. They are most often found on large reservoirs; however, they also use stock tanks and other small bodies of water. Canvasbacks, as with all *Aythya* ducks, have been known to spend the summer in the region. These very unusual records usually pertain to injured birds.

Redhead (*Aythya americana*)

Uncommon to locally common winter resident. Wintering birds can be found from late September to early April. A portion of the wintering population routinely lingers into early summer, when they are generally rare. The reason for this consistent lingering is unknown, and there is no evidence of these birds attempting to breed. As with Canvasbacks, Redheads are most often found on large reservoirs. They appear to use small bodies of water more frequently than do Canvasbacks.

Ring-necked Duck (*Aythya collaris*)

Uncommon winter resident and common migrant throughout the region. The first fall migrants arrive in mid-September, although this species does not become common until the height of fall migration, in late October and early November. Winter residents are present through March, becoming rare in April. Spring migrants pass through the region in late February and early March. This species can be found regularly on stock ponds and other small bodies of water as well as on large reservoirs.

Greater Scaup (*Aythya marila*)

Occasional and local winter resident on some of the large reservoirs in the region. Records of this species for the plateau extend from early November through late March. Most of these records are from Canyon Lake with a few from the Highland Lakes and Lake Amistad. It is likely that the high number of records from Canyon Lake is an artifact of increased observer awareness of the species rather than a highly localized wintering population.

Lesser Scaup (*Aythya affinis*)

Common to abundant migrant and winter resident. Lesser Scaup are present from late October through May. This is the most common *Aythya* duck in the region, occasionally gathering in large mixed flocks with Redheads and, less commonly, Ring-necked Ducks. It is not unusual for individuals of this species to be found during the summer months. There is no evidence of breeding in the region, but Lesser Scaup are casual breeders in the Panhandle and northern South Plains.

Surf Scoter (*Melanitta perspicillata*)

Accidental. There are four reports for the Edwards Plateau. Single immature (or female) birds were on Town Lake in Austin on 4 November 1966 and at Junction on 30 September 1984 and again on 6 December 1984 (TPRF 557). Another was near Mason on 19 October 1999. There have been numerous records from eastern Travis and southeastern Bexar Counties. This species should be expected to occur with greater frequency on the plateau.

White-winged Scoter (*Melanitta fusca*)

Accidental. There are two records for the Edwards Plateau. Single immature (or female) birds were near San Marcos, Hays County, on 4 December 1963 through 8 February 1964 and at Canyon Lake during the winter of 1980–1981. There are fewer records of White-winged Scoter for eastern Travis and southeastern Bexar Counties than for Surf Scoter.

Long-tailed Duck (*Clangula hyemalis*)

Accidental. There are four records for the Edwards Plateau. Single birds were reported at Lake Buchanan on 4 February 1968 and again on 29 December 1979; on Town Lake in Austin on 4 January to 9 March 1990; and at the Inks Lake Fish Hatchery on 10 January to 2 March 1990. As with the scoters, there are several records of Long-tailed Ducks from areas adjacent to the plateau. Formerly known as Oldsquaw.

Bufflehead (*Bucephala albeola*)

Common winter resident throughout the region. Wintering birds arrive in early November, with most departing by the end of March. Many linger through April and are considered uncommon during that month. Buffleheads are diving ducks and, as such, are often associated with deep

found in open grasslands and have a tendency to remain in an area if prey items are abundant.

Mississippi Kite (*Ictinia mississippiensis*)

Uncommon migrant over the eastern plateau, becoming less common westward. Rare migrant in Crockett and Val Verde Counties. Spring migrants can be seen from mid-March to mid-May. Fall migrants typically pass through the area from mid-August to early October. Mississippi Kites are potentially very local breeders in the northwestern plateau. They are most often found in urban areas with mature Pecans and other large trees in the Concho Valley and should be looked for in similar situations in Ozona and Eldorado.

Bald Eagle (*Haliaeetus leucocephalus*)

Locally common winter resident along major river systems of the eastern and central plateau. They are present between early November and late March. The Colorado River drainage, including the San Saba River west to Schleicher County, appears to be the center of the winter population on the plateau. There is also a fairly large wintering population along the Frio River in Real County. Bald Eagles are rare, but regular, visitors to the remainder of the plateau. Those encountered on the western plateau may be individuals from nearby rivers spreading out into the adjacent rangeland in search of prey items. Although primarily fish eaters, Bald Eagles will feed on carrion when available.

Northern Harrier (*Circus cyaneus*)

Common winter resident throughout the live oak–mesquite savannas of the northern and western plateau. Northern Harriers are less common and more local in the Balcones Canyonlands subregion. They are occasional fall migrants from early August until early October, when wintering birds begin to arrive in greater numbers. Most wintering birds depart by the end of March, but spring migrants can still be found until early May. The majority of wintering harriers on the plateau are first-winter birds, which resemble adult females but are more uniform in color, particularly on the underparts.

Sharp-shinned Hawk (*Accipiter striatus*)

Common migrant and winter resident. Fall migration for this species is from mid-September to late October. Spring migrants pass through this region from late March to early May. Migrants are most often seen

DRAWING 3. *Bald Eagle*

singly or in pairs during migration and are only occasionally seen in kettles with other hawks. Wintering birds are frequently encountered in urban areas and are well known for raiding bird feeders for the passerine birds that make up the majority of their diet.

Cooper's Hawk (*Accipiter cooperii*)

Uncommon winter resident and local summer resident throughout the region. Fall migrants begin to appear on the plateau in mid-September with wintering birds remaining through April. As with the Sharp-shinned Hawk, migrants are most often seen singly or in pairs. Cooper's

Hawk occurs throughout the region as a very low density breeding bird. Nest sites are often in secluded canyons, and the same nest is often used for several years.

Gray Hawk (*Asturina nitida*)

Accidental. The one report for the Edwards Plateau was an adult observed at Devils River State Natural Area during April 1993. In Texas, Gray Hawks normally occur only as a rare permanent resident in the Lower Rio Grande Valley and as a rare breeder in Big Bend National Park. However, they may occur in cottonwood stands along the Rio Grande closer to Val Verde County than is currently known. Gray Hawk was recently removed from the genus *Buteo* and placed in the monotypic genus *Asturina*. In addition, some authors split Gray Hawk into two species with the population north of Costa Rica, including Texas, retaining the common name.

Common Black-Hawk (*Buteogallus anthracinus*)

Rare and local summer resident in Val Verde County along the Devils River drainage. Although breeding has been documented and there are several other records from the area, the status of this species is poorly understood. Common Black-Hawks breed in riparian woodlands along permanent streams and rivers. Just to the north of the region, a breeding pair was in Tom Green County from 1993 to at least 2000, when a second pair was discovered nearby. Single Common Black-Hawks have been reported four times in the region away from Val Verde County. Three of these records are from spring: two are from Lost Maples State Natural Area in Bandera County (5 April 1990 and 29 April 1995), and the third is from Colorado Bend State Park, San Saba County (20 March–17 May 1994). The remaining record is from late fall, with one in Bandera County on 25 November 1973. Although not in the region, of interest was an adult collected at Fort Clark, Kinney County, on 13 February 1898.

Harris's Hawk (*Parabuteo unicinctus*)

Uncommon permanent resident in the Live Oak–Mesquite Savannas subregion of the northwestern plateau, east locally to Mason County. Irregular visitor at all seasons to the Balcones Canyonlands, presumably from birds wandering northward from the South Texas Plains, where the species is an uncommon permanent resident.

Red-shouldered Hawk (*Buteo lineatus*)

Common permanent resident in the Balcones Canyonlands, less common and more local over the remainder of the plateau. Within the Balcones Canyonlands subregion, they are primarily found in diverse oak-juniper woodlands as well as along riparian corridors. In the remainder of the region, Red-shouldered Hawks are found almost exclusively in riparian forests. Nesting begins in early March.

Broad-winged Hawk (*Buteo platypterus*)

Uncommon to common migrant over the eastern plateau, becoming increasingly more uncommon westward. Rare migrant in the western tier of counties. Spring migrants are reported between mid-March and early May. Fall migrants typically pass through the area from mid-September to mid-October. Broad-wingeds are also rare and local nesters along the eastern edge of the plateau, with nesting reported in Travis County along heavily wooded drainages in west Austin such as Shoal Creek and the West Lake Hills area.

Short-tailed Hawk (*Buteo brachyurus*)

Accidental. There are three records of light-morph adults for the Edwards Plateau. Two of the records are from Lost Maples State Natural Area, 24 May–16 June 1995 (TBRC 1995-71) and 6–20 April 1999 (TBRC 1999-50). The third record is from near Dripping Springs, Hays County, on 6 June 1995 (TBRC 1995-78). Prior to 1989, there were no documented records for Texas, but since then there have been 11 accepted records. A possible explanation for the sudden increase in Short-tailed Hawk sightings in Texas is that the population in Mexico has grown to the point that there is a temporary range expansion forcing some individuals to seek suitable habitat away from the traditional population centers. Only time will tell if the Short-tailed Hawk will become a regular component of the Texas avifauna. *Review Species*

Swainson's Hawk (*Buteo swainsoni*)

Common migrant, sometimes observed in very large concentrations, over the entire plateau. Migrants can be seen in the spring from late March to late May and in the fall from early September to late October. The largest flight reported from the Edwards Plateau was 5,000 birds over Kerrville on 1 October 1988. Swainson's Hawks are also uncommon summer residents in the live oak-mesquite savannas of the northern and western plateau. Although there are no documented winter records from the region, there is one from Tom Green County. An immature bird was photographed on 2 February 1993 a few miles south of San Angelo. This represents one of the very few well-documented winter records for this species in the state.

White-tailed Hawk (*Buteo albicaudatus*)

Accidental. There is one documented record of this species for the Edwards Plateau. A single bird was photographed as it captured bats at the Frio Bat Cave, Uvalde County, on 23 March 1985 (TPRF 344). There have been three other sightings of this species just south of the plateau in Uvalde and Medina Counties. This hawk, at least on rare occasions, wanders west from the Coastal Plains.

Zone-tailed Hawk (*Buteo albonotatus*)

Uncommon summer resident, primarily in the southwestern and southern plateau. Zone-taileds arrive on the plateau in mid- to late March and remain through mid-September. The breeding range extends east to Bandera County and north to Crockett, Sutton, and Kimble Counties. There is also an isolated breeding record from Burnet County. Zone-tailed Hawks are very rare visitors as far east as Bexar, San Saba, and Travis Counties. On the plateau, Zone-tails typically nest in large trees in secluded canyons, though not necessarily near permanent water sources. Until the late 1800s, this species nested as far east as Bexar and Comal Counties. There are scattered late winter records of this species from the plateau. Whether these are actually wintering individuals or early spring arrivals is unknown. It is possible that this species is an irregular winterer on the plateau along riparian corridors. Zone-tailed Hawks have wintered irregularly to the southeast of the plateau in Bastrop and Gonzales Counties.

Red-tailed Hawk (*Buteo jamaicensis*)

Common to locally abundant winter resident and uncommon summer resident throughout the region. Red-taileds occur in greater densities in the live oak–mesquite savannas of the northern and western plateau than in the Balcones Canyonlands. The "Harlan's" race is a very rare winter visitor to the plateau, where there have been reports from Schleicher and Val Verde Counties eastward to Comal County.

Ferruginous Hawk (*Buteo regalis*)

Rare winter visitor throughout the live oak–mesquite savannas of the northern and western plateau and a very rare visitor to the Balcones Canyonlands. Winter visitors have been reported between early November and early March. Ferruginous Hawks prefer open habitats where they prey on prairie dogs, ground squirrels, and other rodents. This species has been reported during early April on two occasions. These could potentially be birds that wintered farther south or possibly simply misidentifications.

Rough-legged Hawk (*Buteo lagopus*)

Very rare winter visitor, primarily to the northern tier of counties, but occurring throughout the live oak–mesquite savannas of the northern and western plateau. Virtually absent from the Balcones Canyonlands. Rough-legged Hawks have been reported between mid-November and early March. Almost all have been first-winter birds; adults are very rarely encountered.

Golden Eagle (*Aquila chrysaetos*)

Uncommon winter visitor to the western and central plateau, becoming increasingly rare in the eastern counties of the region. This species occurs with the greatest regularity on the live oak–mesquite savannas of the northwestern plateau, east to Kerr and Mason Counties and south to Val Verde and northern Kinney Counties. They generally occur between mid-October and early March. Golden Eagles apparently nested on the plateau in the late 1800s and early 1900s. Vernon Bailey discovered an active nest near Rocksprings, Edwards County, on 13 July 1902. Oberholser (1974) also includes breeding records from Comal and Kerr Counties from prior to 1900.

FAMILY FALCONIDAE: Caracaras and Falcons

Crested Caracara (*Caracara cheriway*)

Irregular visitor to the southern and eastern plateau. The majority of records are from the winter months, but this species is being reported with increasing frequency from all seasons. A small population of Crested Caracaras seems to have become established in western Lampasas and eastern San Saba Counties. It may be only a matter of time before breeding is detected in other areas of the plateau. Caracaras prefer open habitats, and the cleared pastureland present throughout the region provides excellent foraging areas.

American Kestrel (*Falco sparverius*)

Common migrant and winter resident for the entire region. Rare and local breeder in the northwestern plateau. Fall migrants begin to appear in early September and are uncommon until mid-October when the wintering population arrives. They are common in open habitats until late April, when most wintering birds depart. Lingering or late migrants have been reported into late May.

Merlin (*Falco columbarius*)

Rare migrant and winter resident for the entire region. Migrants are present throughout April and May in the spring and from late September through October during the fall. Merlins are less frequently reported during the winter than during the typical migration periods. As with kestrels, Merlins frequent open habitats and are known to frequent Brazilian Free-tailed Bat (*Tadarida braziliensis*) colonies in the fall until the bats migrate south for the winter.

Peregrine Falcon (*Falco peregrinus*)

Occasional migrant and rare winter visitor for the region. Spring migrants pass through the area from mid-April to late May, occasionally lingering into early June. Fall migrants appear from early September through October, with peak migration in late September. Peregrine Falcons are also known to frequent bat caves for an easy meal during their southward migration. A pair of Peregrines were noted at the Frio Bat Cave on 8 July 2000. This species was a rare and local breeder on the plateau until at least the early 1900s. An adult female in breeding condition was collected in Kerr County on 23 May 1902, and a nest with four eggs was discovered on 20 March 1908, also in Kerr County. Both of these records are within the normal nesting period of this species in the Trans-Pecos.

Prairie Falcon (*Falco mexicanus*)

Uncommon to rare winter visitor to the western half of the plateau; very rare in the east. This species is most frequently reported from the area surrounding Lake Amistad and is considered to be uncommon in winter. The winter reports of this species from the remainder of the plateau fall between 11 November and 4 February, with most in late December and early January. This may be an artifact of increased observers during the Christmas Bird Count period. There is one record of a migrating bird, 24 September 1987, from Kendall County, this may actually have been an immature Peregrine.

FAMILY PHASIANIDAE: Grouse and Turkeys

Lesser Prairie-Chicken (*Tympanuchus pallidicinctus*)

Formerly a resident in the northwestern plateau, southeast to Menard County. Early Spanish explorers reported them as fairly common in March and April 1683, including hearing the unusual sounds associated with lek displays. By 1850 the population had fallen to the point that they were very hard to find. William Lloyd (1887) reported that they were winter visitors to the Concho Valley and postulated that they were driven south by prairie fires on the plains. Wintering birds were likely also present in at least Crockett and Schleicher Counties, although Lloyd does not mention areas south of the Concho Valley. Lacey (1911) states that prairie-chickens were very common on his ranch near Kerrville from December 1885 to April 1886. There have been no reports of this species from the plateau since that winter.

Wild Turkey (*Meleagris gallopavo*)

Common to locally uncommon permanent resident in open woodlands over the entire plateau. They can also be found in open shrublands, where woody vegetation has invaded areas that were once grasslands or savannas. In arid parts of the plateau, they are restricted during fall and winter to river drainages and other mesic habitats where oaks and other food sources are more common. Recent population studies have shown a slow decline in the populations on the southern plateau. The factors contributing to this decline are not clear.

FAMILY ODONTOPHORIDAE: New World Quail

Scaled Quail (*Callipepla squamata*)

Declining permanent resident in open grasslands and savannas on the western plateau. Scaled Quail are still a common resident in Crockett and Val Verde Counties. They are uncommon in Schleicher and Sutton

Counties and may still be present locally in western Menard, Kimble, and Edwards Counties. This species was formerly found east to Mason, Llano, western Travis, and Kendall Counties. The factors that have contributed to the decline of Scaled Quail on the Rolling Plains and Edwards Plateau are not known, but this species has become increasingly scarce in all but the most arid portions of the region. Scaled Quail are still fairly common just below the escarpment to the south, but rarely are found on the plateau.

Northern Bobwhite (*Colinus virginianus*)

Common permanent resident in open shrublands and woodlands over entire plateau. In the arid regions of the Live Oak–Mesquite Savannas, this species is frequently restricted to river drainages and other mesic habitats. Northern Bobwhites have experienced a serious decline in the southeastern United States. The population on the plateau appears to be stable at this time, but increased monitoring may be warranted.

Montezuma Quail (*Cyrtonyx montezumae*)

Rare and local resident on the southwestern plateau in open habitats with abundant tall grasses. This species once ranged throughout most of the plateau, occurring east to Bexar, Kendall, and Burnet Counties. Currently the species is restricted to northern Kinney, Edwards, Real, and northwestern Uvalde Counties. Montezuma Quail are sensitive to changes in the quality of the grasslands and savannas they inhabit. Recent research has shown that when 40 to 50 percent of tall-grass cover is removed the quail are extirpated. At Kickapoo Cavern State Park, the population of Montezuma Quail has shown a steady increase since the park was acquired in 1986, as the park has recovered from previous land use.

FAMILY RALLIDAE: Rails

There is very limited habitat available for rails on the plateau. The inaccessibility of much of that habitat has resulted in very few sightings of any species of rail from the region.

King Rail (*Rallus elegans*)

Accidental. There is one documented record of this species on the Edwards Plateau. A pair successfully nested in Crockett County during the summer of 1977. An adult and one of the young was photographed on 30 July (TPRF 119). Despite the lack of records, this species is probably a casual migrant over the eastern third of the plateau.

Virginia Rail (*Rallus limicola*)

Rare migrant throughout the region but probably occurs far more commonly than reports would suggest. Spring migrants have been detected from late March through late April. Fall migrants have been found from late September through late October. Virginia Rails are considered rare winter visitors in areas surrounding the plateau. There are winter records from the San Angelo, Austin, San Antonio, and Uvalde areas. Despite the lack of records from the winter season, it seems likely that Virginia Rail is a rare winter visitor in marshes with abundant emergent vegetation throughout the plateau.

Sora (*Porzana carolina*)

Occasional migrant and rare winter visitor throughout the region. As with the Virginia Rail, Soras likely occur much more frequently than they are found. Spring migrants have been reported between late March and mid-May, with an apparent peak in early May. Fall migrants have been reported from early September to early November. There are only a few winter records for this species from the plateau, including a specimen from Kerrville (20 January 1950).

Purple Gallinule (*Porphyrula martinica*)

Accidental. There are two records of this species from the region. Lacey (1911) was brought a specimen by a local resident. It was reportedly taken, along with two American Coots, from the Guadalupe River near Kerrville on 20 May 1909. The only recent report is a single bird from the Bandera area on 18 June 1996.

Common Moorhen (*Gallinula chloropus*)

Occasional migrant and rare winter visitor to the entire plateau. Spring migrants have been reported during April and early May. Fall migrants have been found between mid-September and early November. Winter reports of this species are primarily from early winter and may actually reflect lingering migrants, rather than wintering individuals. Although unreported, Common Moorhen is probably a rare and local nesting species on the eastern plateau.

American Coot (*Fulica americana*)

Common winter resident and rare summer visitor. Fall migrants begin arriving in mid-September and remain until early May. On the large reservoirs in the region, wintering flocks of several hundred birds are not unusual. The wintering population of coots on Lake Amistad has been estimated to be more than 5,000 birds. Although American Coots have been reported locally throughout the summer on the plateau, there has been no documented evidence of breeding.

FAMILY GRUIDAE: Cranes

Sandhill Crane (*Grus canadensis*)

Common migrant and locally uncommon winter resident. Autumn migrant Sandhill Cranes begin arriving in mid-September but are uncommon until early October. They winter primarily in farming areas of the region, roosting in the fields and wandering over the countryside during the days. Spring migration is from early March to mid-April. Most of these spring migrants are birds that wintered along the coastal plains to the east and south. Small populations winter in central Uvalde and Medina Counties and in Schleicher and McCulloch Counties. Individuals from these population centers can be regularly seen in other nearby areas of the region.

Whooping Crane (*Grus americana*)

Very rare migrant over the eastern third of the region, west to Burnet and Llano Counties. Reports of fall migrating Whooping Cranes are all from the last two weeks of October. Spring reports are from late March and early April. Just south of the escarpment, an adult Whooping Crane was found on 4 January 1999 among wintering Sandhill Cranes near Sabinal in central Uvalde County. The bird could not be relocated but may have wintered locally.

SHOREBIRDS

The status and distribution of shorebirds on the Edwards Plateau is very difficult to assess. For most of the region, shorebird habitat is very limited. In many areas, available habitat is primarily sandbars in rivers and reservoirs. Many of the records referred to here have come from the sewage ponds in the cities of Kerrville and Junction. The ponds in Kerrville no longer exist; the water was diverted into an automated system during the fall of 1988, and currently there is no public access to the Junction ponds. There is virtually no shorebird habitat over much of the western half of the plateau. The exception is in Schleicher and northern Crockett Counties, where shallow playa depressions over sealed limestone are common. During wet years, quality shorebird habitat is present and calidrine sandpipers, yellowlegs, and Common Snipe can be commonly encountered. In general, there is a paucity of reports for many species that should be regular migrants throughout the region. For most of the plateau, the underlying limestone is not sealed. As a result, even after heavy rains shorebird habitat is available only for brief periods. It is very likely that almost all of these birds occur on the plateau more frequently than they have been reported. The National Fish Hatchery near Uvalde is three miles south of the escarpment and produces more shorebird records than almost any location on the plateau.

FAMILY CHARADRIIDAE: Plovers

Black-bellied Plover (*Pluvialis squatarola*)

Rare spring and fall migrant throughout the entire region. Spring migrants have been reported between mid-April and mid-May. Fall migrants have been found from late August to mid-October. There are two winter records from the plateau that likely were lingering migrants. One was photographed at Canyon Lake on 30 November 1987 (TPRF 524), and another was reported from a private ranch in Medina County on 13 December 1984.

American Golden-Plover (*Pluvialis dominica*)

Very rare spring and fall migrant, with almost all records from the spring. Spring migrants have been reported from mid-March to early May. An injured individual lingered into early June at Kerrville in 1988. The only fall records for this species are from the latter half of September. Autumn migrants should be looked for between late August and mid-October.

Snowy Plover (*Charadrius alexandrinus*)

Rare migrant over western plateau, east to Kerr County, becoming very rare farther east. They are also local summer residents at Lake Amistad.

Spring migrants are found between early April and mid-May, and fall migrants are present from early August to early October. Snowy Plover nest on islands at Lake Amistad when water levels are low. There are two documented winter records from the plateau: six birds were found at Lake Buchanan on 7 December 1996 (TPRF 1415), and a single bird was at Brady Reservoir on 1 January 1997 (TPRF 1427).

Semipalmated Plover (*Charadrius semipalmatus*)

Very rare spring migrant and rare to occasional fall migrant throughout the plateau. The few records of spring migrants are all from early May, but this species should occur from early April through mid-May as a rare migrant. Fall migrants have been reported from mid-July to mid-September.

Killdeer (*Charadrius vociferus*)

Common permanent resident throughout the region. Killdeer are present in open habitats along watercourses and at stock ponds, farmlands, and open pastures. Permanent water is not required for this species to be present. They are the most common and widespread shorebird in the region.

Mountain Plover (*Charadrius montanus*)

Rare and local winter resident in Schleicher County. Lloyd (1887) reported that Mountain Plovers were abundant migrants and that some remained through the winter. All of the recent sightings of this species are from midwinter. In the Concho Valley, just to the north of Schleicher County, Mountain Plovers arrive in early September and are present until mid-April. This species has occurred on winter wheat fields and heavily grazed areas that mimic short-grass prairie in other parts of the plateau, particularly in Crockett, Sutton, and Menard Counties. There are records, including specimens, from the 1880s from the Boerne area, but no reports since that time.

FAMILY RECURVIROSTRIDAE: Stilts and Avocets

Black-necked Stilt (*Himantopus mexicanus*)

Occasional migrant and local summer resident throughout the region, although more commonly encountered in the western half of the plateau. Spring migrants occur from early April to mid-May, and fall migrants are found from mid-August to late September, occasionally lingering into October. Black-necked Stilts are irregular breeders on the plateau but regularly nest at nearby locations, such as the fish hatchery in Uvalde and the San Angelo area. A lack of habitat, or at least habitat accessible to birders, is probably the reason for the minimal number of breeding records from the region.

American Avocet (*Recurvirostra americana*)

Rare spring migrant and occasional fall migrant in the western half of the plateau, east to Kerr County. This species is apparently a rare to very rare migrant in the eastern third of the plateau. Spring migrants occur from early April to mid-May, and fall migrants can be encountered from mid-August through October. This species is a common migrant in the San Angelo region and likely occurs more regularly in the western plateau than the records would suggest.

FAMILY JACANIDAE: Jacanas

Northern Jacana (*Jacana spinosa*)

Accidental. There is one documented record of Northern Jacana for the Edwards Plateau. An adult was present at a stock tank on private property near Kerrville from 11 May to 10 June 1986 (TPRF 393). Another report came from a property owner in Real County who reported a bird walking on lily pads at a stock pond on his property from mid-October to mid-November 1979. His brief description mentioned yellow wings; unfortunately the bird was not photographed. *Review Species*

FAMILY SCOLOPACIDAE: Shorebirds and Phalaropes

Greater Yellowlegs (*Tringa melanoleuca*)

Occasional migrant and rare and local winter resident for the entire plateau. Spring migrants occur from mid-March through May. Fall migrants begin appearing in late July, becoming more common from mid-August through early November. Greater Yellowlegs have been reported throughout the winter, when almost all reports involve single individuals.

Lesser Yellowlegs (*Tringa flavipes*)

Occasional spring and uncommon fall migrant. Very rare winter visitor for the entire region. Spring migration for this species occurs from mid-March to mid-May with a peak in late April and early May. Fall migrants begin appearing in mid-July and are present through late October. Winter records of Lesser Yellowlegs are probably lingering fall migrants, rather than winter residents. Records from the plateau extend from mid-November to early January.

Solitary Sandpiper (*Tringa solitaria*)

Occasional spring and fall migrant throughout the region. Spring migrants can be found between mid-March and mid-May. Fall migrants begin appearing in mid-July and occur through early September, becoming increasingly rare through the end of October. This species has been reported in early winter on a number of occasions. These reports are hard to assess for a species that is a relatively early fall migrant. Documentation is needed for any winter sightings of this species.

Willet (*Catoptrophorus semipalmatus*)

Rare spring and fall migrant for the entire plateau. Spring migrants have been reported from late April and early May. Fall migrants have occurred from early August through mid-September. There is one winter report of this species for the plateau, a single bird at Lake Buchanan on 10 January 1985.

Spotted Sandpiper (*Actitis macularia*)

Uncommon migrant and winter resident and rare summer resident for the entire region. Spring migrants occur between late March and mid-May, and fall migrants can be expected from late July through mid-September. Winter residents are not as common as migrants, but can be found along almost any watercourse or body of water. Spotted Sandpipers are present in low numbers during most summers. Concrete evidence of nesting is lacking, but has been suspected by many observers beginning with Lacey in the 1880s. The strongest evidence of local breeding was two adults with flying young at the Kerrville Sewage Ponds on 15 June 1988.

Upland Sandpiper (*Bartramia longicauda*)

Common to abundant spring and fall migrant over the eastern plateau, becoming uncommon in the western plateau. Upland Sandpipers can be heard overhead during spring from late March through mid-May and again in the fall from mid-July to mid-September. Although this species is rather infrequently seen on the ground, its distinctive call can be heard on almost any early morning during its migration periods. When on the ground, Upland Sandpipers prefer open pastures or short-grass prairies. They are occasionally found around stock ponds or other small bodies of water.

Eskimo Curlew (*Numenius borealis*)

Probably extinct, but formerly an uncommon spring migrant through the entire region. Eskimo Curlews used short-grass prairies and heavily grazed pastures as stop-over habitat during migration. There is one specimen record for the region. Three birds were reportedly collected near Boerne in March 1880. One of those specimens, taken on 17 March 1880, is housed at the Museum of Vertebrate Zoology at the University of California at Berkeley. The peak of migration was from early March to mid-April. *Review Species*

Long-billed Curlew (*Numenius americanus*)

Occasional spring and fall migrant on the western plateau, becoming more uncommon in the eastern third of the region. Spring migrants can be expected from late March to early May, and fall migrants pass through the region from late August to early October. Long-billed Curlew is also an irregular winter visitor to the western half of the plateau, east to Kerr County. These winter visitors are mainly lingering migrants, as most of the winter records are from early November to early January. Long-billed Curlews are regular winter residents in agricultural areas along the Rio Grande south of Del Rio and may occur in winter with more regularity in southern Val Verde County.

Marbled Godwit (*Limosa fedoa*)

Casual fall migrant to at least the eastern half of the plateau. All of the records for the plateau for this species are from mid-October. This species is a rare spring and fall migrant to the east of the plateau as well as the San Angelo area and should be expected to occur with greater regularity.

Ruddy Turnstone (*Arenaria interpres*)

Accidental spring and casual fall migrant to the eastern half of the plateau. The lone spring report is of three birds at Kerrville on 9 May 1985.

Fall migrants have been reported from early September to mid-October. However, there is a midsummer report of a single individual near Johnson City on 5 July 1991. There are also two early winter reports that likely pertain to lingering migrants: a single bird at Kerrville on 20 December 1984 that was joined by a second on 28 December and another there on 7 November 1986.

Sanderling (*Calidris alba*)

Casual fall migrant to the eastern half of the plateau. Sanderlings have been reported only during the month of September. This species is a rare migrant in the San Angelo area as well as to the east of the escarpment. Spring migrants have been found primarily during late April and early May in those areas. Fall migrants occur from early August through September.

Semipalmated Sandpiper (*Calidris pusilla*)

Occasional spring and fall migrant over entire region. Spring migrants can be found between late March and mid-May. Fall migrants pass through the region between mid-August and early October. There are no documented records of this species during the winter on the plateau or elsewhere in Texas. Male Western Sandpipers (*C. mauri*) can be very similar to Semipalmated Sandpipers in appearance and are usually the cause of any confusion.

Western Sandpiper (*Calidris mauri*)

Occasional spring and uncommon fall migrant throughout the region. Western Sandpiper is also a rare early winter visitor to the entire Edwards Plateau. Spring migrants pass through the region between early March and mid-May, while fall migrants can be found between mid-July and the end of October. Western Sandpipers routinely linger through the early part of the winter on the plateau. Most of these birds have departed by mid-January.

Least Sandpiper (*Calidris minutilla*)

Common migrant and uncommon winter resident throughout the region. Least Sandpiper is the most common migrant shorebird on the Edwards Plateau. Fall migrants arrive in early July and are common through October. Spring migrants begin arriving in late March and are common through the end of May with a few lingering into June. Least

Sandpipers are present every month of the year, even though they nest in the high arctic.

White-rumped Sandpiper (*Calidris fuscicollis*)

Occasional spring and accidental fall migrant throughout the region. Spring migrants pass through the plateau from late April through early June. The only fall record for this species for the region is a specimen collected near Ingram on 8 August 1915. White-rumped Sandpipers make an elliptical migration, moving northward over the Great Plains and returning southward along the East Coast in the fall.

Baird's Sandpiper (*Calidris bairdii*)

Uncommon to locally common spring and fall migrant over the western half of the region, become less common farther east. Spring migrants can be found between mid-March and late May. Fall migrants pass through the region between late July and early October, rarely lingering into November. Baird's Sandpiper is frequently encountered, sometimes in large numbers, in the Uvalde and San Angelo areas. The general lack of stop-over habitat over the western plateau accounts for the small number of reports of this species from within the region.

Pectoral Sandpiper (*Calidris melanotos*)

Uncommon spring and fall migrant over entire region. Spring migrants arrive in mid-March and can be seen until the end of May. Fall migrants can be found between mid-July and early October, occasionally lingering into early November.

Dunlin (*Calidris alpina*)

Very rare spring and rare fall migrant throughout the region. All of the spring records for the plateau are from early May. Fall migrants have been noted from early August to late September. Dunlins regularly linger through the early winter in the Austin to San Antonio area. They have also been noted in early winter from as far north as White River Lake, Crosby County, and as far west as Imperial Reservoir, Pecos County. Dunlins have not been found on the plateau during this period, but it seems likely that they do occur and should be expected in the early winter.

Stilt Sandpiper (*Calidris himantopus*)

Rare spring and occasional fall migrant through the region. Spring migrants have been found between mid-April and the end of May. Fall migrants occur on the plateau between mid-July and mid-October, with a peak from mid-August to early September.

Buff-breasted Sandpiper (*Tryngites subruficollis*)

Casual spring and fall migrant for entire region. Spring migrants occur on the plateau between mid-April and mid-May. Fall migrants have been reported between mid-August and mid-September. Buff-breasted Sandpipers are grassland species and are probably more common than they have been reported, particularly in the fall. Although often found near water, this bird also uses heavily grazed pastures and short-grass prairie as stop-over habitat during migration.

Short-billed Dowitcher (*Limnodromus griseus*)

Casual spring migrant across at least the eastern half of the plateau. The only reports of this species from the Edwards Plateau are from the Kerrville Sewage Ponds, where up to eight were present from 27 to 28 March 1987. Short-billed Dowitchers are regular spring and fall migrants east of the escarpment in the Austin to San Antonio area and have undoubtedly been overlooked at other locations on the eastern plateau. Although this species has not been reported from the western plateau, one bird was collected at San Angelo on 25 September 1976, and the species should be expected to occur within the region. Spring migrants should pass through the region between late March and mid-May. During fall migration, Short-billed Dowitchers should occur between late July and late October.

Long-billed Dowitcher (*Limnodromus scolopaceus*)

Occasional spring and fall migrant throughout the region. Spring migrants have been noted between mid-April and the end of May. Fall migrants can be found from mid-July through October. As with several other species of shorebirds, Long-billed Dowitchers occasionally linger through the early winter. Most of these birds disperse by the middle of January, but they overwinter on rare occasions.

Common Snipe (*Gallinago gallinago*)

Uncommon migrant and winter resident throughout the plateau. Common Snipe arrive on the plateau in the fall by late September and remain through April. Snipe can be found in moist habitats and are not necessarily found only near permanent bodies of water. Seeps and springs that drain into grassy areas provide perfect habitat for this bird. The Common Snipe is composed of two distinctive populations that are sometimes considered separate species, with the New World populations referred to as Wilson's Snipe (*G. delicata*). Recent genetic studies do not show significant differences between the two groups.

American Woodcock (*Scolopax minor*)

Uncommon winter resident on the eastern plateau, west to eastern Kerr County. Wintering birds first arrive in late October and remain until late February or early March, although one remained at Balcones Canyonlands National Wildlife Refuge until at least 10 May 1997. Woodcocks are very rare to casual winter visitors on the western plateau. The westernmost documented record for the plateau was one at Devils River State Natural Area in Val Verde County, found on 22 February 1996. On the eastern plateau, they are most often detected in late January and February, when the males begin to display prior to departing for the breeding grounds. Recent studies have determined that some portion of the woodcock population may nest during this display period. The only confirmed breeding record for the plateau is provided by a nest discovered on 28 January 1888 in western Comal County.

Wilson's Phalarope (*Phalaropus tricolor*)

Uncommon spring and fall migrant throughout the region. Spring migrants occur between late March and late May. Fall migrants begin arriving in mid-July and can be found through mid-October. There are also two early winter reports of this species: three at Canyon Lake on 18 November 1982 and one at Lake Buchanan on 16 December 1982.

FAMILY LARIDAE: Jaegers, Gulls, and Terns

Pomarine Jaeger (*Stercorarius pomarinus*)

Accidental. There is one record of this species for the Edwards Plateau. A light morph subadult was found dead at Lake Travis following Hurricane Carla on 13 September 1961. The specimen is housed in the Texas Cooperative Wildlife Collection at Texas A&M University. The only other report of a jaeger from the region was one at Lake Buchanan on

3 October 1993. The bird was tentatively identified as a Parasitic Jaeger (*S. parasiticus*) by the observers; however, no documentation is available from which to make a positive identification.

Laughing Gull (*Larus atricilla*)

This species has established a small breeding colony on Lake Amistad. The first evidence of nesting was discovered on 1 June 1995, when two small colonies with active nests were found on small islands when the lake was low (TPRF 1215). This represented the first inland breeding record for the state. The breeding colony persists, and about 25 adults were present during the summer of 1999. For the region, away from Lake Amistad, Laughing Gull is an accidental visitor primarily between mid-July and early October.

Franklin's Gull (*Larus pipixcan*)

Common spring migrant and rare fall migrant throughout the plateau. Franklin's Gulls are also early winter visitors in the region. Spring migrants occur on the plateau between early April and late May, with the majority of the birds being seen in late April and early May. Fall migrants begin to appear in late September, with a peak in migration during the first two weeks of October. Migrant birds routinely linger on the larger reservoirs to early January.

Bonaparte's Gull (*Larus philadelphia*)

Uncommon migrant and winter resident on the large reservoirs in the region. Fall migrants arrive in early November and most depart by the end of February. This small and graceful gull can occasionally be found in flocks, sometimes containing over 100 individuals, on these reservoirs. The Bonaparte's Gull molts into adult plumage during the second fall. First-winter and adult plumaged birds are equally common on the plateau.

Ring-billed Gull (*Larus delawarensis*)

Common migrant and winter resident on the large reservoirs in the region. Fall migrants can be found after mid-October with wintering birds remaining until early April, although most depart by the end of March. Ring-billed Gulls are more often found at the smaller bodies of water on the plateau than are other species of gulls.

Herring Gull (*Larus argentatus*)

Uncommon to rare winter resident on the large reservoirs of the region. Herring Gulls are present from early December to mid-February. Most of the wintering birds in the region are immature, though adults are present. Herring Gulls are usually outnumbered by the much more common Ring-billed Gull.

Black-legged Kittiwake (*Rissa tridactyla*)

Accidental. Black-legged Kittiwake has been documented three times from the region. The first documented record of this species for Texas was an immature bird discovered at a city park in north-central San Antonio on 30 December 1956. The bird was subsequently found dead on 1 January 1957. The specimen is housed at the Witte Museum in San Antonio. The second record from the plateau was an adult on Lake Buchanan on 24 January 1987 (TPRF 480). There are brief, but compelling, details of a second-winter bird from an Upper Guadalupe River Authority Lake in Kerr County from 18 October 1990. The details of this sighting were not submitted to the TBRC before this species was removed from the review list on 20 November 1999.

Sabine's Gull (*Xema sabini*)

Accidental. There is only one record of this species from the Edwards Plateau. An immature Sabine's Gull was documented at Lake Buchanan on 25 September 1988 (TBRC 1988-260). This species is an annual fall migrant in Texas. There are over 50 accepted records for the state, and all but two, one in May and one in July, pertain to fall migrants. There is a high probability that Sabine's Gulls will occur again within the region, and they should be looked for from early September through early November. This species is no longer included on the TBRC's review list.

Caspian Tern (*Sterna caspia*)

Very rare spring and fall migrant primarily over the eastern Edwards Plateau. Spring migrants have been noted from late February through late May. Fall migrants have been reported from mid-September through October. There is only one documented record from Lake Amistad, a single bird photographed on 28 May 1994 (TPRF 1531), although the species probably occurs there more frequently.

Forster's Tern (*Sterna forsteri*)

Uncommon migrant and winter resident over the entire plateau. Fall migrants can be found from early August through October. Spring migrants pass over the plateau between late February and mid-May. Most observations of this tern are from the large reservoirs of the plateau. Forster's Terns nested on islands in Lake Amistad during 1999, providing the first nesting record for the region. The only other known inland nesting location in the state is at Choke Canyon Reservoir in McMullen County.

Least Tern (*Sterna antillarum*)

Uncommon summer resident at Lake Amistad; very rare visitor to the remainder of the region. At Lake Amistad, 15 to 20 pairs of the Federally Endangered Interior Least Tern were discovered nesting on islands in the lake in 1995. Over 100 Least Terns were present during a survey of those islands in June 1999. Individuals in this colony regularly linger through the fall into early winter. Elsewhere in the region, Least Terns are rare visitors between April and December. At this time, there is no discernible pattern to the occurrences. Least Terns are also summer residents on the reservoirs surrounding San Angelo.

Sooty Tern (*Sterna fuscata*)

Accidental. There is one record of this species from the region. An adult Sooty Tern was discovered in a garage in west Austin on 13 September 1961 following Hurricane Carla. The emaciated bird was taken to a wildlife rehabilitater, but died the following day. The specimen was apparently not saved. On the same day, another Sooty Tern was found at Mitchell Lake in southeastern Bexar County.

Black Tern (*Chlidonias niger*)

Occasional spring and fall migrant throughout the region. Spring migrants are present from the end of April through May with the majority of birds passing through in the latter half of May. Fall migrants appear from mid-July through the end of September. There is a definite peak in the number of fall migrants during August and early September.

FAMILY COLUMBIDAE: Pigeons and Doves

Rock Dove (*Columba livia*)

Common permanent resident in urban areas throughout the region. In rural areas, particularly in the western half of the plateau, this species is seldom encountered, even though they are present in every town.

Band-tailed Pigeon (*Columba fasciata*)

Accidental. There are two recent records of this species from the region. Two individuals were at Kickapoo Cavern State Park on 29 December 1989 (TPRF 822), providing the first plateau record since 1915. The second was an individual found dead near Concan, Uvalde County, on 5 November 1999 (TPRF 1761). There is one other historical record of this species from the region: one was collected in northern Uvalde County on 3 December 1915. Although just off the plateau, another Band-tailed was collected at Fort Clark on 18 December 1897.

Eurasian Collared-Dove (*Streptopelia decaocto*)

This non-native dove is rapidly colonizing the eastern half of Texas. During the late 1970s, this bird colonized Florida from the Bahamas, where it had originally been introduced. By the mid-1990s, this bird had expanded over much of the southeastern United States and had reached Texas. Currently, there is a small colony in Johnson City, and collared-doves have been reported in western Travis, Burnet, Kinney, Menard, Uvalde, and Val Verde Counties. It is likely that other colonies are established within the region. This species will undoubtedly become a common resident in urban areas throughout the state over the next 10 to 15 years.

White-winged Dove (*Zenaida asiatica*)

Common to abundant permanent resident in urban areas throughout the region. White-winged Doves were first documented on the Edwards Plateau in the early 1900s. One was collected at Kerrville on 25 November 1910. During the 1990s, White-winged Doves underwent an amazing northward range expansion. Surveys conducted by Texas Parks and Wildlife in 1999 determined that the largest population in the state was in urban San Antonio with an estimated 400,000 individuals. Away from urban areas, they are primarily an uncommon spring migrant and summer resident, but each year more appear to overwinter

DRAWING 4. *White-winged Dove*

away from towns. As populations continue to increase, this species may become a common permanent resident throughout the plateau.

Mourning Dove (*Zenaida macroura*)

Abundant permanent resident throughout the region. Mourning Doves are considered to be the most abundant and widely distributed game bird in North America. They are certainly one of the most commonly found birds on the plateau. Large flocks of Mourning Doves can be encountered on the plateau, especially during migration, when large numbers of birds from the Great Plains pass through Texas on their way to wintering grounds in Mexico.

Passenger Pigeon (*Ectopistes migratorius*)

Extinct. Passenger Pigeons were formerly an uncommon to common migrant and winter resident through much of the region. This species was generally present in Texas from mid-September to early March (Oberholser 1974). The timing of occurrence on the plateau was likely very similar, but specific information from the region is generally lacking. Oberholser was particularly interested in the distribution of this species in Texas. A summary of the information he gathered is presented in *The Bird Life of Texas*. Stanley Casto has recently begun researching the occurrence of this species within the state and has uncovered many county records, including some from the plateau, that were unknown to Oberholser. Passenger Pigeons have been reported from 14 Edwards Plateau counties, including Bandera, Bexar, Burnet, Comal, Edwards, Gillespie, Kendall, Kerr, Llano, Mason, Real, San Saba, Travis, and Uvalde. There were apparently major invasions of Passenger Pigeons into Texas, including the Edwards Plateau, during the winters of 1872–1873 and 1881–1882 (S. Casto pers. comm.). During the winter of 1881–1882, many accounts were published in local newspapers of the enormous flocks of Passenger Pigeons present around Austin. Lloyd (1887) reported an "immense" roost in Frio Canyon, Real County, on 1 February 1882. Another very large roost during that winter was along Pigeon Roost Creek in southwestern Bandera County (S. Casto pers. comm.). The last report from the plateau was from western Travis County in October or November 1885.

Inca Dove (*Columbina inca*)

Uncommon to common permanent resident throughout the region. This species, like the White-winged Dove, has expanded its range northward in recent decades. Inca Doves have shown an affinity for urban areas where they are commonly encountered in city parks and neighborhoods. Away from towns, Inca Doves prefer open habitats, such as shrublands and savannas.

Common Ground-Dove (*Columbina passerina*)

Occasional to locally uncommon breeding species in the southern part of the Edwards Plateau. The breeding range of this species on the plateau extends from Val Verde and southern Crockett Counties in the west to Bexar and Comal Counties in the east. They prefer open shrublands and other arid habitats and are rarely, if ever, found in woodlands. This species is a casual visitor throughout the remainder of the plateau, primarily in fall and early winter. In the spring of 1999, eight to 10 territorial males were found at the Balcones Canyonlands National Wildlife Refuge; whether these birds reflect a northward expansion of the breeding range or a temporary occupation due to climatic conditions is unknown.

White-tipped Dove (*Leptotila verreauxi*)

Casual visitor during the spring and fall to southern Val Verde County, accidental elsewhere. The first record for the county, and region, was one photographed near the Devils River, close to what is now the Devils River State Natural Area, on 17 October 1979 (TPRF 220). In recent years, this species has been found irregularly in the Del Rio area. The range of White-tipped Doves has apparently been slowly expanding northward, at least in the western half of the South Texas Plains. They were first encountered in LaSalle County in 1988 and have been slowly increasing in numbers since. The recent observations near Del Rio may reflect that expansion, and if so, they may occur at other seasons. The only other documented record for the region was one visiting a bird bath at Canyon Lake, Comal County, from 7 to 17 September 2000.

FAMILY PSITTACIDAE: Parrots and Parakeets

Monk Parakeet (*Myiopsitta monachus*)

Introduced and established in Austin. A well-established population of this southern South American parakeet is present along Town Lake and is slowly spreading into other parts of town. This species builds large stick nests and is fond of light stands at softball fields and other large metal structures. The city of Austin has begun removing the large nests, and this may either curtail the population or just move them away from the river. What are probably local escapees have been reported in other towns in the region. A small colony has become established in Temple, Bell County, and so there is always the potential of other colonies getting started.

FAMILY CUCULIDAE: Cuckoos

Black-billed Cuckoo (*Coccyzus erythropthalmus*)

Rare spring migrant over the eastern one-third of the plateau; accidental farther west. Records of spring migrants range from 13 April to 3 June, with all but two falling between 6 and 25 May. Banding records from the Driftwood Banding Station suggest that this species occurs more regularly than has been reported. Almost half of the records for the plateau have come from that banding station. The only record for this species from the western two-thirds of the plateau was a single bird at Junction on 11 May 1990. This species has been recorded only once during fall migration, a single bird was found at Emma Long Metropolitan Park, Travis County, in early October 1976.

Yellow-billed Cuckoo (*Coccyzus americanus*)

Common migrant and summer resident throughout the region. Spring migrants typically arrive on the plateau during the last week of April, although they have been reported as early as 17 April. They are a common summer resident through August, becoming uncommon during September and very rare to mid-October. Yellow-billed Cuckoos are found in woodland habitats ranging from near closed-canopy forests to savannas. In the western third of the plateau where the climate is arid, this species is most often associated with riparian corridors and mesic canyons where more mature and diverse woodlands are found.

Greater Roadrunner (*Geococcyx californianus*)

Common permanent resident throughout the entire plateau. Although roadrunners are often associated with arid environments, they are found in open habitats throughout the region. The only habitat type available on the plateau that roadrunners do not use is closed-canopy forest. In the Balcones Canyonlands subregion, much of the landscape has been modified, and roadrunners are common.

Groove-billed Ani (*Crotophaga sulcirostris*)

Uncommon and local summer resident along the Rio Grande in southern Val Verde County. They arrive in late April and usually are present into late September. Occasionally, birds linger into early October and on very rare occasions have remained through early winter. Groove-billed Anis are regularly encountered elsewhere on the plateau, but are accidental for any particular area. Most of the records of Groove-billed Ani away from the breeding population pertain to postbreeding wanderers, as these records generally fall between late July and early October. There are several spring and early summer records for the southern and western plateau. They have been found as far northeast as Llano County, where one was present on 9 May 2000.

FAMILY TYTONIDAE: Barn Owls

Barn Owl (*Tyto alba*)

Rare and local resident throughout the region. The status of this species is hard to assess. Where the birds are known to occur, they are regular nesters, but those known locations are few. Barn Owls prefer open habitats and are rarely found in heavy woodlands or forests. They are also cavity nesters that have adapted their nesting habits to take advantage of buildings and other man-made structures. Barn Owls have been discovered using deer hunter's stands for nesting sites. Unfortunately, these blinds are usually not available for long-term occupation by the owls.

FAMILY STRIGIDAE: Typical Owls

Flammulated Owl (*Otus flammeolus*)

Accidental. Flammulated Owls have been discovered twice within the region: one was reported from Crockett County on 13 November 1986, and the other was photographed at Devils River State Natural Area in Val Verde County on 16 April 1994 (TPRF 1200). This small western owl is highly migratory and has been repeatedly mist-netted along the front range of the Rocky Mountains in New Mexico. It seems likely that they are a very rare to casual migrant through the extreme western edge of the region. The spring migration period for the species is from late March to early May, while the fall migration period is from late September through mid-November.

Eastern Screech-Owl (*Otus asio*)

Common resident throughout the Balcones Canyonlands and Llano Uplift. Uncommon and more localized throughout the remainder of the region. Eastern Screech-Owls are found in a variety of habitats, including urban neighborhoods, open woodlands, and scattered oak mottes in savannas and open shrublands. In the more arid parts of the plateau, such as the Live Oak–Mesquite Savannas area of the northern plateau and Val Verde County, they are typically found only along riparian corridors. Gray is the dominant color morph on the plateau, with red-morph birds very rarely found.

Western Screech-Owl (*Otus kennicottii*)

Uncommon resident in the Live Oak–Mesquite Savannas region of the plateau. Western Screech-Owls have been found as far east as western Kerr County. They appear to be rare visitors south to northwestern Uvalde and northern Kinney Counties. Western Screech-Owls are the dominant screech-owl in upland habitats within their range. They are found in mesquite and live oak savannas, while Eastern Screech-Owls are more restricted to riparian corridors and other mesic habitats.

Great Horned Owl (*Bubo virginianus*)

Common resident throughout the region. Great Horned Owls can be found almost anywhere within the region. They are the most adaptable owl in terms of habitat preference in North America. On the Edwards Plateau, they can be found in habitats ranging from the open woodlands of the Balcones Canyonlands to the arid canyons of the Devils and Pecos River drainages. The only habitats within the region where they are not routinely found are closed-canopy forests.

Elf Owl (*Micrathene whitneyi*)

Uncommon and local summer resident in Val Verde County. They are also a very low density summer resident in Crockett, Kinney, Edwards, Sutton, and western Uvalde Counties. Elf Owls have been mist-netted in Tom Green County as well and, therefore, may also occur in Schleicher County. They typically are first detected in early April and likely remain through September. The presence of Elf Owl on the Edwards Plateau was unknown until the late 1980s, when territorial birds were located in several locations, including Devils River State Natural Area, Kickapoo Cavern State Park, near Montell (Uvalde County), and near Sonora. On the Edwards Plateau, Elf Owls are found in open woodlands and savannas and frequently occupy old woodpecker holes in utility poles.

Burrowing Owl (*Athene cunicularia*)

Occasional migrant and winter resident in the Live Oak–Mesquite Savannas region of the plateau; very rarely recorded elsewhere in the region. Fall migrants usually pass through the area between mid-September and mid-October with spring migrants present from early March to mid-April. Burrowing Owl is also a rare summer resident in Schleicher and Crockett Counties, and possibly in nearby counties as well. The demise of the Black-tailed Prairie Dog (*Cynomys ludovicianus*) in the northwestern plateau has also likely had a negative impact on the numbers of Burrowing Owls in that area.

Barred Owl (*Strix varia*)

This eastern owl reaches the western extreme of its Texas range on the Edwards Plateau, extending as far west as Val Verde County. It is an

DRAWING 5. *Barred Owl*

occasional and local resident in riparian zones throughout much of the plateau. They are absent from the northwestern corner of the region in Crockett, Schleicher, and Sutton Counties. Barred Owls are primarily found in the remaining gallery forests along the major rivers that drain the region. Interestingly, they are a major predator of screech-owls and can sometimes be attracted to a screech-owl call.

Long-eared Owl (*Asio otus*)

Casual winter visitor throughout the region. There are very few records of Long-eared Owl from the plateau. However, the reclusive habits of this species may account for the lack of sightings. Records from the plateau are from early November to early April. Long-eared Owls were at least formerly a very rare breeding species in the region. An active nest containing eggs was discovered in Comal County on 28 March 1888, and a pair was collected near Ingram on 13 March 1915.

Short-eared Owl (*Asio flammeus*)

Rare winter resident of the entire region. Wintering individuals typically arrive in early November and remain through March. Late spring migrants have been found as late as early May. Short-eared Owls require areas of tall grass for roosting and hunting. This habitat is in short supply on the Edwards Plateau, where most pastures and grasslands are heavily grazed. Migrant birds are occasionally found in road right-of-ways and overgrown fence lines, but these areas do not provide the necessary habitat for wintering birds.

FAMILY CAPRIMULGIDAE: Nightjars

Lesser Nighthawk (*Chordeiles acutipennis*)

Rare and irregular wanderer over the western and southern plateau from spring through fall. This species is an uncommon summer resident in the open shrublands along the floodplain of the Nueces River in western Uvalde County. Lesser Nighthawks have been reported between early April and late September; however, no evidence of nesting has been discovered away from Uvalde County. In most cases, the birds involved were found only on a single occasion and did not appear to remain in the area. They have been reported as far east as Kerr, Kendall, and Bexar Counties. They are common to abundant summer residents just south of the escarpment from Val Verde County east to Gonzales County.

Common Nighthawk (*Chordeiles minor*)

Abundant migrant and summer resident throughout the region. Spring migrants arrive on the plateau in late April, but have been recorded as early as 12 April. Summer residents and fall migrants have usually departed by mid-September with a few individuals lingering through October. On rare occasions, Common Nighthawks may linger into early winter. Common Nighthawks are found in open habitats, including urban areas, throughout the plateau. They are known for nesting on gravel-covered, flat-topped roofs in urban areas.

Common Poorwill (*Phalaenoptilus nuttallii*)

Common summer resident throughout the region and occasional winter resident on the southern half of the plateau. This species inhabits dry hillsides and open shrublands in the eastern plateau and is widespread in the more arid western part of the region. Poorwills arrive on the plateau in late February and early March and depart by the end of October. In the southwestern portion of the plateau, northeast to Kimble County, this species is a regular winter resident and can be heard on most warm nights.

Chuck-will's-widow (*Caprimulgus carolinensis*)

Common summer resident in the Balcones Canyonlands west to Kinney and Edwards Counties and very locally in Val Verde County. They are rare migrants in the remainder of the region. Chuck-will's-widows arrive on the plateau in mid-April and are common through July. They probably remain through early September but are rarely reported after they stop calling. Chuck-will's-widows are found primarily in dense woodlands and forests, but often use more open woodlands along the western edge of their range on the plateau. In Val Verde County, they are restricted to riparian corridors.

Whip-poor-will (*Caprimulgus vociferus*)

Occasional spring and fall migrant over the eastern half of the plateau; rare in the western half. Spring migrants have been reported from late March through early May. Fall migrants have been found from late August through September. Whip-poor-wills have been detected as far west as the Devils River drainage in central Val Verde County. There are two vocally distinct populations of this species in Texas that may represent separate species. The eastern birds, *C. v. vociferus,* are the migrants found on the eastern plateau. The western birds, *C. v. arizonae*, nest in the mountains of the Trans-Pecos north through central New Mexico. The migrants detected in Val Verde County could belong to either subspecies, but are likely from the eastern subspecies.

FAMILY APODIDAE: Swifts

Chimney Swift (*Chaetura pelagica*)

Abundant to common summer resident in urban areas and uncommon to occasional in the remainder of the region. Spring migrants begin arriving on the plateau in mid-March with the majority of the summering population arriving during April. This species congregates in large roosts in late summer, often numbering in the several hundreds to a few thousand at favored sites. Fall migrants begin departing in late September, becoming increasingly uncommon through October. Chimney Swifts are declining throughout their range. The availability of suitable nesting locations is a primary factor in this decline, as increasingly, chimneys are being covered to exclude these birds.

White-throated Swift (*Aeronautes saxatalis*)

Rare winter resident to the Devils River drainage in Val Verde County. This species has been reported between mid-October and early April at this location. White-throated Swifts should be looked for at other seasons. They are permanent residents just to the west along the Pecos River, including at Seminole Canyon State Historical Park. White-throated Swift is an accidental fall migrant elsewhere in the region, with reports from Austin, San Antonio, and Brady.

FAMILY TROCHILIDAE: Hummingbirds

Green Violet-ear (*Colibri thalassinus*)

Casual late spring and summer visitor to the southeastern quarter of the plateau. There are 15 documented records for the plateau with the farthest west records from Kerr County. All of the records from the region fall between 14 May and 18 September. This tropical hummingbird is documented almost annually somewhere in Texas. The first documented record for the United States was in 1961 at Santa Ana National Wildlife

Refuge in the Lower Rio Grande Valley. It now appears that one may have been in northwestern Bexar County in May 1959 (see Magnificent Hummingbird account in the Species of Uncertain Occurrence section of this book). *Review Species*

Broad-billed Hummingbird (*Cynanthus latirostris*)

Accidental. There are four documented records from the plateau for this western hummingbird. Two of the records are from Val Verde County, with males at Del Rio from 9 to 10 April 1990 (TBRC 1990-90) and Dolan Falls Preserve on 18 April 1993 (TBRC 1994-166). There is also one record from Kinney County, a female on 24 July 1999 (TBRC 1999-83). The other record for the region was a female near Buchanan Dam that first appeared between 22 November 1993 and 7 April 1994 (TBRC 1993-154). Amazingly, it returned on 2 October 1994 and remained for 17 months before departing on 7 April 1996. *Review Species*

White-eared Hummingbird (*Hylocharis leucotis*)

Accidental. This species has been documented from the plateau once. An adult male was at Fredericksburg, Gillespie County, from 31 July to 4 August 2000. It was photographed during its stay, providing a very unexpected record for the region. The White-eared Hummingbird is extremely rare in Texas with most of the previous records coming from the mountains in the Trans-Pecos. *Review Species*

Buff-bellied Hummingbird (*Amazilia yucatanensis*)

Accidental. There are four records from the southeastern part of the Edwards Plateau. This species has been documented twice at Helotes, Bexar County, with single individuals present from 19 to 24 September 1990 and on 1 June 1997. The other two records from the plateau also involved single individuals: one in northwest Austin on 21 December 1990, and the other near Bulverde, Comal County, on 30 December 1998. Although it was just off the plateau, a Buff-bellied Hummingbird was photographed in Uvalde from 2 to 4 October 1996.

Violet-crowned Hummingbird (*Amazilia violiceps*)

Accidental. There is one record of this species for the Edwards Plateau. A Violet-crowned Hummingbird was photographed at Lake Amistad near the Rough Canyon Recreational Area on 31 October 1996 (TBRC 1996-145). This represented the third record for Texas and, at the time, was the easternmost record for the species in the United States. Since that time, however, this species has been documented even farther east in the state. *Review Species*

Blue-throated Hummingbird (*Lampornis clemenciae*)

Accidental. There are four documented records from the Edwards Plateau. A female was found on 10 April 1988 at Lost Maples State Natural Area, where it remained until 2 May when it was joined by a male. Another male was at Lost Maples State Natural Area from 20 July to 5 November 1996 (TPRF 1421). The final two records were females: one was in northwestern San Antonio on 7 April 2000, and another was at Junction, Kimble County, on 5 July 2000. This species has been reported, without supporting details, from the plateau on at least three other occasions.

Lucifer Hummingbird (*Calothorax lucifer*)

Casual fall visitor; accidental during late spring to early summer on the Edwards Plateau. This species has been documented five times between early August and mid-October. A male Lucifer Hummingbird was photographed near Kyle, Hays County, on 5 September 1993 (TPRF 1194), providing the first photographically documented record away from the Trans-Pecos in Texas. This species also has been reported, with details, from the Prade Ranch, Real County, on 12 September 1962; Wimberley, Hays County, on 4 October 1962; Del Rio from 3 to 5 August 1993; and San Antonio on 21 October 1999. There are single well-documented records from the spring and early summer. An adult male was present at the Tierra Linda Ranch, southwestern Gillespie County, from 14 to 23 May 2000 (TPRF 1763), and an immature male was at San Antonio from 26 June to 1 July 1995.

Ruby-throated Hummingbird (*Archilochus colubris*)

Occasional spring and uncommon fall migrant except in the eastern tier of counties, where it is a common migrant. Spring migrants pass through the region from late March through mid-May. Fall migrants can be found between early August and late October, with the majority passing through during September, after most Black-chinned Hummingbirds (*A. alexandri*) have departed. Ruby-throated Hummingbirds are a locally common breeding species to the east of the escarpment. They may be a rare, but overlooked, nester along the escarpment from Travis County south to northeastern Bexar County.

DRAWING 6. *Black-chinned Hummingbird*

Black-chinned Hummingbird (*Archilochus alexandri*)

Abundant migrant and summer resident throughout the region. Spring migrants first appear in early March and are abundant by early April. The summer population begins to migrate in early August, and most have departed by mid-September. Black-chinned Hummingbirds are by far the most common hummingbird in the region. This species is a casual winter visitor on the eastern plateau; all winter records are at hummingbird feeders.

Anna's Hummingbird (*Calypte anna*)

Casual with records from midsummer through early winter. Most records of Anna's Hummingbird from the plateau are between late September and early November. On three occasions, individuals lingered at feeders into the winter. Perhaps the most interesting record from the plateau was of an immature male and a female coming to feeders near Kerrville from 17 June to 18 September 1985. During this period, pink feathers continued to fill in the gorget and crown of the male, until it was almost complete. Although just out of the region, another summer record was provided by a male in Irion County from 10 to 12 June 1995.

Costa's Hummingbird (*Calypte costae*)

Accidental. There is a single record of this desert hummingbird in the region. The first documented record for Texas was of a male near San Marcos from 6 February to 2 March 1974 (TPRF 56). There are now six documented records for the state. *Review Species*

Calliope Hummingbird (*Stellula calliope*)

Very rare fall migrant throughout the region. Adult males are the first to migrate, passing through the region in late July. Female-plumaged individuals, the majority of which are probably hatch-year birds, have been recorded from mid-August through early November. On very rare occasions, individuals have lingered through the winter at feeders. This species is not expected in Texas during the spring, but there is one report of a male in Kerr County on 14 April 1987. Calliope Hummingbirds have been reported most often in the eastern half of the plateau. One in Menard from 17 to 27 July 1995 provided one of the few records from the western plateau. There are at least three records, including one specimen, from the San Angelo region as well. The small number of reports from the western plateau is likely due to a lack of observers present. Calliope Hummingbird probably occurs annually through the western third of the region.

Broad-tailed Hummingbird (*Selasphorus platycercus*)

Rare spring and occasional fall migrant over the entire plateau. Spring migrants have been reported between late March and late May, with almost all of the records from the first half of April. Fall migrants have been reported between late July and early November. On at least four occasions, fall migrants have lingered through the winter at feeders, two of which were in Austin suburbs. There are two summer reports of this species from the plateau. A male was photographed while visiting feeders at Kickapoo Cavern State Park from 14 to 16 June 1988. The other is a report of a successful nest at Lost Maples State Natural Area in 1960; however, there is no supporting documentation.

Rufous Hummingbird (*Selasphorus rufus*)

Uncommon fall migrant over the western plateau; less common in the eastern half. Fall migrants begin to appear in late July and early August and continue to pass through the area until early October. Rufous Hummingbirds have lingered through the winter at feeders. Wintering Rufous Hummingbirds are reported regularly along the Texas Coast and occasionally below the escarpment in the Austin and San Antonio areas. Overwintering is a rare occurrence on the plateau, presumably because of the harsher climatic conditions. There is one report of a spring migrant from Lake Buchanan on 7 April 2000. This bird was probably a lingering bird that wintered locally, since Rufous Hummingbirds migrate up the West Coast of North America during spring.

Allen's Hummingbird (*Selasphorus sasin*)

Accidental. This species has been documented from the region three times. An adult male was at Helotes, Bexar County, from 6 November to 20 December 1987, and an immature male was at Kerrville on 7 August 2000. In both cases, the birds were captured and measured in order to confirm the identification. Documenting the occurrence of Allen's Hummingbird requires examining retrix 2 and measuring retrix 5 (the outermost tail feather) to eliminate "green-backed" Rufous Hummingbirds (see Stiles 1972, McKenzie and Robbins 1999). The third record was a fully-gorgeted adult male in San Antonio from 26 July 1996 to 27 February 1997 and returning 3 August 1997 to 22 February 1998 (TBRC 1996-114). Another adult male was present in San Antonio from September 1977 to 21 February 1978 (TPRF 129), but critical examination of the photographs has not led to an undisputed identification. Although this bird is very likely an Allen's Hummingbird, it was not captured and therefore does not represent a documented record for the state. *Review Species*

FAMILY ALCEDINIDAE: Kingfishers

Ringed Kingfisher (*Ceryle torquata*)

Rare visitor to the southern half of the Edwards Plateau. They are an uncommon permanent resident along the Rio Grande below Lake Amistad in Val Verde County. They may also be rare permanent residents along the Nueces River in Uvalde County and the Guadalupe River in Kerr and Kendall Counties. Ringed Kingfishers have been found with increasing regularity along the major river systems on the plateau during the past 15 years. The majority of sightings are between mid-September and late April. There are, however, sightings from all months. There has been no evidence of nesting away from the Rio Grande.

Belted Kingfisher (*Ceryle alcyon*)

Uncommon migrant and winter resident throughout the region. Belted Kingfishers are occasional to rare summer residents. Fall migrants arrive on the plateau in early October and remain until mid-April. Belted Kingfishers nest in burrows along secluded stretches of rivers and larger creeks.

Green Kingfisher (*Chloroceryle americana*)

Locally uncommon permanent resident in the southern half of the Edwards Plateau. Green Kingfishers are rare as far north as Menard and San Saba Counties. They are typically found along clear-running creeks and streams, but can be seen along major rivers, such as the Guadalupe and Rio Grande. Populations appear to fluctuate according to the severity of the winter. After particularly cold winters, the northernmost populations may disappear.

FAMILY PICIDAE: Woodpeckers

Lewis's Woodpecker (*Melanerpes lewis*)

Accidental. There are three documented records from the Edwards Plateau. Two Lewis's Woodpeckers were at separate locations in the Kerrville area during the winter of 1987–1988. The first was present from 1 December to 26 April (TPRF 605), and the other, from 10 December to 26 March (TPRF 693). The third record pertains to one in Mason County from 10 to 14 March 1998 (TBRC 1998-103). Although these are the only records from the plateau, there are many records from the surrounding area, and it should be expected to occur again. This species has been documented twice at Fort Clark, in central Kinney County. The first documented record for Texas was a specimen taken there on 8 January 1898, and two were present at the same location from 25 December 1987 to 25 April 1988. There have been 12 reports of this species, four of which are documented, from Midland. There are also two documented records from San Angelo. *Review Species*

Red-headed Woodpecker (*Melanerpes erythrocephalus*)

Casual winter visitor, primarily to the eastern half of the plateau. This species has been reported throughout the plateau, but most frequently in the eastern third. During "invasion" years, Red-headed Woodpeckers

can be found in gallery forests and urban areas. These irregular incursions onto the plateau rarely involve large numbers of birds and often
coincide with incursions of Blue Jays. In recent decades, the largest
invasion year was the winter of 1980–1981. During that winter, they
were commonly encountered as far west as Kerrville and were present
in smaller numbers west to Val Verde County. When present, they have
been found between mid-October and mid-April.

Acorn Woodpecker (*Melanerpes formicivorus*)

Formerly an uncommon and local permanent resident in southwestern
Kerr County. Since 1985 the number of sightings of this species has
dropped dramatically. The current status of this disjunct population is
unknown. Most recent sightings have been along State Highway 39
between Hunt and the Real County line. Lacey (1911) considered this
species to be fairly common in the uplands along the divide between the
Guadalupe and Medina Rivers.

Golden-fronted Woodpecker (*Melanerpes aurifrons*)

Common permanent resident throughout the region. Golden-fronted
Woodpeckers are found in arid to semiarid upland habitats, including live oak and mesquite savannas. They can also be found in open
woodlands that have been maintained by human disturbance. Golden-
fronteds are occasionally found in open riparian woodlands that border
more typical habitat.

Red-bellied Woodpecker (*Melanerpes carolinus*)

Rare resident along the Colorado River drainage as far west as Colorado
Bend State Park. Very rare winter and spring visitor to the eastern third
of the plateau; accidental farther west. Red-bellied Woodpeckers are
found in the gallery forests along major waterways. These riparian corridors are typical of the mesic habitats this species frequents throughout the remainder of its range to the east. Although out-of-range birds
can be found in almost any habitat, this species is most often found in
mature forests on the plateau.

Yellow-bellied Sapsucker (*Sphyrapicus varius*)

Uncommon to locally common winter resident throughout the region.
This species arrives on the plateau in mid-October and typically remains through March. Individuals have been known to linger well into

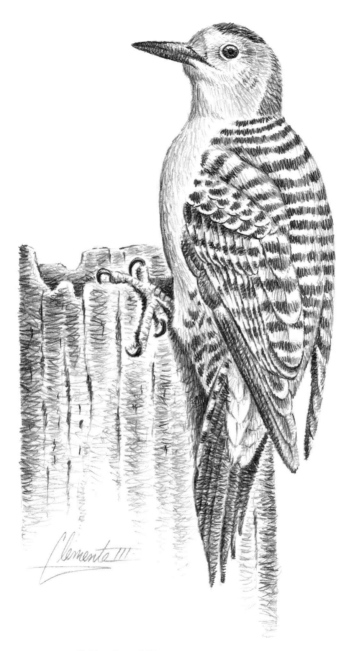

DRAWING 7. *Golden-fronted Woodpecker*

April. They use a wide variety of habitats, including riparian woodlands, Ashe Juniper–oak woodlands and live oak savannas.

Red-naped Sapsucker (*Sphyrapicus nuchalis*)

Rare winter visitor to the western half of the plateau, becoming very rare in the eastern half. Records from the plateau extend from early November through March. Red-naped Sapsuckers are found in habitats similar to those used by the Yellow-bellied. Careful examination of wintering sapsuckers is needed to differentiate Red-naped from Yellow-bellied Sapsuckers. The presence of red feathers on the nape is not a diagnostic feature. The pattern of the back and throat are important characteristics for identifying these closely related species. The majority of wintering Red-naped Sapsuckers in Texas are male. As with the Yellow-bellied Sapsucker, the sexes segregate in winter with females moving south into northern Mexico.

Williamson's Sapsucker (*Sphyrapicus thyroideus*)

Accidental. William Lloyd (1887) was the first to report this species from the Edwards Plateau. He reported finding the species along the Nueces River in northern Uvalde County during the winter of 1883. Lacey (1911) collected a male on his ranch near Kerrville on 24 October 1898. Oberholser (1974) lists a winter specimen taken in Kimble County, but the location of the specimen and details are not known. There are no recent records from the region, but this species has been reported off of the Edwards Plateau in eastern Travis County on three different occasions, including one documented record.

Ladder-backed Woodpecker (*Picoides scalaris*)

Common resident throughout the region. Although more characteristic of arid areas, this species is found in almost every type of wooded habitat. They are found in Ashe Juniper–oak woodlands as well as live oak and mesquite savannas. This species is the most widely distributed of the breeding woodpeckers on the plateau.

Downy Woodpecker (*Picoides pubescens*)

Uncommon and local permanent resident along the Colorado River drainage. Downy Woodpeckers are a rare and local permanent resident along the Guadalupe River, west to Kerrville, and along the San Gabriel watershed. This species inhabits mesic gallery forests that border the rivers and extend up protected canyons. Elsewhere in the region, this species is a rare to very rare winter and spring visitor. Winter reports of this species away from the breeding range are primarily from mature woodlands and urban areas. These reports range from early October to late March.

Hairy Woodpecker (*Picoides villosus*)

Very rare winter and spring visitor to the eastern half of the Edwards Plateau. Winter reports from the plateau fall between mid-December and late February. Spring reports are from late March and early April. There appears to have been a small incursion of Hairy Woodpeckers onto the eastern plateau during the winter of 1992–1993. There were several reports from that winter, including from the Boerne and Burnet Christmas Bird Counts.

Northern Flicker (*Colaptes auratus*)

Common winter resident throughout the plateau. Flickers typically arrive in the region in early October, occasionally as early as late September. Wintering birds remain until late March and early April. There is a single summer report of a flicker in Burnet County on 31 July 2000, but they have never been documented as breeding. Flickers inhabit a wide variety of open habitats on the plateau, ranging from woodland edges in the Balcones Canyonlands to live oak savannas in the western part of the region. The majority of wintering flickers on the plateau are "Red-shafted" with "Yellow-shafted" birds being an irregular visitor. "Yellow-shafted" Flickers are more commonly encountered in the eastern half of the plateau, but have been noted throughout the region.

Pileated Woodpecker (*Dryocopus pileatus*)

Accidental. There are four reports of this species from the Edwards Plateau. In all four cases, the birds were observed along major drainages. This is to be expected because the gallery forests that remain along these rivers provide the only potential habitat for this large woodpecker. The first report of Pileated Woodpecker for the plateau was a single bird in Kerr County on 30 November 1986. Since then, single birds have been reported from Lake Travis (4 April 1994) and Colorado Bend State Park (2 May–5 June 1997), and two birds were seen flying along the Guadalupe River near Ingram on 28 July 1999. These represent the westernmost records in the state.

FAMILY TYRANNIDAE: Tyrant Flycatchers

Olive-sided Flycatcher (*Contopus cooperi*)

Uncommon to occasional migrant throughout the plateau. Spring migrants pass through the region from late April to late May. Fall migrants are typically found from late August through late September with a few stragglers into early October. Olive-sided Flycatchers are true canopy birds, even as migrants. They are almost always found on exposed perches in the tops of the tallest trees, often on exposed snags. The specific epithet of this species was changed from *borealis* to *cooperi* in the seventh edition of the A.O.U. checklist.

Greater Pewee (*Contopus pertinax*)

Accidental. There is one accepted sight record of this species from the Edwards Plateau. A Greater Pewee was discovered on private property in northwestern Bexar County on 7 April 1991 (TBRC 1991-62). There are only five accepted Texas records, and this is the easternmost of those records. *Review Species*

Western Wood-Pewee (*Contopus sordidulus*)

Occasional migrant in Val Verde and Crockett Counties. A rare to very rare migrant through Schleicher, Sutton, Edwards, and Kinney Counties. Spring migrants have been recorded between mid-April and late May. Fall migrants have been reported between early September and mid-October. This species may occur farther east on the plateau, and observers should be aware of the differences in the call notes and songs of these two wood-pewees.

Eastern Wood-Pewee (*Contopus virens*)

Uncommon migrant and summer resident throughout the region. The migration periods for Eastern Wood-Pewees are from late April to late May in the spring and mid-August to late September in the fall. As a breeding bird, Eastern Wood-Pewees are found along riparian corridors and, in the Balcones Canyonlands subregion, in upland oak-elm savannas. This species is present along all of the major river systems, including tributaries to the Pecos River.

Yellow-bellied Flycatcher (*Empidonax flaviventris*)

Occasional to rare migrant over the eastern third of the plateau, casual farther west. Spring migrants pass over the plateau from late April to late May with a few late migrants regularly found during the first few days of June. Fall migration occurs between late August and late September. The only record of Yellow-bellied Flycatcher from the western third of the plateau was a bird banded at Kickapoo Cavern State Park on 11 May 1989 (TPRF 752).

Acadian Flycatcher (*Empidonax virescens*)

Very local summer resident in riparian corridors throughout the region. Acadian Flycatchers arrive on the breeding grounds in late April and have generally departed by early August. Despite being a localized breeder, this species is very rarely encountered as a migrant on the plateau. Breeding Acadian Flycatchers occupy well-developed forests along watercourses on the plateau. Even in good habitat, they seem to be very local. They can be found in most of the major river drainages from the Colorado River west to the Nueces. They are present, but rare, along the West Nueces and Devils Rivers.

Alder Flycatcher (*Empidonax alnorum*)
Willow Flycatcher (*Empidonax traillii*)

The status of Alder and Willow Flycatchers is confused by difficulty in correctly identifying these sister species. These two species were formerly considered as one, the Traill's Flycatcher. Traill's-type flycatchers are uncommon migrants through the region. Spring migrants can be found between very late April and late May, with the peak of migration between 5 and 20 May. It is not uncommon to encounter migrants as late as the first few days of June. Fall migrants begin arriving in late July and can be seen through October. These two extremely similar species can be safely identified only by voice in the field. Call notes and songs are diagnostic, but these species rarely sing in Texas and are often silent for long periods of time. Traditionally, Traill's-type flycatchers encountered on the plateau were generally considered to be Willows. In recent years, the knowledge of *Empidonax* flycatcher identification has increased greatly, and ideas about Traill's-type flycatchers are changing. It appears that Alder Flycatchers are uncommon migrants over the eastern third of the plateau and may outnumber Willows. For the remainder of the plateau, Willows appear to be the more common species, and Alders are considered casual at best. Pyle (1997) has also developed better criteria for separating hand-held birds. Data from the Driftwood Banding Station support the idea that Alders are more common than Willows on the eastern plateau.

Least Flycatcher (*Empidonax minimus*)

Common migrant throughout the region. Least Flycatcher is the most common migrant *Empidonax* on the Edwards Plateau. Spring migrants pass through the region between mid-April and late May. The first fall migrants reach the plateau in late July, with records as early as 18 July. The peak of fall migration is from late August through mid-September, but migrants can still be found through October.

Black Phoebe (*Sayornis nigricans*)

Uncommon to rare and local permanent resident in the western plateau, casual visitor farther east. Permanent residents occur as far east as Real and western Bandera Counties. Black Phoebes are found exclusively along clear-running rivers and streams with at least some remnant of riparian woodland. There may be seasonal movements within the Edwards Plateau population. The vast majority of the records of this species from the eastern plateau have been during the winter. Whether these are migrants from more northerly populations or are local movements within the plateau population is unknown.

Eastern Phoebe (*Sayornis phoebe*)

Common winter and uncommon summer resident in the southern and eastern plateau. Common as a summer resident and rare during winter in the northwestern quarter of the region. Fall migrants reach the southern plateau in late September and remain until early March. During winter, Eastern Phoebes are found in the open woodlands of the Balcones Canyonlands. During the breeding season, they are typically found along watercourses, but are not restricted to that habitat. In the more arid western and northern parts of the plateau, this species is more closely tied with riparian zones throughout the year. Breeding activities can begin as early as March, and multiple nesting attempts by a single pair are not uncommon. The first fledglings of the year can be seen in mid- to late May.

Say's Phoebe (*Sayornis saya*)

Uncommon winter resident in Crockett, Schleicher, Sutton, and Val Verde Counties. An occasional winter visitor east to Kerr and Bandera Counties and rare farther east. They arrive in mid-October and are present until mid-April. Say's Phoebes are typically found in open habitats, such as savannas and arid shrublands. They are rarely, if ever, found in woodlands. In the eastern plateau, they are most often found in agricultural areas, farmlands in particular. This species is occasionally found in central Val Verde County during the summer, particularly in the arid foothills between the Pecos and Devils Rivers and around Lake Amistad.

Vermilion Flycatcher (*Pyrocephalus rubinus*)

Common summer resident in the western half of the plateau, becoming uncommon and more localized in the eastern half. Occasional to rare on the Llano Uplift, but regular in small numbers at Balcones Canyonlands National Wildlife Refuge at the northeastern limit of its range. Vermilion Flycatchers are generally present from mid-March to mid-September on the breeding grounds. During mild winters, they will linger into early winter and occasionally remain until spring. It is likely that other factors, such as food availability rather than the severity of the weather, are involved when Vermilion Flycatchers overwinter on the plateau.

Ash-throated Flycatcher (*Myiarchus cinerascens*)

Uncommon to locally common summer resident throughout the region. Ash-throated Flycatchers are among the first summer residents to return in the spring. They begin arriving in mid- to late March, with the majority of the breeding population present by mid-April. Breeding birds begin dispersing by the end of July, but a small percentage of the population remains until late September. Ash-throated Flycatchers occupy open, primarily upland, habitats on the plateau. They are found in a variety of dry habitats, from open shrublands and savannas to mesquite woodlands to mixed desert scrub in Val Verde County. As with the other *Myiarchus*, Ash-throated Flycatchers are cavity nesters. They most frequently use abandoned woodpecker cavities for nesting, but they will also use nest boxes if the opening is large enough.

Great Crested Flycatcher (*Myiarchus crinitus*)

Uncommon summer resident in the Balcones Canyonlands; occasional to rare in appropriate habitat in the remainder of the region. As a breeding bird, Great Crested Flycatchers are found almost exclusively in riparian woodlands or in mesic shaded canyon heads on the Edwards Plateau. They are ecologically separated from the upland habitats favored by the other regularly breeding member of the genus on the pla-

DRAWING 8. *Ash-throated Flycatcher*

teau, the Ash-throated Flycatcher. They begin to arrive on the breeding grounds in early April and remain through September.

Brown-crested Flycatcher (*Myiarchus tyrannulus*)

Uncommon summer resident in Val Verde County along the Rio Grande and the Devils River drainage and along the Nueces River in western Uvalde County. Rare and irregular elsewhere in the southern half of the plateau; accidental north to Balcones Canyonlands National Wildlife Refuge. At the northern extreme of their range, Brown-crested Flycatchers are found primarily in oak woodlands bordering riparian corridors and other areas where large trees are prevalent. They are not typically found in open shrublands that are inhabited by Ash-throated Flycatchers. They are present in breeding areas from early March to late August. There are isolated breeding records for this species from several locations in the southern and central plateau, including near Concan in Uvalde County, along the Frio River in Real County, Kerrville, and Kickapoo Cavern State Park.

Great Kiskadee (*Pitangus sulphuratus*)

Uncommon and local permanent resident along the Rio Grande and San Felipe Creek in the Del Rio area; a rare visitor north to the Devils River drainage. This species is probably best considered accidental elsewhere in the region. There are single records from Bandera, Burnet, Medina, northern Kinney, and western Uvalde Counties and three from northwestern Bexar County. Great Kiskadee has slowly expanded its range northward along the Rio Grande and its tributaries. In addition to the Del Rio population, this species has become a permanent resident along Las Moras Creek in southern Kinney County.

Couch's Kingbird (*Tyrannus couchii*)

Uncommon and local summer resident along the Rio Grande and San Felipe Creek in the Del Rio area; a rare visitor during spring and fall to the Devils River drainage in northern Val Verde County. There are only five records, primarily from April, of Couch's Kingbirds from the plateau away from Val Verde County, and all involve single birds. One was collected by Lacey (1911) near Kerrville (11 September 1908), and more recently, single individuals have been found at Kickapoo Cavern State Park (11–13 April 1988), Austin (23–26 April 1991), Park Chalk Bluff (10 May 1995 and 12–26 April 1999), and Concan (26 April 1999). It is possible that this species occurs more regularly along the floodplain of the Nueces River in western Uvalde County, since the ranges of many South Texas species extend up this river valley. This species is also a local summer resident along Las Moras Creek in southern Kinney County.

Cassin's Kingbird (*Tyrannus vociferans*)

Casual spring vagrant to the Edwards Plateau. Cassin's Kingbird has been reported eight times from the Edwards Plateau, with all of the records falling between 5 April and 14 May. The majority of these reports come from the central plateau with single reports from Bandera, Kendall, Kerr, and Real Counties. The easternmost record is a detailed sight report from near Helotes, Bexar County, on 5 May 1988. Although there are only three records from the Del Rio area, this kingbird is probably a rare to very rare migrant through Val Verde and Crockett Counties.

Western Kingbird (*Tyrannus verticalis*)

Common summer resident throughout the region. Breeding birds arrive on the plateau in early to mid-April along with northbound migrants. Although nesting activities may begin by early May, migrants are still common through the month. Large migrating flocks of kingbirds are occasionally encountered in late April and early May. Most of the breeding population has dispersed by the end of August. A few lingering individuals and autumn migrants can be found through the end of September. As a breeding bird, Western Kingbirds inhabit very open habitats. They are frequently found in open shrublands with scattered trees, savannas, around farmhouses, and in urban areas.

Eastern Kingbird (*Tyrannus tyrannus*)

Uncommon spring and occasional fall migrant for all but the extreme western edge of the plateau, where this species is rare to occasional in both seasons. Spring migrants can be found between early April and late May with the peak of migration during the first three weeks of May. Autumn migrants pass through the region between late July and mid-September. Eastern Kingbirds formerly bred, at least locally, throughout the eastern half of the plateau. Lacey (1911) reported them as uncommon with a few nesting pairs. Currently, they are an uncommon breeding bird just east of the escarpment and in the Lampasas Cut Plains to the northeast. In those areas, they use parklands and open pastures with scattered trees as nesting habitat. It is possible that this species is a rare and local nester in San Saba County.

Scissor-tailed Flycatcher (*Tyrannus forficatus*)

Abundant migrant and summer resident throughout most of the region, uncommon along the extreme western edge of the plateau. Spring migrants make their way to the plateau by mid- to late March. Scissor-taileds begin to gather in flocks in preparation for migrating in the latter half of September. Lingering birds and migrants are present on the plateau through October and few linger into November. Scissor-taileds prefer open habitats and adapt well to disturbed areas, such as agricultural lands. This elegant bird is well adapted to these open habitats. Its slender build and long tail are adaptive advantages for flycatching in a savanna-like environment.

FAMILY LANIIDAE: Shrikes

Loggerhead Shrike (*Lanius ludovicianus*)

Common winter resident and uncommon to rare summer resident throughout the region. Fall migrants begin to arrive on the plateau in mid-September, becoming common by mid-October. Winter residents and spring migrants remain in the region through late April and often into early May. Loggerhead Shrikes are found in open habitats, rarely venturing into woodland or forest habitats. One of the subspecies, *L. l. migrans,* has declined precipitously throughout the northeastern United States. This subspecies occurs as a nesting bird in northeast Texas, where the population appears to be stable, and may occur as a migrant along the eastern third of the plateau. Two other subspecies occur on the plateau: *L. l. excubitorides* is a permanent resident, and *L. l. gambeli* only occurs as a migrant and winter resident.

FAMILY VIREONIDAE: Vireos

White-eyed Vireo (*Vireo griseus*)

Common summer resident throughout the Balcones Canyonlands, becoming rare in the Live Oak–Mesquite Savannas region of the northern and western plateau. They are permanent residents along the Devils River drainage and along the Rio Grande in southern Val Verde County. The breeding population of White-eyed Vireos arrives on the southern plateau in late March with the majority of the population on the breeding grounds by mid-April. Summer residents begin to disperse in late August with a few remaining until mid-September. They are found in a wide variety of habitats on the plateau. In the southwestern part of the plateau, they can be found in open shrublands and savannas with large live oak mottes. In this arid region and in the Live Oak–Mesquite region, they are also found in the dense scrub along dry washes and in riparian corridors. Throughout the Balcones Canyonlands and along the

Colorado River drainage, they are found in almost any habitat with a developed understory or shrubby component, including riparian zones, diverse juniper-oak woodlands, and occasionally in open shrublands.

Bell's Vireo (*Vireo bellii*)

Common to locally abundant summer resident in the western plateau, becoming increasingly uncommon and local farther east. Spring migrants arrive on the breeding grounds on the southwestern plateau in late March and by early April in the remainder of the region. Breeding birds remain until mid- to late September, rarely lingering into early October. The plateau populations of Bell's Vireo are found in open shrublands where vegetation reaches the ground. If the habitat is heavily browsed, either by livestock or deer, it is generally unsuitable.

Black-capped Vireo (*Vireo atricapillus*)

Uncommon to rare, and generally local, summer resident throughout the region. Black-capped Vireos are particularly local in the Llano Uplift and westward through the northwestern portion of the plateau. This species has not been reported from Schleicher County and is very localized in Menard and Sutton Counties. However, there are several apparently stable populations in Crockett County. The stronghold of the species on the plateau is in the southwest, from Kerr and Bandera Counties west to Val Verde County. Spring migrants arrive on the breeding grounds in the southwestern plateau in mid- to late March, the average arrival date is the twenty-second, but they have been found as early as the eighteenth. For the remainder of the region, they generally arrive before 1 April. The breeding population begins to migrate south in late August and is gone by 20 September. The latest documented fall record was a hatch-year bird captured at Kickapoo Cavern State Park on 14 October 1992 (TPRF 1049). Black-capped Vireos are habitat specialists, but it is the structure and not the species composition that is important. They are found in open shrublands where the vegetation reaches the ground. This habitat is found on dry hillsides throughout much of the region. In the western plateau, Black-capped Vireo habitat exists in areas of deeper soil, such as floodplains and canyon bottoms. Heavy browsing, by livestock or deer, alters the structure of the habitat and makes it unsuitable for the vireo. The U.S. Fish and Wildlife Service lists this species as Endangered.

Gray Vireo (*Vireo vicinior*)

Uncommon to occasional and local summer resident in the western third of the Edwards Plateau. Gray Vireos are found in portions of Val Verde, Crockett, Kinney, Edwards, Uvalde, and Real Counties. They probably also occur in western Schleicher and Sutton Counties. There is one record of a singing male in north-central Kerr County from 19 May 1991, providing the easternmost record for the state. In the southwestern United States, Gray Vireos are associated with arid scrub in canyons and ravines. On the Edwards Plateau, they are found primarily in savannas and open shrublands. In all cases, the common component is continuous tree and shrub foliage cover from the ground up to about two meters. Most nesting attempts are within this zone, although Gray Vireos will occasionally nest higher above the ground. Spring migrants arrive on the breeding grounds in late March. Summer residents remain until late September. Although Gray Vireos were known from Terrell County since the 1950s, the presence of this species on the southwestern plateau was generally unknown until the late 1980s. Whether this is a result of an actual range expansion or if they were simply overlooked is open to speculation.

Yellow-throated Vireo (*Vireo flavifrons*)

Uncommon to locally common summer resident along the river systems throughout the region. Breeding birds arrive on the southern plateau in late March and are present through late August, becoming rare during the first half of September. On the Edwards Plateau, Yellow-throated Vireos are restricted to riparian corridors along river systems. They are present along every river system, including the Colorado River to the north and the Devils River to the west. They use forest habitats, such as pecan-sugarberry and sycamore–bald cypress communities. They are rarely found, as a breeding bird, away from these riparian habitats.

Plumbeous Vireo (*Vireo plumbeus*)

Rare migrant and winter visitor to the entire region. The status of Plumbeous Vireo on the Edwards Plateau is almost unknown. This is one of three species that were previously treated as subspecies of the Solitary Vireo (*V. solitarius*). Since that taxonomic revision, birders have focused greater attention on the complex. As a result, there have been several well-documented sightings of this species from the plateau. Fall migrants should be looked for between mid-September and late October, and spring migrants should occur between early April and mid-May. Plumbeous Vireo will probably prove to be a more regular migrant in the western half of the region.

Cassin's Vireo (*Vireo cassinii*)

Rare migrant through the western portion of the plateau. As with the Plumbeous Vireo, this member of the Solitary Vireo complex probably occurs more regularly on the plateau than current records indicate. Cassin's Vireos probably occur more regularly, and in greater numbers, in the fall than in the spring, which is the pattern noted in the Trans-Pecos and New Mexico. Spring migrants should be looked for between early April and mid-May. Fall migrants should pass through the region between mid-August and early October. The status of this species in the region is almost unknown at this time. Little attention was paid to the Solitary Vireo complex in Texas prior to the taxonomic revisions that elevated the three subspecies groups to the species level in 1997. Although this species has been reported several times on the plateau, there are only two documented records for the region: an adult male was mist-netted at Kickapoo Cavern State Park on 11 May 1991 (TPRF 1753), and another adult male was observed at Government Canyon State Natural Area, Bexar County, on 2 May 2000. Cassin's Vireos were present during the winter of 1990–1991 in the oak woodlands along Las Moras Creek in southern Kinney County. This species has the potential to be a rare and local winter resident in riparian woodlands in the western half of the plateau.

Blue-headed Vireo (*Vireo solitarius*)

Uncommon spring and fall migrant throughout the region. Blue-headed Vireos are also an occasional winter visitor on the plateau, although most birds appear to depart during January. Spring migrants are present on the plateau from late March to mid-May, with the peak of migration between early April and early May. Returning autumn migrants arrive on the plateau as early as late August, but typically are not found until after mid-September. Fall migrants are present until early November and frequently linger into the early winter, but true winter residents are rare. Blue-headed Vireos use almost any woodland habitat as migrants and winter visitors. This species is the most likely of the Solitary Vireo complex to be encountered on the plateau.

Hutton's Vireo (*Vireo huttoni*)

Accidental. Prior to 1999, there were only two records of Hutton's Vireo from the Edwards Plateau. Amazingly, the first record for the region was of a breeding pair on the Prade Ranch, Real County, found during the spring of 1990 (TPRF 801). These birds were again present at the same location in 1991. During the spring of 1999, three different individuals were discovered: singles near Kerrville on 29 March, Concan on 13 April, and Government Canyon State Natural Area, Bexar County, on 26 April. Hutton's Vireos were again discovered on the plateau during the spring of 2000. At least one returned to the same location near Kerrville, where this species was found in 1999, and remained through early July. Another Hutton's Vireo was discovered on a private ranch in southeastern Edwards County on 30 March 2000. There is also a winter record from the plateau; one was discovered at Balcones Canyonlands National Wildlife Refuge on 14 December 2000. This dramatic increase in sightings, coupled with some apparent site fidelity, suggests at least the possibility that Hutton's Vireo could be a very low density resident on the plateau.

Warbling Vireo (*Vireo gilvus*)

Occasional spring and fall migrant through the eastern third of the region, becoming increasingly less common westward. This species is a rare to very rare summer visitor to the Concho Valley northwestward to the Midland region and may be present in northern Crockett and northwestern Schleicher Counties. Spring migrants pass through the region between late April and late May. Warbling Vireos have been banded between 18 April and 18 May at the Driftwood Banding Station. Fall migrants pass through the region between early September and early October, with a few still present into late October. Recent work has suggested that the Warbling Vireo may actually be two species, the Eastern (*V. gilvus*) and Western (*V. swainsonii*) Warbling-Vireos. The two groups differ in many respects, including morphologically, vocally, genetically, and ecologically. Both groups may occur on the plateau, but the identity of the breeding birds to the northwest and migrants through the western plateau is unknown.

Philadelphia Vireo (*Vireo philadelphicus*)

Rare spring migrant to the eastern third of the plateau; very rare to accidental farther west. Spring migrants pass through the area between late

April and late May, with the peak in early May. They have been banded between 21 April and 24 May at the Driftwood Banding Station. The only documented record from the western half of the region was a bird banded at Kickapoo Cavern State Park on 16 May 1990 (TPRF 804). Philadelphia Vireos may occur as casual fall migrants in the eastern third of the region as well. They should be looked for during September. The only autumn report of this species was one near Dripping Springs on 22 August 1994.

Red-eyed Vireo (*Vireo olivaceus*)

Uncommon summer resident along the river systems and mesic canyons throughout the region. Breeding birds arrive on the southern plateau in early to mid-April and are present through most of September. They are present from the Colorado River west to the Devils River. Red-eyed Vireos are found in the same ecological situations as the Yellow-throated Vireo on the Edwards Plateau. They are primarily restricted to riparian corridors with mature trees along the major river systems. As with the Yellow-throated, they use forest habitats, such as pecan-sugarberry and sycamore–bald cypress communities, although they are also an uncommon breeding bird in mature oak-juniper woodlands in the Balcones Canyonlands region.

FAMILY CORVIDAE: Jays and Crows

Steller's Jay (*Cyanocitta stelleri*)

Accidental. There are three reports of Steller's Jays from the Edwards Plateau. Two birds were found in Bandera County on 5 November 1955, and a single bird was discovered in western Travis County on 24 October 1961. The third record was associated with a major invasion of Steller's Jays into West Texas during the winter of 1972–1973. During that winter small numbers of these jays wandered across the Pecos River into Crockett County. They likely were present in eastern Val Verde County as well, although none were reported.

Blue Jay (*Cyanocitta cristata*)

Common permanent resident in urban areas in all but the southwestern corner of the region, where they are irregular in winter. Uncommon permanent resident in riparian woodlands along the eastern edge of the Balcones Canyonlands region. Blue Jays are irregularly irruptive visitors during the winter, varying widely in the number of birds present from year to year, occasionally involving large numbers of birds. These "invasions" generally begin in late September with most of the birds departing by May. During these major invasions, they can be found throughout the region. Blue Jays tend to remain in riparian corridors and well-developed forests where hardwoods are plentiful.

Green Jay (*Cyanocorax yncas*)

Very rare to rare winter visitor to southeastern Val Verde County, casual at other seasons. During the past 10 years, Green Jays have occurred with increasing frequency in the Del Rio area, primarily during winter. A similar pattern has been noted along Las Moras Creek in southern Kinney County. They typically arrive in mid- to late October and remain through February. There is a summer report from Del Rio, a single bird along San Felipe Creek on 29 July 1998.

Western Scrub-Jay (*Aphelocoma californica*)

Common permanent resident throughout the Balcones Canyonlands west to eastern Val Verde County, becoming more uncommon and local to the north, including the Llano Uplift. They are generally absent from the most arid habitats found in central Val Verde and Crockett Counties. Western Scrub-Jays are found in woodland habitats. They are most frequently encountered in open juniper-oak woodlands and oak savannas, rarely in gallery or other closed-canopy forests. Scrub-Jays are a relatively new addition to the avifauna of the eastern plateau. The species underwent a major range expansion in the late 1950s and early 1960s. Prior to that, the eastern edge of their range was central Kerr County. The subspecies on the Edwards Plateau, *A. c. texana*, has the drabbest coloration of any subspecies. Western Scrub-Jay was previously combined with the Florida (*A. coerulescens*) and Island (*A. insularis*) Scrub-Jays as a single species. Additionally, the Western Scrub-Jay may actually consist of three species. There are several disjunct populations of this jay that differ in plumage and voice. Should this taxon be further split, Woodhouse's Scrub-Jay would be the likely name for the populations in Texas.

Pinyon Jay (*Gymnorhinus cyanocephalus*)

Accidental. The status of Pinyon Jay in Texas is not well understood. There have been irregular incursions into the western half of the state, including the extreme western plateau. During such invasions, Pinyon Jays were present from as early as August and remained as late as May. Specimens were collected in Crockett, Sutton, and Val Verde Counties between 1910 and 1940, when the species would probably have been considered casual. Major incursions into the Trans-Pecos occurred during the late 1970s and early 1980s and again during the fall of 2000; however, no Pinyon Jays were reported on the plateau during that period.

American Crow (*Corvus brachyrhynchos*)

Uncommon to rare visitor to the eastern half of the plateau; most often encountered during the winter. American Crows have become a common permanent resident within the urban areas along the Interstate Highway 35 corridor. American Crows wander onto the eastern plateau at all seasons from these urban areas and from the large populations found on the Blackland Prairies. Farther from the escarpment, as far west as Junction, they occur primarily as a rare winter visitor between late September and mid-March, although there are scattered reports throughout the year. Winter visitors are frequently found in Pecan bottoms where they feed on the nuts.

Chihuahuan Raven (*Corvus cryptoleucus*)

An occasional fall and rare spring migrant over the western plateau; accidental farther east. Chihuahuan Ravens pass through the western plateau during the late fall, primarily in October. Flocks of up to 50 birds have been encountered. Spring migrants, usually single birds or small flocks of about four or five individuals, pass through the region between mid-March and late April. The seasonal movements of this species are not well understood. They are found only as migrants on the plateau, even though the species is generally considered to be resident within its range. Chihuahuan Ravens may also be an occasional to rare permanent resident in the Live Oak–Mesquite Savannas region of the northwestern plateau in Crockett, Schleicher, and northwestern Sutton Counties. Confusion with Common Raven (*C. corax*) clouds the status of this bird on the plateau.

Common Raven (*Corvus corax*)

Uncommon and local permanent resident throughout the Balcones Canyonlands; becoming more local in occurrence in the remainder of the region. Common Ravens are found primarily in open habitats, but are also frequently seen in juniper-oak woodlands. They are quite nomadic and can be found almost anywhere. They generally nest in abandoned hawk nests or in small caves or on ledges, but they also occasionally nest on telephone poles and other man-made structures.

FAMILY ALAUDIDAE: Larks

Horned Lark (*Eremophila alpestris*)

Uncommon permanent resident in the Live Oak–Mesquite Savannas region of the northwestern plateau south to Val Verde County. This species is primarily encountered along the shorelines of Lake Amistad and in areas converted for agricultural uses, farming in particular, all across the region. They may also be present in short-grass prairies or overgrazed pastures that mimic that habitat type. This species is a casual to accidental winter visitor elsewhere on the plateau.

FAMILY HIRUNDINIDAE: Swallows and Martins

Purple Martin (*Progne subis*)

Common to locally abundant migrant and summer resident, mostly in urban areas, throughout the region. Generally, Purple Martins are uncommon to rare visitors away from urban centers. They can be attracted to martin houses in rural areas, suggesting that suitable nesting cavities are the limiting factor in the species' distribution on the plateau. Spring migrants generally arrive on the plateau in mid-February, but have been reported as early as late January. The bulk of the population does not arrive until early March. They are present on the plateau until mid-August, when they begin to disperse. A few individuals typically linger into September. As with all of the swallows that occur as breeding species on the plateau, Purple Martins frequent open habitats.

Tree Swallow (*Tachycineta bicolor*)

Rare spring and uncommon fall migrant throughout the region. Spring migrants have been reported between early March and early May. Fall migrants pass through the region from mid-August to mid-November with the peak of migration occurring between mid-September and mid-October. An unusually early report of fall migrants was five individuals at Kerrville on 23 July 1992. These birds may have summered locally, although that would be equally unusual, since the closest breeding population is in northeastern Texas. Tree Swallows frequently linger into early winter, and occasionally through the winter in areas surrounding the plateau. Although there is only one winter report from the plateau, a bird near Ingram during January 1973, they should be looked for, particularly around reservoirs at that season.

Violet-green Swallow (*Tachycineta thalassina*)

Casual migrant throughout the region. Violet-green Swallows are probably a more regular migrant in Val Verde County, where they have been reported during April and September. There have been only two reports of this species from the central plateau, both from Kerr County. A flock of 12 was observed south of Kerrville on 21 April 1973, and a single individual was found near Kerrville on 23 October 1986. However, Violet-greens have been reported during April and from late August through September in the Austin area.

Northern Rough-winged Swallow (*Stelgidopteryx serripennis*)

Uncommon spring and common fall migrant. Rough-wingeds are also locally uncommon summer residents and early winter visitors throughout the region. Spring migrants pass through the region between late February and early May, with the peak of migration from late March to late April. Fall migrants begin to arrive in mid-August and can be seen until late October. The peak of migrants in the fall occurs from mid-September through early October. Rough-winged Swallows are local breeders throughout the region. Suitable nesting sites, which are earthen banks where burrows can be dug, are probably a limiting factor. Most of the winter reports of this species from the plateau are associated with water. Apparently, their prey base continues to thrive during the winter months around these reservoirs and rivers.

Bank Swallow (*Riparia riparia*)

Uncommon and local breeder along the Rio Grande in Val Verde County; very rare breeder elsewhere on the plateau. Otherwise, an uncommon to occasional migrant throughout the region. There has been a breeding colony of Bank Swallows on the Rio Grande at Del Rio since at least the late 1970s. There have been isolated breeding records from other locations on the plateau. Usually these involve small colonies, or single pairs in some cases, and are often in temporarily available sites, such as in fresh road cuts in areas where the soil type is conducive to burrowing. Spring migrants pass through the region between mid-April and mid- to late May. Fall migrants are often more common and pass through from early August to late September.

Cliff Swallow (*Petrochelidon pyrrhonota*)

Common migrant and summer resident throughout the region. Spring migrants begin to arrive in early March, and most of the breeding population are present by mid-April. Breeding birds begin to disperse in late July, with most departing by late August. They are an uncommon migrant through September with a few lingering into early October. Cliff Swallows still nest in traditional colonies on bluffs along the Colorado River above Lake Buchanan and at a few other locations on the plateau. As in other parts of the Cliff Swallow's range, the majority of the population now uses man-made structures such as bridges and overpasses for nesting. Direct competition with Cave Swallows for nesting sites is occurring with Cliff Swallows being displaced in some areas.

Cave Swallow (*Petrochelidon fulva*)

Common migrant and locally common summer resident in all but the northeastern portion of the plateau. Cave Swallows have undergone an amazing range expansion over the past 15 to 20 years. Nesting sites were once restricted to limestone caves, but this is no longer the case. They can now be found over almost all of the plateau and are common fall migrants as far east as the Austin and San Antonio areas. Cave Swallows arrive on the breeding grounds in late February and remain until mid-September. Fall migrants have been detected away from breeding areas from mid-August through late September. Cave Swallows have even begun to winter locally. Winter records have come from Bexar, Edwards, Travis, Val Verde, and Williamson Counties. The expanding population of Cave Swallows has displaced both Cliff and Barn Swallows, at least locally. How these species will be impacted if the Cave Swallow populations continue to grow is unknown.

Barn Swallow (*Hirundo rustica*)

Common migrant and summer resident throughout the region. Spring migrants arrive on the plateau in early March. Breeding Barn Swallows are found nesting almost exclusively on man-made structures. Nesting activities continue into early August. Fall migrants pass through the region from late July through October and are occasional through the first half of November. This is normally the most common migrant swallow on the plateau, although there can be large concentrations of other species of swallows at times.

FAMILY PARIDAE: Chickadees and Titmice

Carolina Chickadee (*Poecile carolinensis*)

Common permanent resident throughout the Balcones Canyonlands and eastern plateau. Generally absent west of the West Nueces River in eastern Kinney County. In the Live Oak–Mesquite Savannas region of the northwestern plateau, the species is rare and local except along the San Saba River and its tributaries, where they are uncommon. Away from the Balcones Canyonlands where the species is widespread, Carolina Chickadees are generally confined to riparian corridors and well-developed juniper-oak woodlands. They wander away from their typical haunts during the winter months, but are not irruptive.

Tufted Titmouse (*Baeolophus bicolor*)

Abundant permanent resident throughout the region. They can be found in a wide variety of habitats, from juniper-oak woodlands to oak savannas. The Tufted Titmice that occur on the plateau are "Black-crested" (*B. b. sennetti*). "Black-crested" Titmouse was formerly considered a separate species (*B. atricristatus*) and may be classified as such again. Considerable research has focused on this question with mixed results. It has been shown that the "Eastern" versus "Black-crested" are genetically distinct, but they freely interbreed in a narrow zone just to the east of the escarpment. In this zone, hybrid individuals far outnumber the parental types. There are no records of "Eastern" Tufted Titmice (*B. b. bicolor*) on the plateau, although hatchling "Black-crested" Titmice do have gray crests until the postjuvenile molt.

FAMILY REMIZIDAE: Verdins

Verdin (*Auriparus flaviceps*)

Uncommon to rare permanent resident throughout the Edwards Plateau. Verdins are most common in arid habitats; for most of the plateau, that translates into dry hillsides and open shrublands. They are most common through the western plateau and become increasingly uncom-

DRAWING 9. *Tufted (Black-crested) Titmouse*

mon eastward. In the eastern third of the region, Verdins are uncommon and local. Verdins defend territories throughout the year and build nestlike roosting structures that are usually smaller than the actual nests used during the breeding season.

FAMILY AEGITHALIDAE: Long-tailed Tits

Bushtit (*Psaltriparus minimus*)

Uncommon resident in the Balcones Canyonlands, becoming more localized in the remainder of the region. Bushtits are most commonly found in mature juniper woodlands on the plateau. They seem to prefer areas with high concentrations of juniper, although they also can be found in open oak woodlands. "Black-eared" Bushtits are regularly encountered on the Edwards Plateau. These black-eared individuals are primarily immature males, and the trait is rarely held into adulthood. Despite extensive collecting of birds in Texas from 1890 to 1930, only a few "Black-eared" Bushtits were collected on the plateau. Oberholser (1974) lists one each from Kinney and Kerr Counties. It is possible that these black-eared individuals were present all along and for some reason were not represented in historical collections. It is also possible that the genes that control the expression of the black "ears" have slowly moved through the population from the black-eared population in the Trans-Pecos.

FAMILY SITTIDAE: Nuthatches

Red-breasted Nuthatch (*Sitta canadensis*)

Irregular fall and winter visitor throughout the region. Fall migrants have been recorded as early as 20 September. Wintering individuals frequently linger into the early spring, with most departing by early April. The latest spring record for the plateau was one at Colorado Bend State Park that lingered from the previous winter until 7 May 1996. Red-breasted Nuthatches do not occur annually on the Edwards Plateau and when present are usually found only in small numbers. There have been major incursions into the region, such as the one during the winter of 1974–1975, when large numbers were present. One of the more notable concentrations during that winter was 40 individuals in and around Brady, McCulloch County.

White-breasted Nuthatch (*Sitta carolinensis*)

Very rare to casual winter visitor to the Edwards Plateau. Most White-breasted Nuthatch records from this region are from early to midwinter. The range of these records falls between mid-October and early January. This species has been found primarily along riparian corridors, but there are also reports from urban habitats. Although the few records for the region do not suggest this, it is likely that these birds remain through the winter. The White-breasted Nuthatch was once a more common winter visitor to the plateau. Simmons (1925) reports that this species was an uncommon to occasional winter resident in the Austin area. Lacey (1911) also reported observing them, but considered them rare winter visitors. This species was documented in 1997 as nesting east of the escarpment at Webberville Park, Travis County. Although this location continues to host this species, the only other known nesting location in central Texas is at Temple, Bell County. There is, however, a recent summer record from the plateau: one bird in northwestern Travis County on 23 July 1998. White-breasted Nuthatches may have formerly nested on the plateau. Three individuals were collected during July 1937 near Ingram, although nesting was not documented.

FAMILY CERTHIIDAE: Creepers

Brown Creeper (*Certhia americana*)

Uncommon to occasional winter resident throughout the region. Brown Creepers begin to appear on the plateau as fall migrants in mid-October. They are present throughout the winter and generally migrate northward by mid-March. This species occurs in open woodlands, including diverse Ashe Juniper–oak woodlands and along riparian corridors. They are less frequently encountered in oak savannas. This species likely occurs more commonly than reported, as they are easily overlooked.

FAMILY TROGLODYTIDAE: Wrens

Cactus Wren (*Campylorhynchus brunneicapillus*)

Common permanent resident in the western half of the plateau, becoming uncommon eastward. Cactus Wrens are typically found in open, arid to semiarid habitats. In the northern plateau, they are found in mesquite savannas with a brush component. In the eastern plateau, the Cactus Wren is very local in open shrublands and semiopen grasslands. They maintain territories throughout the year and build smaller dome-like structures for roosting during the nonbreeding season.

Rock Wren (*Salpinctes obsoletus*)

Uncommon permanent resident in Val Verde and southern Crockett Counties, becoming increasingly uncommon eastward. In the eastern half of the plateau, Rock Wrens are highly localized and occur with greater frequency in the winter months. This western wren is found in very open and rocky arid habitats. It reaches the eastern edge of its range on the plateau and is a peripheral species throughout most of the region. Although Rock Wrens are permanent residents in Texas, they are also migratory. Fall migrants normally reach the plateau in late September and early October and remain until late March.

DRAWING 10. *Cactus Wren*

Canyon Wren (*Catherpes mexicanus*)

Uncommon permanent resident throughout most of the region, rare and local in the live oak–mesquite savannas of the northern plateau, including the Llano Uplift. Canyon Wrens, as their name implies, are found along canyon bluffs and rocky outcrops on steep hillsides. On the plateau, this habitat type is most often associated with river drainages. Canyon Wrens also occur in open arid habitats where large rocky outcrops are found.

Carolina Wren (*Thryothorus ludovicianus*)

Common to abundant permanent resident throughout most of the region; becoming more local in the arid habitats of the southwestern plateau. Carolina Wrens are found in a wide variety of mesic habitats, ranging from riparian corridors to mature juniper-oak woodlands. They are generally not found in upland areas where they are replaced by Bewick's Wren (*Thryomanes bewickii*). There is considerable overlap in the habitat use of these two wrens. On the southwestern plateau, Carolina Wrens are restricted to riparian zones, including the dense brush along dry arroyos. They can be locally common in such habitats. They are one of the more conspicuous members of the plateau's avifauna.

Bewick's Wren (*Thryomanes bewickii*)

Abundant permanent resident throughout the plateau. Bewick's Wren is found in more arid habitats than the Carolina Wren, although there is considerable overlap. They are found in upland habitats including savannas, open shrublands, and even areas of dense brush. Bewick's Wren can be found almost anywhere on the plateau, although they are seldom encountered in mesic habitats such as riparian corridors. Resident populations on the plateau are entirely the western or gray-backed form of the Bewick's Wren. The eastern or red-backed form is a rare winter visitor just to the east of the escarpment in the Blackland Prairies region and is a casual winter visitor to the eastern third of the plateau.

House Wren (*Troglodytes aedon*)

Uncommon migrant and occasional winter resident on the Edwards Plateau. Fall migrants pass through the region between mid-September and early November. Spring migrants arrive on the plateau in early April and can be found through mid-May. Wintering House Wrens are generally found in protected areas, such as canyon bottoms, and most often in brushy habitats. The number of wintering individuals varies widely from year to year.

Winter Wren (*Troglodytes troglodytes*)

Occasional fall migrant and rare winter resident throughout the plateau. Winter Wrens migrate through the region in the late fall, between early October and mid-November. As winter residents, they are present through late March. Winter Wrens are found in brushy habitats, most often along watercourses. They can also be found in protected areas, such as along canyon walls in dense underbrush. Recent studies have suggested that Old World and New World Winter Wrens may be different species. It has also been suggested that there may be more than one species in North America based on differences in habitat preference and call notes between populations.

Sedge Wren (*Cistothorus platensis*)

Rare to locally uncommon migrant and winter resident in the eastern third of the plateau; casual farther west. Fall migrants have been found between mid-September and early November. Winter residents remain until late March, and spring migrants can be encountered into early May. Sedge Wrens inhabit wet or moist grasslands most often, although they are found in sedges and grasses in marshes as well. They are generally found in the same grasslands as Le Conte's Sparrows (*Ammodramus leconteii*). Sedge Wrens also occur in South America; however, many recent authors have considered those populations to be a separate species, the Grass Wren. If this taxonomy is adopted then the scientific name of Sedge Wren would become *C. stellaris*.

Marsh Wren (*Cistothorus palustris*)

Rare to uncommon, but very local, migrant and winter resident throughout the region. Fall migrants begin to appear on the plateau in early October with winter residents remaining through early April. Marsh Wrens, as their name implies, are restricted to cattail marshes or the edges of lakes or ponds with emergent vegetation. Migrants can be found in a wider range of habitats and have been found using brushy areas as stop-over habitat. Recent work suggests that there are actually two species of Marsh Wren. The two groups are different vocally and morphologically. If these groups were elevated to species status, Edwards Plateau birds would be the Eastern Marsh-Wren (*C. palustris*). The Western Marsh-Wren (*C. paludicola*) would occur in Texas only in the western Trans-Pecos.

FAMILY REGULIDAE: Kinglets

Golden-crowned Kinglet (*Regulus satrapa*)

Occasional winter resident throughout the region. Golden-crowned Kinglets are present on the plateau from late October through late March. They are most frequently found along riparian corridors and in diverse woodlands, including Ashe Juniper–oak forests. The number of wintering birds fluctuates greatly, but during most years the number of individuals present is fairly low. Golden-crowned Kinglets are more common to the east in the Post Oak Savannah and Pineywoods regions of Texas. During most years, as in most of Texas, Golden-crowneds are far outnumbered on the plateau by Ruby-crowned Kinglets.

Ruby-crowned Kinglet (*Regulus calendula*)

Common to abundant migrant and winter resident throughout the plateau. Fall migrants arrive on the plateau in late September. At the Driftwood Banding Station, the first Ruby-crowned Kinglet of the fall is usually banded about 25 September. Interestingly, this species typically can be found by mid-September in woodlands of the Blackland Prairies region east of the plateau. By early October, this species is a common sight in all woodland habitats on the plateau. Most of these kinglets depart the plateau by mid-April, but some linger into early May. The latest documented record for the region was one mist-netted at Kickapoo Cavern State Park on 19 May 1996.

FAMILY SYLVIIDAE: Gnatcatchers

Blue-gray Gnatcatcher (*Polioptila caerulea*)

Common migrant and uncommon summer resident throughout the region. Blue-gray Gnatcatchers are also rare to locally uncommon winter residents in the Balcones Canyonlands subregion. Spring migrants arrive on the plateau in mid-March and are present through early May. Summer residents have already begun nesting activities during this time. Fall migration peaks during September, with a few individuals lingering as late as mid-October. Winter residents are most common along riparian corridors and in areas protected from severe weather, such as narrow canyons. During the breeding season, Blue-gray Gnatcatchers are found in open woodlands and savannas. In the more arid portions of the plateau, such as central Val Verde County, they are frequently restricted to riparian zones. They are usually not present in mature forests except along edges.

Black-tailed Gnatcatcher (*Polioptila melanura*)

Uncommon permanent resident along the extreme western edge of the plateau in central Val Verde and western Crockett Counties. This species appears to be increasing in eastern Val Verde, northern Kinney, and southern Edwards Counties. Black-tailed Gnatcatchers are found in arid habitats, including mixed desert scrub along arroyos. A pair successfully nested along a dry wash at Kickapoo Cavern State Park in 1998, providing the first confirmed breeding record on the plateau away from Val Verde and Crockett Counties. During 1999 and 2000, this species has become increasingly more common at this location. The easternmost reports for the plateau are from Park Chalk Bluff, where a male was discovered on 17 May 1995, and apparently territorial birds have been noted during the spring in subsequent years. Black-tailed Gnatcatchers may occur more regularly along the southwestern edge of the plateau than is currently known.

FAMILY TURDIDAE: Thrushes

Eastern Bluebird (*Sialia sialis*)

Common permanent resident throughout all but the southwestern part of the region. Eastern Bluebirds inhabit open habitats, including pastureland and savannas. They are also found throughout the year in Pecan bottoms and other riparian woodlands that have a closed canopy and, therefore, do not have an understory. On the southwestern plateau, and locally elsewhere in the region, Eastern Bluebirds are common winter residents and rare and local breeders. They are generally present between late September and early May. Bluebirds are cavity nesters and have benefited from nest box programs undertaken in the region.

Western Bluebird (*Sialia mexicana*)

Very rare and irregular winter visitor to the western plateau. This species is casual to accidental in the eastern third of the region. When present, Western Bluebirds have not been reported before mid-November. These reports are generally of small flocks with some remaining through early March. These birds are somewhat nomadic and wander locally. They use open habitats such as pastures, shrublands, and juniper woodlands.

Mountain Bluebird (*Sialia currucoides*)

Irregular winter visitor to the western half of the plateau; rarely wandering into the eastern third of the region. This species is an uncommon winter resident in Crockett and western Schleicher Counties of the northwestern plateau, but may be abundant during invasion years.

During invasion years, Mountain Bluebirds reach the plateau as early as mid-October and remain as late as early April. These birds are generally nomadic during their stay on the plateau with flocks wandering locally. They use open habitats such as pastures, second-growth juniper woodlands, and shrublands. They typically use low perches, such as shrubs or fences.

Townsend's Solitaire (*Myadestes townsendi*)

Rare and irregular winter visitor throughout the region, occurring with greater frequency on the western half of the plateau. When present, these winter visitors are generally first detected in early November. These birds are often nomadic during their stay and, therefore, do not remain in one location throughout the period. They occasionally remain on the plateau into late April. A few have remained into mid-May, but the latest date reported was a bird found in Mason County on 5 June 1999. Townsend's Solitaires use a wide variety of habitats when present. They are most frequently found along riparian corridors, but can be found in open shrublands with scattered live oak mottes as well.

Veery (*Catharus fuscescens*)

Rare spring migrant and casual fall migrant along the eastern third of the plateau. This species has not been reported in the remainder of the region. Almost all records of this species from the region have been of birds mist-netted at the Driftwood Banding Station. Between 1982 and 1998, 14 Veeries were banded at that location, and one, at Mansfield Dam, Travis County. Spring migrants have been netted between 26 April and 12 May. The only fall records are from late September. This species has been reliably reported only three times at other locations on the plateau during the spring. These sight records fall within the dates listed above. Attwater (1892) collected one at San Antonio on 18 May 1891, but the precise location of the specimen is unknown; it probably was not from the plateau.

Gray-cheeked Thrush (*Catharus minimus*)

Occasional spring migrant through the eastern third of the plateau; casual to accidental farther west. As with the Veery, most of the records for this species come from the Driftwood Banding Station. There are, however, more sight records of this species than of Veery for the region. Spring migrants pass through the region between 23 April and 14 May with the latest spring migrant recorded on 23 May. There are two fall reports for the region, single birds in Kendall County on 18 October 1989 and northwestern San Antonio on 11 October 1999.

Swainson's Thrush (*Catharus ustulatus*)

Uncommon spring and very rare fall migrant in the eastern half of the plateau, occasional spring migrant in the western half. Spring migrants pass through the region between mid-April and late May, although lingering migrants have been reported as late as 6 June. All fall records from the plateau are from the latter half of September. Swainson's Thrush can be divided into two distinctive groups of subspecies. These groups were originally described as distinct species, the Olive-backed Thrush (*C. swainsoni*), found throughout most of North America, and the Russet-backed Thrush (*C. ustulatus*) of the West Coast. Continuing studies may reveal that they are indeed two species. The Swainson's Thrushes reported from the Edwards Plateau belong to the eastern subspecies group and apparently are *C. u. swainsoni*. Attwater (1892) reported collecting a specimen of *C. u. ustulatus* in Bexar County on 25 April 1890. The exact location where the specimen was taken is unknown, but it probably was not from within the boundaries of the plateau. The location of the specimen is also unknown. Although Attwater had collected Swainson's Thrushes and Veeries in the past, there is the possibility that it was a misidentified Veery.

Hermit Thrush (*Catharus guttatus*)

Common migrant and winter resident throughout the region. Fall migrants are first detected on the plateau in mid- to late October. Winter residents remain in the area until mid-April with a few lingering as late as early May before departing. There are several morphologically distinctive subspecies of Hermit Thrush. Wintering birds on the plateau come from the eastern United States and from the Rocky Mountains. The birds from the East tend to be more rufous in color and smaller than those from the Rockies. The differences in appearance between these two populations could potentially cause confusion, particularly between the "Rocky Mountain" Hermit Thrushes and Swainson's Thrush. Hermit Thrush is the only *Catharus* thrush to occur on the Edwards Plateau during the winter, despite reports of the other species.

Wood Thrush (*Hylocichla mustelina*)

Very rare spring migrant and casual fall migrant in the eastern half of the plateau. This species has not been reported west of Kerr County on the plateau, but is considered a very rare spring migrant in the San Angelo area. Spring migrants on the plateau have been reported between 20 April and 10 May. This species has been reported twice in the fall: both were single birds in Kendall County (25 October 1986 and 16 November 1975).

American Robin (*Turdus migratorius*)

Common to abundant migrant and winter resident throughout the region, although the number of birds present fluctuates widely from year to year. Uncommon and local breeding species in urban settings throughout the eastern plateau as far west as Junction, Kimble County. American Robins nest in San Angelo, and therefore nesting may occur in other communities on the western plateau. Fall migrants arrive on the plateau in early November and remain until mid-March. During winters when the population is high, flocks of several thousand can be encountered in the region. An amazing count of one million birds was recorded on the Burnet Christmas Bird Count on 20 December 1983. Robins prefer open habitats, but can be found in open second-growth juniper feeding on the berries.

FAMILY MIMIDAE: Thrashers

Gray Catbird (*Dumetella carolinensis*)

Uncommon spring migrant and occasional fall migrant in the eastern plateau; rare farther west. Gray Catbirds are also casual winter visitors to the region. Spring migrants pass through the region between early April and late May, with the peak between 20 April and 10 May. Fall migrants have been reported from late September through October. Individuals have lingered into early winter and on rare occasions have overwintered. When they are present on the plateau, catbirds frequent brushy habitats along riparian corridors and dry washes.

Northern Mockingbird (*Mimus polyglottos*)

Abundant permanent resident throughout the region. Northern Mockingbirds occupy a wide range of habitats ranging from pastures and savannas to open woodlands. The only habitats where they are not found are dense, contiguous forests. Not only are mockingbirds one of the most common birds on the plateau, but their remarkable mimicry and consistent singing also make them one of the most conspicuous. Northern Mockingbirds are migratory in the northern parts of their range, and there may be seasonal movements within Texas. Individuals mimicking species that do not occur locally suggest such seasonal movements.

Sage Thrasher (*Oreoscoptes montanus*)

Uncommon winter resident in the northwestern quarter of the plateau. Sage Thrashers are irregular winter visitors throughout the remainder of the western half of the region and are casual to the eastern third. This species is very irruptive, with large numbers present some years and absent during others. When present, they are most frequently encountered in juniper woodlands and other open habitats interspersed with dense vegetation. On the northwestern plateau, and elsewhere during irruptive years, they begin arriving in late October and remain until early April.

Brown Thrasher (*Toxostoma rufum*)

Occasional migrant and winter resident in the eastern half of the region; rare in the western half. Fall migrants pass through the plateau from early October through mid-November. Spring migrants have been reported from mid-March to late April. Wintering birds are normally found in brushy habitats, including overgrown fence rows and riparian corridors with dense undergrowth. This species is more common as a winter resident east of the escarpment.

Long-billed Thrasher (*Toxostoma longirostre*)

Rare and local permanent resident along the southern edge of the Edwards Plateau from Val Verde County east to western Bexar County. Long-billed Thrashers are most common in the western half of this area, where they occur as far north as southern Edwards County and northern Uvalde County. Casual visitor to the remainder of the region, with reports from all seasons. Long-billed Thrasher is an uncommon permanent resident just south of the escarpment in the northern portion of the South Texas Plains that encroaches onto the southern edge of the plateau. Vagrants have been reported from virtually every part of the plateau. During the late 1980s, they were found regularly in a few places in Kerr County, fueling speculation that they might be expanding northward. However, there does not appear to be an established population in the central plateau.

Curve-billed Thrasher (*Toxostoma curvirostre*)

Uncommon permanent resident in the western half of the plateau, becoming increasingly uncommon and local in the east. This western thrasher is found in arid, mostly open habitats. On the plateau, they frequent shrublands, mesquite savannas containing brushy areas, and other upland habitats. They are also present in the dense undergrowth along dry washes.

Crissal Thrasher (*Toxostoma crissale*)

Rare permanent resident in extreme northwestern Crockett County. Crissal Thrashers were discovered during the 1960s along Howard Draw and the Pecos River in Crockett County and have since been found considerably farther east in Irion County. Observations were made from all seasons, but nesting remains unconfirmed. There have been no recent sightings, but birders have not regularly visited this part of the plateau since the early 1970s. Whether Crissal Thrashers are still present in this area is unknown. There is also an undocumented report by an experienced observer from northern Uvalde County (7 November 1993).

FAMILY STURNIDAE: Starlings

European Starling (*Sturnus vulgaris*)

Abundant permanent resident in urban areas throughout the region. This introduced species is ubiquitous in urban areas, including small towns. Starlings congregate in large flocks during the late fall and winter and are more likely to be encountered in rural areas during those seasons. These cavity nesters compete with woodpeckers and other species for available nest sites. For this reason, they are the most problematic of the introduced European birds that have become widely established in the United States.

FAMILY MOTACILLIDAE: Wagtails and Pipits

American Pipit (*Anthus rubescens*)

Common migrant and winter resident throughout the region. Fall migrants can be found on the plateau beginning in early October, although the main winter population does not arrive until early November. Winter residents remain through April with a few lingering until mid-May. American Pipits use shorelines of ponds and lakes, wet pastures, and other agricultural lands. Although they are most frequently found near water, they are not confined to shorelines. Formerly known as the Water Pipit, which was split into two species with the Old World population retaining that name.

Sprague's Pipit (*Anthus spragueii*)

Rare migrant and winter resident throughout the region. Sprague's Pipits arrive on the plateau during mid-October and remain until late March. They inhabit grazed grasslands and pastures that resemble short-grass prairie. Sprague's Pipits occur with the greatest frequency in open pastures in the northwestern plateau. This elusive bird is difficult to find and is more commonly encountered in the Blackland Prairies region to the east of the escarpment.

FAMILY BOMBYCILLIDAE: Waxwings

Cedar Waxwing (*Bombycilla cedrorum*)

Common to locally abundant migrant and winter resident throughout the region. Although Cedar Waxwings occur annually on the plateau, their numbers fluctuate greatly from year to year. Some years, it is not uncommon to see flocks with over 100 individuals in an area, while the next year is almost devoid of waxwings at the same location. They frequent open woodlands, including juniper second growth. They arrive on the plateau in mid-November, with numbers slowly building until early December, when most of the wintering birds have arrived. Winter residents remain through mid-May with many lingering to the end of the month. A few individuals routinely linger into early June, with the latest reported being three birds in Real County on 19 June 1992.

FAMILY PTILOGONATIDAE: Silky-flycatchers

Phainopepla (*Phainopepla nitens*)

Casual visitor to the southwestern plateau, accidental elsewhere in the region. This species has been reported on the plateau from all seasons. The majority of the records fall between late October and mid-May. There are summer reports from Val Verde and Edwards Counties, with single individuals found near Devils River State Natural Area on 8 June 1989 and near Carta Valley on 22 July 1998, respectively. The first record for the plateau was of a bird collected near Kerrville on 9 February 1895.

FAMILY PARULIDAE: Wood-Warblers

Blue-winged Warbler (*Vermivora pinus*)

Rare spring migrant over the eastern third of the plateau; casual to accidental farther west. Spring migrants have been reported between mid-April and early May. Reports of this species are fairly evenly distributed between 17 April and 13 May. Only one of the reports is photographically documented: a bird banded at the Driftwood Banding Station on 22 April 1986 (TPRF 381). There is only one report from the fall: a single bird found near Wimberley, Hays County, on 7 September 1961.

Golden-winged Warbler (*Vermivora chrysoptera*)

Very rare spring migrant over the eastern half of the plateau; accidental farther west. Spring migrants have been reported between mid-April and early May. There is only one photographically documented record from the plateau in the Texas Photo Record File, a female at Guadalupe River State Park, Kendall County, on 8 May 1995 (TPRF 1752).

Tennessee Warbler (*Vermivora peregrina*)

Occasional to uncommon spring migrant and rare fall migrant over the eastern third of the plateau; rare farther west. Spring migrants pass through the region between early April and late May. The peak in spring migration is between 20 April and 15 May. Fall migrants pass through the region from mid-September to mid-October. A Tennessee Warbler was reported during the Boerne Christmas Bird Count on 31 December 1972, providing the only winter report for this species from the plateau. This species is regularly found, in small numbers, during winter along the Texas Coast and in the Lower Rio Grande Valley.

Orange-crowned Warbler (*Vermivora celata*)

Common spring and fall migrant and uncommon winter resident throughout the region. Fall migrants begin to appear in the region in mid-September and are present through October with many remaining through the winter months. Spring migrants move through the plateau from late March through early May. The Orange-crowned Warbler is one of the most common migrant warblers through the region. Individuals from the western subspecies tend to be much brighter and are olive-yellow above with yellowish underparts. Eastern subspecies have much grayer upperparts, particularly the head and back and are duller yellow below. The brightly plumaged western birds are occasionally misidentified as Yellow Warblers.

Nashville Warbler (*Vermivora ruficapilla*)

Common to abundant spring and fall migrant throughout the region. Nashville Warbler is the most common migrant wood-warbler on the plateau. Spring migrants begin to arrive in late March and are present until late May. The peak of spring migration is between 15 April and 5 May. Fall migrants pass through the area from mid-September to late October and even into November. The peak in fall migration takes place during the first half of October, but large numbers can be encountered throughout the month. The most surprising record of Nashville Warbler on the plateau was an early fall migrant banded at the Driftwood Banding Station on 14 July 1989. Occasionally, individuals linger into early winter and have been reported on the Del Rio Christmas Bird Count.

Northern Parula (*Parula americana*)

Occasional to rare spring migrant and uncommon and local summer resident on the plateau. Spring migrants pass through the region between mid-March and early May. Summer residents are present until late July, but are more difficult to locate after mid-June, when they quit singing. As summer residents, Northern Parulas are most common along the Guadalupe River drainage, but are present along most of the major river systems west to the Devils River. They are notably absent from the Frio River drainage. Northern Parulas are also very local along the Colorado River and its tributaries. Spanish Moss (*Tillandsia usneoides*) is well-known as the preferred nesting material of this species, but it does not occur widely on the plateau. For most of the region, Northern Parulas nest in clumps of Ball Moss (*Tillandsia recurvata*) in Plateau Live Oaks (*Quercus fusiformis*). As a result, even though they are found primarily along river corridors, they are not strictly confined to the riparian woodlands. Along the westernmost rivers where the Northern Parula nests, such as the Devils and West Nueces, these live oaks are common just above the floodplain.

DRAWING 11. *Northern Parula*

Tropical Parula (*Parula pitiayumi*)

Casual spring and summer visitor to the southwestern portion of the plateau. Tropical Parula was first reported from the plateau at Garner State Park, Uvalde County, on 19 April 1980. There are well-documented records from Bandera, Medina, Uvalde, and Val Verde Counties. The first photographically documented record from the plateau was a male found at Garner State Park on 9 May 1996 (TPRF 1350). Another male of this species was found at Lost Maples State Natural Area on 15 April 1998 (TPRF 1566). A territorial male Tropical Parula was along the Devils River, Val Verde County, between mid-April and mid-June in 1997. During this period, the male was reported to have a mate, but nesting could not be confirmed. Another territorial male was located at Hill Country State Natural Area, Medina County, where it remained from 6 April to 21 May 2000. During the spring of 2000, at least three Tropical Parulas were discovered on a private ranch near the headwaters of the Devils River. To date, there has been no evidence of breeding on the Edwards Plateau. However, these recent discoveries show that more work is needed to determine the status of this species.

Yellow Warbler (*Dendroica petechia*)

Common spring and fall migrant throughout the region. Yellow Warbler is one of the more common migrants on the plateau. Spring migrants can be found between mid-April and late May. The peak of spring migration for this species is during the first 10 days of May. Fall migrants pass through the region between mid-August and late September, with a few lingering into early October. The peak of fall migration is during the first half of September. Yellow Warbler, *D. p. sonorana*, was formerly a rare and local breeding species on the Edwards Plateau. The last documented nesting was near Kerrville in 1938. The last reported nesting was in 1967 near Lake Austin, Travis County, where two adults were observed feeding a Brown-headed Cowbird (*Molothrus ater*) fledgling.

Chestnut-sided Warbler (*Dendroica pensylvanica*)

Occasional spring migrant through the eastern third of the plateau; rare to casual farther west. Chestnut-sided Warblers have been found between mid-April and late May, with a few noted as late as early June. The peak of migration for this species on the plateau is during the first two weeks of May. This species has not been reported during the fall on the plateau, but probably occurs as a rare to very rare migrant.

Magnolia Warbler (*Dendroica magnolia*)

Occasional to uncommon spring migrant and rare fall migrant through the eastern third of the plateau; casual farther west. Spring migrants pass through the region between late April and late May. The peak of spring migration is between 5 and 20 May. Fall migrants can be found between early September and late October. Magnolia Warbler is one of the more commonly encountered eastern warblers that migrate through the region.

Black-throated Blue Warbler (*Dendroica caerulescens*)

Casual along the eastern edge of the region; accidental farther west. There are three documented sight records from the western two-thirds of the plateau. The first was an adult male discovered at the Lacey Ranch near Kerrville on 11 September 1911. The second, also a male, was near Sheffield, Crockett County, on 7 May 1988. The most recent record was an adult male below the dam at Lake Amistad on 16 October 1999.

Yellow-rumped Warbler (*Dendroica coronata*)

Common to locally abundant migrant and winter resident throughout the region. Fall migrants reach the plateau in mid-October, becoming common by early November. Winter residents begin to disperse northward by mid-April, and spring migrants have departed by early May. Winter residents are widespread through the Balcones Canyonlands and in riparian corridors throughout the region. They are more uncommon and local in upland habitats on the western plateau during midwinter. The vast majority of migrant and wintering Yellow-rumped Warblers on the Edwards Plateau are of the eastern or "Myrtle" form. The western or "Audubon's" form is an occasional migrant and winter resident in the western third of the region, becoming rare farther east.

Black-throated Gray Warbler (*Dendroica nigrescens*)

Very rare spring and fall migrant over the entire plateau. This species is probably an occasional migrant through Val Verde County. Spring migrants have been reported between early April and mid-May. Fall migrants have been found between early September and late October. There are two winter reports, one documented, of this species for the plateau. A male was in northwestern San Antonio on 9 December 1995, and another was in Del Rio on 6 February 1999. This species has overwintered along Las Moras Creek in southern Kinney County, and there are winter records from western Bastrop County. Most of the records of this species are from the eastern plateau, probably reflecting the larger number of observers present rather than an actual increased abundance.

Townsend's Warbler (*Dendroica townsendi*)

Very rare fall migrant through the western third of the plateau; accidental farther east. Fall migrants have been reported between mid-August and early November. There is also one winter record for the region: one was present in a Kerrville neighborhood from 11 January through early

February 1978. This species is a regular migrant, sometimes in large numbers during the fall, through the Trans-Pecos. Townsend's Warblers should occur more regularly, including during spring migration, along the western edge of the plateau than records indicate.

Hermit Warbler (*Dendroica occidentalis*)

Accidental. There are two reports of this western warbler from the Edwards Plateau. The first was a female discovered in northwestern Bexar County on an early date of 6 April 1993. A well-described male was found at Lost Maples State Natural Area on 7 May 1996. Hermit Warblers are extremely rare east of the Trans-Pecos, but might be expected to occur on the plateau again and should be looked for during their peak migration periods. They are rare, but annual, migrants through the upper elevations of the Chisos Mountains and probably occur with similar regularity in the Davis Mountains as well. During the spring, they occur from mid-April through mid-May, but are found with greater frequency during the fall. They are early migrants in the fall and are found primarily from late August through mid-September.

Black-throated Green Warbler (*Dendroica virens*)

Occasional to uncommon spring migrant and rare fall migrant through the eastern half of the plateau; rare farther west. Black-throated Green Warbler has one of the longest migration periods, both spring and fall, of any warbler that is found on the plateau. Spring migrants pass through the region between late March and late May. The peak of spring migration is between 20 April and 20 May. Late spring migrants have been reported in early June, and two have been banded at the Driftwood Banding Station in mid-June (17 and 20 June 1990). Fall migrants have been reported between early September and early November. On very rare occasions, Black-throated Greens have lingered into early winter. The latest date reported was of one found on the Boerne Christmas Bird Count on 1 January 1986.

Golden-cheeked Warbler (*Dendroica chrysoparia*)

Uncommon and local summer resident throughout the Balcones Canyonlands and very local elsewhere on the eastern plateau. Golden-cheeked Warblers can be common in suitable habitat. This species nests exclusively on the Edwards Plateau and is the quintessential Texas specialty. They normally arrive on the breeding grounds in early to mid-March and depart by early August. The record early arrival date is

2 March, and the late date is 18 August. Away from the Balcones Canyonlands, this species is found along the Colorado River drainage north through San Saba County, and there are isolated populations north and west to Kimble County. Golden-cheeked Warblers are habitat specialists and are found only in mature Ashe Juniper–oak woodlands. Nests are constructed exclusively from the bark of mature Ashe Juniper, but are often placed in other species of trees. Diverse closed-canopy forests provide the highest quality habitat for this Federally Endangered species.

Blackburnian Warbler (*Dendroica fusca*)

Rare spring migrant and very rare fall migrant over the eastern half of the plateau; casual farther west. Spring migrants have been reported between late April and late May with the majority of spring records falling in the first two weeks of May. There are a small number of fall records of this species from the plateau. These records all fall between mid-September and late October.

Yellow-throated Warbler (*Dendroica dominica*)

Rare spring and fall migrant through the eastern third of the region. Yellow-throated Warbler is also an uncommon and local summer resident in the Balcones Canyonlands. Spring migrants have been detected between early March and mid-May. The earliest spring migrant recorded was of one near Burnet on 13 February 1998. Fall migrants have been found between late August and late September. As a breeding species on the Edwards Plateau, Yellow-throated Warblers are almost exclusively found in riparian corridors where Bald Cypress (*Taxodium distichum*) is present. They are most common along the Guadalupe, Frio, Sabinal, and Nueces Rivers.

Grace's Warbler (*Dendroica graciae*)

Accidental. There are two records of this western warbler from the region. A Grace's Warbler was reported, with details from multiple observers, from west Austin on 28 October 1979. Another was reported, with details, from the Boerne Christmas Bird Count on 22 December 1990. Grace's Warbler has been documented in California during the winter, but the Boerne sighting represents the only winter report for Texas.

Pine Warbler (*Dendroica pinus*)

Rare to very rare winter visitor throughout the region. This species has been reported between late October and early April. Most of the records are from early winter, although some individuals are known to have spent the entire winter at a given location. Most wintering Pine Warblers are found in riparian corridors and are most often found associating with Yellow-rumped Warblers or in mixed species flocks. Pine Warbler was first documented on the plateau by a specimen taken in western Travis County on 18 December 1912. The closest breeding population of this species to the plateau is found east of the escarpment in the Lost Pines Region of Bastrop County.

Prairie Warbler (*Dendroica discolor*)

Casual spring and fall migrant on the plateau with records as far west as Kinney County. Spring migrants have been found between mid-April and mid-May, and fall migrants have been reported from mid-August through September. The only photographically documented record for the plateau was a singing male at Kickapoo Cavern State Park on 16 May 1990 (TPRF 805).

Palm Warbler (*Dendroica palmarum*)

Very rare migrant and casual winter visitor throughout the region. The only reports of spring migrants have been during the last two weeks of April. Fall reports are from late September through late October. Some of the winter reports probably pertain to fall migrants lingering into early winter. The only midwinter reports of this species are single individuals at Kerrville on 16 February 1990 and in southeastern Gillespie County on 20 February 2000.

Bay-breasted Warbler (*Dendroica castanea*)

Rare spring migrant and very rare fall migrant over the eastern half of the plateau; casual farther west. Spring migrants have been reported between late April and late May. The majority of spring records are from 25 April to 10 May. There are only a few fall records from the region, and they are all from early October.

Blackpoll Warbler (*Dendroica striata*)

Accidental. This species has been reported on the plateau on three occasions during spring migration. The first two reports of Blackpolls are from the same day, with one found at Lost Maples State Natural Area, and another near Comfort, Kendall County, on 3 May 1990. The third report was of a singing male at Kickapoo Cavern State Park on 9 May 1992.

Cerulean Warbler (*Dendroica cerulea*)

Casual spring migrant in the eastern third of the region, but has not been reported from farther west. Single Cerulean Warblers have been reported four times from the plateau, only one of which was documented. The first was at Marble Falls, Blanco County, on 5 May 1967. Since then they have been reported in Kerr County on 3 May 1976 and in western Travis County on 28 April 1997. The lone documented record from the region was a bird banded at the Driftwood Banding Station on 22 April 1983 (TPRF 297).

Black-and-white Warbler (*Mniotilta varia*)

Uncommon spring migrant and occasional fall migrant throughout the region. Uncommon and local summer resident in the Balcones Canyonlands. Spring migrants are present on the plateau from late March through late May. Fall migrants pass through the region between mid-August and mid-October. Black-and-white Warblers occasionally linger into early winter and have been reported on plateau Christmas Bird Counts twice. Summer residents arrive in late March and are present through early August. Breeding pairs are found along riparian corridors and in mature, diverse Ashe Juniper–oak woodlands.

American Redstart (*Setophaga ruticilla*)

Uncommon to occasional spring migrant and rare fall migrant over the eastern third of the plateau; occasional to rare farther west. Spring migrants pass through the region between late April and late May. The peak of spring migration is during the first two weeks of May. Late spring migrants have been reported as late as 1 June. Fall migrants have been reported between early September and early November.

Prothonotary Warbler (*Protonotaria citrea*)

Rare spring and fall migrant in the eastern half of the region; casual farther west. Spring migrants have been noted between late March and late May. The majority of the records are from late April and early May. Fall migrants have been reported between late August and late September. Prothonotary Warbler may be a very rare and local breeding species on the southeastern portion of the plateau. Oberholser (1974) reports a breeding record from Medina County, but there is no additional information. A male Prothonotary Warbler was observed singing and taking nesting material to a nest box in Kendall County from 1 to 9 May 1993.

Worm-eating Warbler (*Helmitheros vermivorus*)

Very rare spring and casual fall migrant over the entire plateau; probably more commonly occurring in the eastern third. Spring migrants have been reported between early April and early May, with most of the record from mid-April. This species has been reported, without details, as late as early June. All fall reports are from early September. There are two records of Worm-eating Warbler for the plateau in the Texas Photo Record File: an individual banded at the Driftwood Banding Station on 24 April 1986 (TPRF 383), and another banded at Devils River State Natural Area on 8 September 1996 (TPRF 1833).

Swainson's Warbler (*Limnothlypis swainsonii*)

Accidental. There are two spring reports, one documented, of this species from the Edwards Plateau. The documented record was a singing male at Wild Basin Preserve, western Travis County from 3 to 6 May 1981. The other sighting was of a single bird from Kendall County on 5 May 1990.

Ovenbird (*Seiurus aurocapillus*)

Uncommon to occasional spring migrant and rare fall migrant over the eastern third of the plateau; rare farther west. Spring migrants occur in the region between late April and late May. The peak of spring migration is during the first two weeks of May. Lingering spring migrants have been reported as late as 6 June. Fall migrants have been reported between mid-September and late October.

Northern Waterthrush (*Seiurus noveboracensis*)

Uncommon to occasional spring migrant and very rare fall migrant over the eastern third of the plateau; occasional to rare farther west. Northern Waterthrush, in general, migrates later than Louisiana Waterthrush (*S. motacilla*) during both spring and fall migration periods. Spring migrants occur in the region between mid-April and late May. The peak of spring migration is between 25 April and 15 May. The earliest record for a spring migrant was at Balcones Canyonlands National Wildlife Refuge on 28 March 2000. Fall migrants have been reported between late August and mid-October.

Louisiana Waterthrush (*Seiurus motacilla*)

Uncommon to rare spring and fall migrant through the entire region. Spring migrants are found on the plateau between late March and mid-April. Fall migrants pass through the region between mid-July and late August. Louisiana Waterthrush is also an occasional to rare, but local, summer resident within the Balcones Canyonlands subregion. They are found along most of the major drainages between the Colorado and Frio Rivers. They may also occur along the Nueces River, although no breeding records are known from that system. They are primarily found in heavily wooded canyons with clear-running streams. Summer residents arrive on the breeding grounds in late March and have usually completed nesting activities by late June. Most of the breeding population departs by late July.

Kentucky Warbler (*Oporornis formosus*)

Rare spring and fall migrant through the eastern half of the region; casual farther west. Spring migrants have been reported between mid-April and late May. Fall migrants occur between early September and mid-October. Kentucky Warbler was formerly an uncommon to occasional summer resident along the Guadalupe River drainage. Lacey (1911) reported that they were "rather common in the river and creek bottoms" in Kerr County; he also reported finding nests on several occasions. There are numerous specimens from along the Guadalupe River in Kerr County between the late 1880s and 1937. They were known to breed as recently as the late 1960s in western Travis County and may still be a casual breeder. The most recent summer record was a bird near Hunt in Kerr County on 20 June 1976.

Connecticut Warbler (*Oporornis agilis*)

Accidental. There is one documented record for the Edwards Plateau. A male Connecticut Warbler was present at the Driftwood Banding Station from 3 to 14 May 1986 (TPRF 387). The bird was captured in the same mist net on three occasions during this period, but was never seen otherwise despite extensive searching. This was the second documented record for the state. *Review Species*

Mourning Warbler (*Oporornis philadelphia*)

Common to uncommon spring migrant and occasional to uncommon fall migrant over the eastern half of the plateau; very rare to casual farther west. Spring migrants pass through the region between late April and early June. The peak of migration occurs between 10 and 25 May. The latest spring record for the plateau is 8 June 1998. Fall migrants have been reported between late August and mid-October, with a few stragglers present into late October.

MacGillivray's Warbler (*Oporornis tolmiei*)

Uncommon to common spring and uncommon fall migrant through the western half of the region. Occasional spring migrant and very rare to rare fall migrant through the remainder of the region. This species is annual during spring in the eastern third of the plateau. Spring migrants have been reported between mid-April and early June. The peak of spring migrants is between 1 and 20 May. Fall migrants pass through the region between late August and mid-October.

Common Yellowthroat (*Geothlypis trichas*)

Common spring and uncommon fall migrant throughout the region. Common Yellowthroat is also an occasional winter resident and a very rare and local summer resident. Spring migrants pass through the region between early April and late May. The peak of spring migrants is typically in early and mid-May. Fall migrants can be found between mid-September and early November. Migrant birds can be found in a variety of habitats, although they are most frequently encountered near water. Wintering and breeding individuals are almost exclusively found in cattail marshes or other areas with abundant emergent vegetation that is tall enough to provide cover and nesting habitat.

Hooded Warbler (*Wilsonia citrina*)

Rare to very rare spring migrant in the eastern third of the region; accidental farther west. Spring migrants have been reported between late March and early May. Hooded Warbler has not been reported during fall migration on the plateau, but should be looked for between early September and mid-October.

Wilson's Warbler (*Wilsonia pusilla*)

Common to locally abundant spring and fall migrant throughout the region. Spring migrants can be found on the plateau between mid-April and late May, with the peak from late April to mid-May. Fall migrants return to the region in mid-August, becoming common during September and departing by mid-October. On rare occasions, individuals have lingered into early winter.

Canada Warbler (*Wilsonia canadensis*)

Uncommon to occasional spring migrant and rare fall migrant through the eastern third of the plateau; casual farther west. Spring migrants pass through the region between late April and late May, with the peak of spring migrants between 1 and 20 May. The latest spring record was a bird banded at the Driftwood Banding Station on 4 June 1990. Fall migrants have been reported between mid-August and early October.

Painted Redstart (*Myioborus pictus*)

Accidental. There have been two reports of this species for the Edwards Plateau. One was seen by several observers in Kendall County on 8 September 1988. Another was photographed at Lost Maples State Natural Area on 15–16 March 1999 (TPRF 1734). Although just outside the region, another Painted Restart was documented along Las Moras Creek, southern Kinney County, during the winter of 1989–1990 (TPRF 807).

Rufous-capped Warbler (*Basileuterus rufifrons*)

Accidental. There are eight documented records of this species from the plateau. The first was one from near Boerne from 3 to 12 January 1982 (TPRF 259). Rufous-capped Warblers have since been documented in Bexar, Medina, Uvalde, and Val Verde Counties. The Medina County record was a bird found along the Medina River on 19 August 1998 (TBRC 1998-134). In Uvalde County, one was at Park Chalk Bluff from 20 April to early August 1995 (TBRC 1995-55). One in San Antonio on 20 December 1998 (TBRC 1999-13) provided the Bexar County record. Between 1993 and 2000, there have been five well-documented records from Val Verde County. Four of these are from Texas Nature Conservancy's Dolan Falls Preserve located along the Devils River drainage. On 13 June 1999, a Rufous-capped Warbler was banded at this location. During the spring of 2000, the banded individual was relocated on 25 March at the same location where it had been captured the previous year. This bird maintained a territory through the spring, and on 12 May it was joined by a second bird. No signs of nesting were observed. The final Val Verde County record was in a dry tributary of Lake Amistad. These birds have been found during the winter, spring, and summer.

This has fueled speculation that the species may be a low-density permanent resident in this region of the state.

Yellow-breasted Chat (*Icteria virens*)

Common summer resident in the western half of the plateau, becoming uncommon and more local in the east. Spring migrants reach the plateau in early April, and breeding birds begin to defend territories almost immediately. Summer residents remain until late July and early August before dispersing. Fall migrants from northern populations are rare, but pass through the region in late August and September. On the southern plateau, breeding Yellow-breasted Chats are typically found in savannas where areas of dense brush occur. This habitat is strongly correlated with that used by Black-capped Vireos in the eastern plateau. They typically nest fairly low, often in patches of brush. From Val Verde County northward through the northwestern plateau, this species is more restricted to riparian zones and is often found in hackberry thickets.

FAMILY THRAUPIDAE: Tanagers

Hepatic Tanager (*Piranga flava*)

Accidental. There are two summer records of this western tanager for the region. The first was a male found at Lost Maples State Natural Area on 14 June 1986. Another male was banded at Devils River State Natural Area on 20 June 1998 (TPRF 1567). Interestingly, this species has been found on a number of occasions just outside of the region in eastern Travis, Bastrop, and Gonzales Counties. All of those records are from winter and early spring. Hepatic Tanagers are found as far north as southern Colorado during the breeding season. This species has the potential to occur as a migrant along the Pecos and Devils Rivers. Migrants could occur between late April and mid-May and late August and early October.

Summer Tanager (*Piranga rubra*)

Uncommon to locally common summer resident throughout the region. Spring migrants arrive on the breeding grounds in early April and are present through September. They are found primarily in open woodland habitats throughout the region, including savannas. In the more arid parts of the plateau, they are more restricted to riparian corridors, including pecan-sugarberry communities.

Scarlet Tanager (*Piranga olivacea*)

Very rare spring migrant through the eastern third of the region; accidental farther west. Spring migrants have been reported between late April and mid-May. The westernmost report was of a male at Kickapoo Cavern State Park on 9 May 1992. One entry from the plateau of this species is in the Texas Photo Record File: a male banded at the Driftwood Banding Station on 10 May 1982 (TPRF 275). Scarlet Tanager has been reported twice during fall migration. Single individuals near Wimberley, Hays County, on 21 August 1991 and Concan on 12 September 1992.

Western Tanager (*Piranga ludoviciana*)

Occasional to rare spring and fall migrant through the western third of the region; very rare to casual farther east. Spring migrants have been recorded between mid-April and late May, with most reports from the first two weeks of May. Fall migrants pass through the region between late August and mid-October. Western Tanagers frequently descend into lowland areas after the breeding season. These postbreeding wanderers have been encountered between early July and late August when fall migration begins. They are very rare visitors on the extreme western plateau during this period. There is one winter report from the region: a single individual found on the Burnet Christmas Bird Count on 19 December 1990.

FAMILY EMBERIZIDAE: Sparrows and Buntings

Olive Sparrow (*Arremonops rufivirgatus*)

Uncommon to rare and very local permanent resident along the southwestern edge of the Edwards Plateau from Val Verde County east to Uvalde County; casual east to Bexar County. They have been found close to the escarpment and along the floodplains of the Devils, Frio, and Nueces Rivers. They are typically found in areas of dense shrublands, such as along dry washes or in areas that have been heavily disturbed and are lined with dense brush. Olive Sparrow is an uncommon permanent resident just south of the escarpment in the northern portion of the South Texas Plains that encroaches onto the southern edge of the plateau. This species has rarely been encountered away from known breeding locations.

Green-tailed Towhee (*Pipilo chlorurus*)

Occasional winter resident to the western third of the region, becoming increasingly uncommon farther east. Fall migrants arrive in early October with wintering birds remaining through March. A few individuals linger through mid-April. Wintering Green-tailed Towhees are found in shrublands ranging from fairly open savanna-like habitats with areas of heavy brush to dense thickets along dry washes and fences. They are also found in brushy areas along riparian corridors. Green-tailed Towhees appear to be somewhat irruptive on the eastern plateau. During some winters, they appear to be much more numerous than would normally be expected.

Eastern Towhee (*Pipilo erythrophthalmus*)

Occasional to rare winter resident to the eastern third of the region. Current information would suggest that Eastern Towhees are casual visitors to the western half of the plateau. The westernmost reports of this species on the plateau include one near Concan, Uvalde County, during April 1999 and a female collected in western Kerr County on 19 January 1915 (Smith 1916). Eastern Towhees have been documented much farther west and could occur anywhere in the region. Fall migrants arrive on the plateau in late October, and wintering birds remain through early April, rarely lingering until late April. As with other towhees, Eastern Towhees are found in brushy habitats in the same areas that are frequented by Spotted Towhees. This species, as with other towhees, is more often heard than seen.

Spotted Towhee (*Pipilo maculatus*)

Common to abundant winter resident throughout the region. The first fall migrants arrive on the plateau in early to mid-October, although the species is not common until mid-November. Winter residents remain in the region until mid-April, but lingering individuals have been noted as late as early May. There is one summer record for the region, a wintering bird near Dripping Springs, Hays County, remained through the summer of 1997. Spotted Towhees are found in brushy habitats, as are the other towhees.

Canyon Towhee (*Pipilo fuscus*)

Common to locally abundant resident through the western two-thirds of the plateau. This species is uncommon and more localized in the eastern third of the region, reaching its eastern range limit in western

Travis County. Canyon Towhees are found in similar habitats as the other towhees found on the plateau, but they tend to occupy more arid, often rocky, open areas. They are more common in upland habitats, although other towhees can be found in these same areas. They are less likely to be found along riparian corridors than are the other species.

Cassin's Sparrow (*Aimophila cassinii*)

Common summer resident in the western half of the region; uncommon to rare and local in the eastern half. Occasional to rare winter resident within the breeding range. Summer residents arrive on the plateau in late March and early April and remain through October. Winter residents are more commonly encountered in the western third of the region. Cassin's Sparrow is found in open grasslands and savannas with minimal invasion by woody shrubs. They are most often found in mid- to short-grass prairies or pastures where medium height grasses are still present.

Rufous-crowned Sparrow (*Aimophila ruficeps*)

Uncommon to locally common permanent resident throughout the region. Rufous-crowned Sparrows are found in open, semiarid habitats. On the plateau, they are most often found in canyons and savannas and, to a lesser extent, upland areas with scattered trees and a well-developed understory of shrubby vegetation. A Rufous-crowned Sparrow was found well east of the escarpment at Monument Hill in Fayette County on 1 January 1998. Monument Hill is a limestone outcrop and may host a small population of this species.

American Tree Sparrow (*Spizella arborea*)

Formerly a very rare or casual winter visitor to the western half of the region. American Tree Sparrow has not been reported from the Edwards Plateau since the 1950s. They were occasionally reported, primarily on Christmas Bird Counts, during the 1940s and early 1950s. The southern edge of the winter range of this species appears to have moved northward. They were formerly regular winter visitors to the Lubbock area and to counties along the Red River until the early 1980s and have since become increasingly rare.

Chipping Sparrow (*Spizella passerina*)

Common to locally abundant migrant and winter resident throughout the region. Chipping Sparrows are an uncommon and local summer

resident within the Balcones Canyonlands and occasional to rare elsewhere in the region. Fall migrants arrive on the plateau in late September and are common through November. Chipping Sparrow is a
common winter resident throughout the southern half of the plateau,
becoming uncommon farther north. Spring migration begins in early
April and extends through May. On the plateau, Chipping Sparrows
are found in open woodland habitats, including savannas.

Clay-colored Sparrow (*Spizella pallida*)

Common spring migrant and uncommon fall migrant throughout the
region. This species is an irregular winter visitor to the western portion
of the plateau, particularly in Crockett and Val Verde Counties. Spring
migrants pass through the region between early April and late May. The
peak of migration is usually between 25 April and 10 May. Fall migrants
can be found between mid-September and late October.

Brewer's Sparrow (*Spizella breweri*)

Rare migrant and irregular winter visitor to the western third of the plateau, casual to accidental farther east. Fall migrants have been noted between late September and early November. Spring migrants are present
between early April and early May. Brewer's Sparrows frequently flock
with other *Spizella* sparrows, particularly Chipping Sparrows, during
the winter. Recent studies have suggested that the two subspecies of
Brewer's Sparrow, *S. b. breweri* and *S. b. taverneri*, should be considered separate species; there are morphological and ecological differences
between the two subspecies. The status of the two subspecies on the
plateau is unknown. Most are presumed to be *S. b. breweri*; however,
S. b. taverneri has been documented in Irion County as a spring migrant.
If elevated to species status, *S. b. taverneri* would be called Timberline
Sparrow.

Field Sparrow (*Spizella pusilla*)

Common permanent resident and abundant winter resident throughout
the region. Field Sparrows are found in open habitats, primarily savannas, open shrublands, and overgrown old fields. Migrants from northern
populations augment the wintering population. They arrive in mid- to
late October and remain until early April. Oberholser (1974) described
the breeding population on the plateau and north-central Texas as a distinct subspecies, *S. p. vernonia*. This subspecies has not been included
in subsequent works dealing with Field Sparrows.

Vesper Sparrow (*Pooecetes gramineus*)

Common migrant and abundant winter resident throughout the plateau. Fall migrants begin to arrive in the region in mid-October. By early November, Vesper Sparrows are abundant in grasslands and pastures. Spring migrants begin to leave by early March, and most have departed by late April. Vesper Sparrow is a grassland species, but it can be found in small woodland openings and in very open shrublands where grasses are plentiful.

Lark Sparrow (*Chondestes grammacus*)

Common to abundant summer resident and occasional to rare winter resident throughout the region. During the spring and summer, Lark Sparrows are most common in the mesquite and live oak savannas of the western and northern plateau. However, they occur more frequently during the winter in the Balcones Canyonlands subregion of the plateau. Lark Sparrows are found in open habitats where woody vegetation is common. They arrive on the breeding grounds in late March and are present through September. During most winters, Lark Sparrows are difficult to find and may be absent in the Live Oak–Mesquite Savannas subregion.

Black-throated Sparrow (*Amphispiza bilineata*)

Uncommon to common permanent resident throughout the plateau. Black-throated Sparrows are found in arid habitats. On the plateau, they are most frequently encountered in open shrublands. They are more common in the western third of the region than farther east. Black-throated Sparrows are uncommon and local in the Balcones Canyonlands, particularly so from Burnet County southward along the eastern edge of the plateau.

Lark Bunting (*Calamospiza melanocorys*)

Common winter resident in the western half of the region; rare farther east. The number of Lark Buntings on the plateau each winter fluctuates greatly. They are rare and irregular summer residents in Crockett and Schleicher Counties. Fall migrants arrive on the plateau in late September and early October and are present until early to mid-May. During most years, small flocks of this species can be found along roadsides and in grasslands during the winter in the western half of the region. Lark Buntings can be found in grasslands that have been encroached upon by woody vegetation, but they are not typically found in shrublands.

Savannah Sparrow (*Passerculus sandwichensis*)

Abundant winter resident throughout the region. Savannah Sparrows reach the plateau in late September, but are uncommon until mid-October, when the majority of the wintering population arrives. Savannah Sparrows are, by far, the most common wintering grassland sparrow found on the plateau. They remain on the wintering grounds until late April; lingering individuals can often be found as late as mid-May. There is one summer record for the region. This unexpected record was provided by a single individual found at Balcones Canyonlands National Wildlife Refuge on 15 June 1999.

Grasshopper Sparrow (*Ammodramus savannarum*)

Rare to uncommon winter resident throughout the region. Uncommon to locally common summer resident of the Live Oak–Mesquite Savannas subregion of the plateau; rare elsewhere. Wintering Grasshopper Sparrows are present between early October and early April. Spring migrants pass through the region from early April through mid-May. Grasshopper Sparrows are found primarily in open grasslands, but not in heavily grazed pastures. This is a true grassland species, and they require areas with tall grass for suitable breeding habitat. During migration, they can be found in woodland openings and other small patches of tall grass.

Le Conte's Sparrow (*Ammodramus leconteii*)

Occasional to locally common winter resident in the eastern third of the region; rare farther west. They arrive on the plateau in mid-October and are present through April. Le Conte's Sparrow is another grassland species that requires areas of tall grass. On the plateau, they are most frequently found in grasslands that contain stands of Little Bluestem (*Schizachyrum scoparium*) and Indian Grass (*Sorghastrum avenaceum*).

Fox Sparrow (*Passerella iliaca*)

Uncommon winter resident throughout the region, generally absent from the arid southwestern portion of the plateau. Fox Sparrows arrive on the plateau in early November and are present through February, becoming rare through mid-March. They are found in brushy areas, such as along washes and fences. Considerable taxonomic research has been devoted to the subspecies groups of the Fox Sparrow. The results of those studies suggest that there may be three or four species involved. The subspecies *P. i. zaboria* occurs on the plateau and is part of the eastern subspecies group and, if elevated to the species level, would likely be called the Red Fox-Sparrow. There are no records of members of any of the other subspecies groups from the plateau.

Song Sparrow (*Melospiza melodia*)

Uncommon to locally common winter resident throughout the region. Song Sparrows are present on the plateau from mid-October through mid-March. A few individuals occasionally linger into early April. They are found in brushy habitats throughout most of the plateau, although they are most common along riparian corridors and other mesic habitats where there is a well-developed understory. In the arid southwestern portion of the region, they are much more restricted to these mesic habitats.

Lincoln's Sparrow (*Melospiza lincolnii*)

Common to locally abundant winter resident throughout the region. Fall migrants arrive on the plateau in early October and remain through early May. Wintering individuals occasionally linger to late May. Lincoln's Sparrow is one of the most common migrant, as well as wintering, sparrows in the region. This species appears to be more common during severe winters on the Great Plains. Lincoln's Sparrows occupy brushy or weedy habitats throughout the region and are more likely to be found in upland, and otherwise more arid, habitats than other species of *Melospiza*.

Swamp Sparrow (*Melospiza georgiana*)

Occasional to rare and local winter resident throughout the region. Swamp Sparrows arrive on the plateau in late October and remain through April, rarely lingering into May. Swamp Sparrows are typically found in mesic and, most often, marshy habitats. Cattail marshes around small ponds or lakes provide the best wintering habitat for this species. They can also be found in brushy or weedy habitat that has been flooded. Swamp Sparrows occasionally use other habitats, particularly brushy areas along riparian corridors. They are less frequently found in these drier habitats and can be overlooked because of their skulking habits.

White-throated Sparrow (*Zonotrichia albicollis*)

Common winter resident in the eastern third of the plateau. This species is uncommon in the central plateau and rare in the western third.

DRAWING 12. *White-throated Sparrow*

White-throated Sparrows arrive on the plateau in mid-October, but are not common until early November. They remain in the region through April, with a few lingering into early May. As with other members of the genus *Zonotrichia,* this species is found in brushy and weedy habitats, including small patches of dense brush.

Harris's Sparrow (*Zonotrichia querula*)

Uncommon to locally common winter resident in the eastern half of the region; rare to casual farther west. Harris's Sparrows arrive in early November and are uncommon through early March, becoming rare through early April. The eastern plateau is the western edge of the species' range. Harris's Sparrows are found in the same habitats as White-crowned Sparrows. They are most frequently encountered in brushy and weedy habitats, such as along washes and fences. This species also uses small patches of dense brush for cover in more open habitats.

White-crowned Sparrow (*Zonotrichia leucophrys*)

Common to abundant winter resident throughout the plateau. Fall migrants arrive in early October, and wintering birds depart by mid-May, although a few individuals normally linger through the month. White-crowned Sparrows typically occupy brushy and weedy habitats, including the edges of woodlands. Three identifiable subspecies winter on the plateau. The white-lored *Z. l. gambelii* breeds in the Rockies and winters throughout the plateau, but is much more common in the western half of the region. There are two black-lored subspecies: *Z. l. leucophrys* is commonly encountered throughout the region, and *Z. l. oriantha*, which appears to be a rare visitor to the western third of the plateau. The subspecies *Z. l. oriantha* has brownish upperparts, particularly the nape and back, when compared to the grayer *Z. l. leucophrys*.

Golden-crowned Sparrow (*Zonotrichia atricapilla*)

Accidental. There is one documented record of this species from the Edwards Plateau. A Golden-crowned Sparrow was present near Junction from 25 October 1986 through 10 February 1987 (TBRC 1988-56). There is also an accepted record of this species from just outside the region; one was found in Uvalde on 31 January 1995 (TBRC 1995-64). *Review Species*

Dark-eyed Junco (*Junco hyemalis*)

Common to uncommon winter resident throughout the region. They arrive on the plateau in late October and early November, but are not common until late November. They remain on the wintering grounds until mid-April, but are less common after mid-March. Dark-eyed Juncos are found in open shrublands as well as brushy or weedy habitats. The majority of Dark-eyed Juncos encountered on the eastern plateau are "Slate-colored." On the western plateau, "Oregon" Juncos, including the "Pink-sided" race, are generally more common. The "Gray-headed" Junco is a casual winter visitor to the region. The only photographically documented record from the plateau was one at Ingram on 4 February 1999 (TPRF 1719). This form has been found more frequently in the Concho Valley and is probably of more regular occurrence in the northwestern quarter of the region.

McCown's Longspur (*Calcarius mccownii*)

Uncommon and local winter resident throughout the region. Winter residents begin to arrive on the plateau in early to mid-November and remain until late March. McCown's Longspurs appear to be somewhat nomadic and frequently have not remained in a specific area for long periods of time. They are found in short-grass prairies, pastures, and farmlands, particularly where grain sorghum had been grown during the previous season. McCown's Longspurs are well known for their tendency to flock with other species, particularly Lapland Longspurs (*C. lapponicus*) and Horned Larks.

Smith's Longspur (*Calcarius pictus*)

Accidental. There is only one record of this species from the plateau that is substantiated with details. One individual was at the Preston Prairie Dog Town in northwestern Schleicher County from 24 to 25 November 1978. This Smith's Longspur was observed by about 30 people during the two-day period. Oberholser (1974) also lists a winter report from Schleicher County, but the details of that sighting are unknown.

Chestnut-collared Longspur (*Calcarius ornatus*)

Uncommon and local winter resident throughout the region. Winter residents are present on the plateau from late October to early April. As with the McCown's Longspur, Chestnut-collared Longspurs appear to be nomadic and frequently don't remain in the same location all winter. They are found in short-grass prairies, pastures, and in farmlands, particularly where grain sorghum was grown during the previous season. Chestnut-collared Longspurs rarely flock with other species. The flight call of this species is very different from other longspurs and is an aid to identifying this species.

FAMILY CARDINALIDAE: Grosbeaks and Buntings

Northern Cardinal (*Cardinalis cardinalis*)

Abundant permanent resident throughout the region. Northern Cardinals are found in almost all of the terrestrial habitats on the plateau, being present in both upland and riparian habitats. Northern Cardinals are typically not found in mature closed-canopy forests except along edges or areas where a well-developed understory exists. This species is one of the most obvious members of the plateau's avifauna.

Pyrrhuloxia (*Cardinalis sinuatus*)

Uncommon permanent resident in the western half of the plateau. Pyrrhuloxias are found in open shrublands and mesquite savannas. In general, they tend to inhabit more arid areas than do their close relative Northern Cardinals. On the plateau, however, habitat used by the two species is almost totally overlapping. On the eastern half of the plateau, Pyrrhuloxias appear to be somewhat irruptive, but are generally rare to very rare winter visitors. When present, they arrive in late October or early November and remain through March.

Rose-breasted Grosbeak (*Pheucticus ludovicianus*)

Occasional spring migrant and rare fall migrant through the eastern third of the plateau. In the western half of the region, this species is a rare spring migrant. Rose-breasted Grosbeaks have been found between early April and mid-May; the peak of migration for this species on the plateau is during the first 10 days of May. Fall migrants have been noted between mid-September and late October. There is also a report from early November.

Black-headed Grosbeak (*Pheucticus melanocephalus*)

Occasional spring migrant and rare fall migrant through the western third of the plateau; very rare to casual farther east. Black-headed Grosbeaks migrate through the region between early April and mid-May. Like the Rose-breasted Grosbeak, the peak of migration for this species on the plateau is during the first 10 days of May. Fall migrants have been noted between mid-September and late October. Black-headed Grosbeaks have been found during the winter season on several occasions. Whether these are lingering migrants or overwintering individuals is unknown. There is also one midsummer record for this species from the region: one was found at Government Canyon State Natural Area, Bexar County, on 18 July 1999.

Blue Grosbeak (*Guiraca caerulea*)

Uncommon to common summer resident throughout the region. Blue Grosbeaks arrive on the breeding grounds in mid-April and are present through August. They disperse after breeding and are rare through early October. They are found in open shrublands and savannas. Blue Grosbeaks are somewhat secretive, making them more difficult to observe than other grosbeaks. Male Blue Grosbeaks do not reach adult plumage until their second year. First-year males are generally brown with patches of blue, particularly on the head.

Lazuli Bunting (*Passerina amoena*)

Rare to occasional spring migrant over the western half of the region; rare to very rare farther east. Spring migrants pass through the region between early April and late May. The peak of migration appears to be between 25 April and 15 May. Surprisingly, Lazuli Bunting has not been reported from the plateau during fall migration. This species is more common as a fall migrant in the central Trans-Pecos and should occur on the plateau between early August and early October. Howard Lacey (1911) listed this species as an occasional nester in Kerr County. He reportedly collected egg sets from two nests in 1903. These are the only reported nesting records away from the Panhandle for this species in Texas.

Indigo Bunting (*Passerina cyanea*)

Uncommon migrant and rare summer resident throughout the region. Spring migrants pass through the region between mid-April and late May. Fall migrants have been noted between mid-August and mid-October. Indigo Buntings are local breeders in riparian corridors along the major river systems on the plateau. They are most frequently encountered where some disturbance has left more open habitats in the floodplains of these rivers. Indigo Buntings frequently sing from exposed perches high in the canopy of trees bordering these open habitats.

Varied Bunting (*Passerina versicolor*)

Uncommon and local summer resident on the southwestern portion of the plateau. Varied Buntings occur locally from Val Verde County east to Bandera County and north to Kimble County. They are most common in Val Verde, Kinney, and Edwards Counties. Varied Buntings are found in canyons with areas of dense brush, although they also occur in more open shrublands. They arrive on the breeding grounds in late April and depart by mid-September.

Painted Bunting (*Passerina ciris*)

Common to locally abundant migrant and summer resident throughout the region. Painted Buntings arrive on the breeding grounds in late April and remain until early September. Late migrants or lingering summer residents have been reported through October, although these are usually hatch-year individuals. The latest fall date for the plateau was one near Center Point, Kerr County, on 17 November 1986. Painted Buntings are found in open shrublands and savannas. They are often one of the most common breeding birds in these habitat types, but can be easily overlooked despite the male's brilliant colors. Adult males are the first to arrive in the spring and generally depart during the first half of August. As with all *Passerina* buntings, male Painted Buntings do not attain the unmistakable plumage of an adult until the second year. First-year males have plumage similar to an adult female. They are consistent singers, which identifies them as males, since the females do not sing.

Dickcissel (*Spiza americana*)

Common to abundant spring migrant and uncommon fall migrant throughout the region. Dickcissels are more frequently heard than seen as migrants. Their harsh flight calls, which might be confused with the less stringent buzz of an Indigo Bunting, can be heard overhead from mid-April throughout May. Fall migrants pass through the region between late July and late September, occasionally lingering into early October. The latest fall record for the region was an immature female at Balcones Canyonlands National Wildlife Refuge on 6 November 1999. The Dickcissel is also an irregular summer resident in the region. If there are sufficient rains during the winter and early spring for lush stands of grass, then they breed locally, sometimes in large numbers. During years when conditions are not as favorable, they continue their migration northward. Dickcissels are most frequently encountered in old fields and other areas with weeds and tall grasses, such as Johnson Grass (*Sorghum halepense*).

FAMILY ICTERIDAE: Blackbirds and Orioles

Red-winged Blackbird (*Agelaius phoeniceus*)

Common to abundant permanent resident in the eastern half of the region. They are uncommon and more localized on the western plateau. During the breeding season, Red-winged Blackbirds are more localized in distribution due to general lack of nesting habitat on the plateau. They are widespread and sometimes found in large flocks during the remainder of the year. On the southwestern plateau, this species is restricted in distribution to mesic habitats along rivers and to agricultural areas where water is present. They are occasional visitors to the drier upland habitats.

Eastern Meadowlark (*Sturnella magna*)

Common permanent resident in the eastern third of the region. Eastern Meadowlarks are uncommon permanent residents over the live oak-mesquite savannas of the northern plateau and are uncommon migrants and winter residents across the southern plateau from Bandera County westward. Meadowlarks are a common sight along roadsides, pastures, and grasslands on the plateau during the winter months. The presence of both species of meadowlark makes determining the status of either species difficult. Recent taxonomic studies have suggested that the southwestern subspecies of Eastern Meadowlark, *S. m. lilianae,* may be a separate species. If elevated to species status, it would be called Lilian's Meadowlark. This subspecies has been documented on the southwestern plateau in eastern Val Verde and Kinney Counties.

Western Meadowlark (*Sturnella neglecta*)

Abundant to common winter resident in the western half of the plateau, becoming more uncommon eastward. The Western Meadowlark is an uncommon summer resident in the grasslands and mesquite savannas of the northern plateau. Winter residents are present from early October through April. In the eastern plateau, spring migrants seem to depart in March and are rarely found by late April. Western Meadowlarks are a common sight along roadsides on the western plateau during the winter months. The presence of Eastern Meadowlarks, and a general lack of scrutiny of meadowlarks, makes determining the status of either species more difficult.

Yellow-headed Blackbird (*Xanthocephalus xanthocephalus*)

Common to abundant spring and fall migrant through the western half of the plateau, becoming uncommon in the east. Spring migrants pass through the region between early April and late May. The earliest spring record was provided by three birds near Burnet on 11 February 1998. It is possible that these were actually birds that had wintered locally rather than spring migrants. There is also one summer record for the Edwards Plateau, an adult male was observed in north-central Mason

County on 25 June 2000. Fall migrants are present from late August to early November. On rare occasions, a few individuals may linger into early winter. Yellow-headed Blackbirds are most frequently found around water sources, such as stock ponds, and in agricultural areas, including corrals and feed lots.

Rusty Blackbird (*Euphagus carolinus*)

Rare winter visitor to the eastern third of the plateau; casual farther west. Rusty Blackbirds appear to have been more common on the plateau in the late 1960s and early 1970s, when they were frequently reported on the Boerne and Burnet Christmas Bird Counts. They have been rarely encountered since. When present, Rusty Blackbirds are found almost exclusively in wetlands or along river systems. The primary habitat of this species includes wet creek bottoms with mature hardwoods, but they can sometimes be found in marshes and even flooded fields. Rusty Blackbirds have been found on the plateau between mid-October and mid-March.

Brewer's Blackbird (*Euphagus cyanocephalus*)

Common winter resident throughout the region. Brewer's Blackbirds are present on the plateau from late October through early April. They can be found along roadsides, in pastures, feed lots, and other agricultural areas, as well as around city parks. Brewer's Blackbird is the most common blackbird in upland habitats for much of the western plateau.

Common Grackle (*Quiscalus quiscula*)

Common winter resident and uncommon and local summer resident throughout the region. Common Grackles are found almost exclusively in urban areas on the plateau. They are rarely encountered in rural areas except during the winter and early spring, when they tend to wander more frequently. Common Grackles have recently expanded their breeding range westward to include the western half of the plateau. This species was not a summer resident there until the early 1970s. Prior to that, Common Grackles were only occasional winter visitors.

Great-tailed Grackle (*Quiscalus mexicanus*)

Abundant permanent resident throughout the plateau. Great-tailed Grackles have expanded their range across the Edwards Plateau and are now found in urban areas in every part of the region. They were first detected on the western plateau in the late 1960s, and by the late 1970s they were firmly established. Great-tailed Grackles are occasional and irregular visitors to rural areas, particularly in the western two-thirds of the plateau. In urban areas, they roost in very large numbers, often in the thousands during the winter.

Bronzed Cowbird (*Molothrus aeneus*)

Uncommon summer resident in the western half of the plateau, becoming less common and more local farther east. Bronzed Cowbirds arrive on the plateau in late March and remain until late August. They are found in open habitats, such as shrublands and savannas. They are a brood parasite, primarily affecting Hooded Orioles (*Icterus cucullatus*) and other similar-sized species that build open-cup nests.

Brown-headed Cowbird (*Molothrus ater*)

Common to locally abundant summer resident and uncommon winter resident throughout the plateau. Brown-headed Cowbirds leave most of the upland habitats during winter. In these areas, they are present from early April until early October. Brown-headed Cowbirds can be locally abundant during the winter, with large roost sites estimated to hold up to 80,000 individuals. Banding data has shown that Brown-headed Cowbirds, like most species, show considerable site fidelity for breeding locations. Brown-headed Cowbirds are also brood parasites to many open-cup nesters. This species is considered a major threat to the Black-capped Vireo, and cowbird management efforts are under way at many locations where the vireo is being protected.

Orchard Oriole (*Icterus spurius*)

Uncommon migrant and summer resident throughout the region. Spring migrants arrive on the plateau in early April and are present until mid-May. Breeding Orchard Orioles are very local and are present on the plateau between mid-April and early August. This species is frequently more common during fall migration than at other times of the year. Fall migrants pass through the area from late August through September. Breeding pairs are found along riparian corridors and in oak and mesquite savannas.

Hooded Oriole (*Icterus cucullatus*)

Uncommon and local summer resident in the southwestern quarter of the plateau. Hooded Orioles are present from Val Verde County east to Bandera County. They are rare and local during the summer as far north as Sutton and Kerr Counties. Hooded Orioles are found primarily in very open Ashe Juniper–oak woodlands and oak savannas. This species appears to be more common around human habitations, often taking advantage of hummingbird feeders as food sources. They arrive on the plateau in mid-March and remain until mid-September, occasionally lingering into early October. Hooded Orioles are casual spring visitors to other areas of the plateau. They have been noted as far north as Schleicher County (TPRF 265) and as far east as Bexar County. The Hooded Orioles found in South Texas and the Edwards Plateau belong to the brightest plumaged subspecies found in the United States, *I. c. sennetti*.

Bullock's Oriole (*Icterus bullockii*)

Uncommon spring and occasional fall migrant through the western half of the region; rare farther east. Bullock's Oriole is also a common summer resident in the mesquite savannas of the northern plateau and local in similar habitats in other areas of the western plateau. Spring migrants reach the plateau in late March and early April and are present through mid-May. Summer residents remain on the plateau through mid-September. Fall migrants pass through the region between late August and late October, although they are generally rare after early October. Formerly considered conspecific with Baltimore Oriole.

Audubon's Oriole (*Icterus graduacauda*)

Accidental. There are four spring reports of this species, three of which are documented, from the Edwards Plateau. An Audubon's Oriole was collected in western Bexar County on 27 March 1890. There is another specimen from San Antonio collected on 3 March 1932. The exact locations of the collections are unknown and possibly were from below the escarpment. There are two more recent reports: the first was from Lost Maples State Natural Area, where a single individual was present from 22 April to 8 May 1986. The second was a singing male tape-recorded along FM 674 in southern Edwards County on 28 April 1993. There is a report of two nests of this species found in Val Verde County on 28 June 1941. Without supporting documentation, it seems more likely that this report pertains to Scott's Orioles (*Icterus parisorum*).

Baltimore Oriole (*Icterus galbula*)

Uncommon spring and occasional fall migrant through the eastern half of the region; rare farther west. Spring migrants pass through the region between mid-April and late May. The peak of spring migrants is between 20 April and 20 May. Fall migrants can be found between late August and early October. On rare occasions, Baltimore Orioles have been known to linger into the early winter. Formerly considered conspecific with Bullock's Oriole (*I. bullockii*) under the name Northern Oriole.

Scott's Oriole (*Icterus parisorum*)

Uncommon summer resident in the southern half of the Edwards Plateau. Scott's Oriole can be found in Ashe Juniper–oak woodlands and oak savannas from Crockett and Val Verde Counties eastward across the southern plateau to western Bexar and Comal Counties. They are rare to casual north to Burnet, Llano, Mason, and Travis Counties. They arrive on the plateau in late March and early April and are present through late September. There are several records of birds lingering through the early winter on the plateau, but they do not remain past mid-January. An adult female was banded at Kickapoo Cavern State Park on 13 February 1993. This individual may have been a very early migrant or possibly have wintered in the area.

FAMILY FRINGILLIDAE: Finches

Purple Finch (*Carpodacus purpureus*)

Irregular winter visitor, primarily to the eastern half of the plateau. Since the late 1970s, Purple Finches have been very rare to casual visitors to the region. When present, Purple Finches have been noted between mid-November and mid-March. Lingering individuals have been reported as late as mid-April. Between the 1940s and 1970s, Purple Finches were reported almost annually from the eastern Edwards Plateau, sometimes in large numbers. The number of Purple Finches present on the plateau steadily declined during the early 1980s, and they have been rarely reported during the 1990s. During the period when they were more common, Purple Finches were found in urban areas and woodland habitats, including riparian corridors.

Cassin's Finch (*Carpodacus cassinii*)

Casual winter visitor with most records from the western and central plateau. Cassin's Finch has been reported a number of times from the plateau, but has rarely been well documented. Reports extend from early November to mid-February. There are only two well-documented records from the region. A male from Travis County on 27 January 1963 near Mansfield Dam and a small flock near Junction, Kimble County, from 1 to 5 January 1984 (TPRF 1762). There have also been reports from Bandera, Kerr, Real, Uvalde, and Val Verde Counties. Many reports of this western finch probably pertain to the more common House Finch (*C. mexicanus*).

House Finch (*Carpodacus mexicanus*)

Common permanent resident throughout the region. House Finches are found primarily in woodland habitats, such as oak savannas and open juniper-oak woodlands. They are also common to abundant in urban areas. House Finches are a relatively recent colonizer of the Edwards Plateau; once they appeared on the plateau, they rapidly spread. They were first noted in the region during the early 1930s, and within 10 years colonies were established as far east as Austin.

Red Crossbill (*Loxia curvirostra*)

Very rare and irregular winter visitor throughout the region. Red Cross-bills have been noted between early November and late March. Lingering individuals have been reported as late as mid-April, and an extraordinarily late male was observed near Kerrville on 11 May 2000. During most winters, Red Crossbills are absent from the region. There have been small invasions onto the plateau by this species during the winters of 1983-1984 and 1996-1997. Even during these winters, very few crossbills were found in the region. Those that were noticed were mostly visiting feeding stations.

Pine Siskin (*Carduelis pinus*)

Uncommon and irregular winter resident throughout the region. The number of Pine Siskins present on the plateau in a given winter varies from locally abundant to virtually absent. Fall migrants arrive in early November and remain through April. Lingering individuals have been noted into late May. Pine Siskins frequent open woodlands, urban areas, old fields, and other weedy locations.

Lesser Goldfinch (*Carduelis psaltria*)

Common summer resident and uncommon to occasional winter resident throughout the region. Summer residents are present from early March to mid-October. Lesser Goldfinches are found in savannas and open shrublands. They are also present along riparian corridors and along edges of mature forests. All of the Lesser Goldfinches that occur on the Edwards Plateau, as well as the rest of Texas, are the black-backed subspecies, *C. p. psaltria*. The green-backed subspecies, *C. p. hesperophilus,* has never been documented in Texas. First-summer males of the black-backed subspecies have green upperparts and are superficially similar to the green-backed subspecies. Although there are two varieties that differ morphologically, some authorities consider the species to be monotypic, therefore having no subspecies. Others have suggested that there are actually two species involved.

American Goldfinch (*Carduelis tristis*)

Common winter resident throughout the region. American Goldfinches are present on the plateau from early November through early May. They are uncommon after late March, when they begin to migrate back to the breeding grounds. Lingering individuals molt into breeding plumage before departing. Some of these lingering birds have been noted as late as early June. American Goldfinches are found in almost any woodland or forest habitat. They are also common in urban areas where mature trees are present.

Evening Grosbeak (*Coccothraustes vespertinus*)

Casual winter visitor throughout the region. Evening Grosbeaks were first reported from the plateau, and apparently new for the state, on 31 January 1905 by Howard Lacey. Recent records fall between late November and early April. There are two documented records from the plateau: up to 25 were at the Driftwood Banding Station from 4 January to 4 March 1986 (TPRF 371), and 10 were at Kickapoo Cavern State Park from 31 March to 1 April 1990 (TPRF 808).

FAMILY PASSERIDAE: Old World Sparrows

House Sparrow (*Passer domesticus*)

Abundant permanent resident throughout the region. House Sparrows are primarily found in urban areas on the plateau. Unlike some of the other urban-adapted species, they will establish small colonies around isolated man-made features such as ranch houses and bridges, particularly those not far from large urbanized areas. House Sparrows are rarely encountered in more remote rural areas or in forest habitats.

SPECIES OF UNCERTAIN OCCURRENCE ON THE EDWARDS PLATEAU

This section includes species needing more conclusive evidence of their occurrence on the Edwards Plateau. Some of the reports included here are believed to be valid, but in all cases no supporting documentation is available. Included here are reported sightings of *Review Species* that have either not been reviewed by the TBRC or the submitted records were not accepted by the committee. Many of these sightings were made prior to the development of the review list. In some cases, specimens have been reported in the literature, but their location is unknown. Some of the species on this list may be encountered again on the Edwards Plateau and should be carefully documented.

Fulvous Whistling-Duck (*Dendrocygna bicolor*)

Oberholser (1974) includes a report of this species nesting on the plateau. An adult and two small young were reported on 22 June 1950 from southwestern Gillespie County. Within Oberholser's unpublished materials, there is also a sight record from Kerr County on 24 June 1896 by Howard Lacey. This sighting is not included in Lacey's 1911 publication.

Black Scoter (*Melanitta nigra*)

An individual of this species was reported at the Boerne City Lake, Kendall County, on 28 February 2000. The details accompanying this report were suggestive of an immature male Surf Scoter. There are two undocumented reports of Black Scoters from areas adjacent to the plateau. One was reportedly taken by a hunter at Chacon Lake in southern Medina County during the winter of 1947–1948. Another Black Scoter was reported from southeastern Bexar County on 27 December 1964.

Northern Goshawk (*Accipiter gentilis*)

Oberholser (1974) reports six specimens from Kerr County collected by Howard Lacey. Apparently, Oberholser examined a specimen collected by Lacey during the winter of 1916–1917. The location of these specimens is unknown. It seems unlikely that Lacey could have collected six Northern Goshawks in Kerr County, including four during November 1916. *Review Species*

PLATE 1 Government Canyon State Natural Area, Bexar County

PLATE 2 Devils River State Natural Area, Val Verde County
(photo by Kelly B. Bryan)

PLATE 3 Lost Maples State Natural Area, Bandera County

PLATE 4 Kickapoo Cavern State Park, Kinney County
(photo by Kelly B. Bryan)

PLATE 5 Honey Creek State Natural Area, Comal County

PLATE 6 West Nueces River, Edwards County
(photo by Kelly B. Bryan)

PLATE 7 Green Heron, *Butorides virescens*

PLATE 8 Black-bellied Whistling-Duck, *Dendrocygna autumnalis*

PLATE 9 Montezuma Quail, *Cyrtonyx montezumae*

PLATE 10 Greater Roadrunner, *Geococcyx californianus*

PLATE 11 Eastern Screech-Owl, *Otus asio*

PLATE 12 Common Poorwill, *Phalaenoptilus nuttallii*

PLATE 13
Black-chinned
Hummingbird,
Archilochus alexandri

PLATE 14
Green Kingfisher,
Chloroceryle americana
(photo by Timothy W.
Cooper)

PLATE 15 Vermilion Flycatcher, *Pyrocephalus rubinus*
(photo by Timothy W. Cooper)

PLATE 16 Scissor-tailed Flycatcher, *Tyrannus forficatus*

PLATE 17 Bell's Vireo, *Vireo bellii* (photo by Greg W. Lasley)

PLATE 18 Black-capped Vireo, *Vireo atricapillus*

PLATE 19 Western Scrub-Jay, *Aphelocoma californica*

PLATE 20 Cave Swallow, *Petrochelidon fulva*

PLATE 21 Verdin, *Auriparus flaviceps*

PLATE 22 Cactus Wren, *Campylorhynchus brunneicapillus*

PLATE 23 Bewick's Wren, *Thryomanes bewickii*

PLATE 24
Golden-cheeked Warbler,
Dendroica chrysoparia—male

PLATE 25
Golden-cheeked Warbler,
Dendroica chrysoparia—female

PLATE 26 Summer Tanager, *Piranga rubra*

PLATE 27 Canyon Towhee, *Pipilo fuscus*

PLATE 28 Harris's Sparrow, *Zonotrichia querula*

PLATE 29 Pyrrhuloxia, *Cardinalis sinuatus*

PLATE 30 Varied Bunting, *Passerina versicolor*

PLATE 31 Painted Bunting, *Passerina ciris*

PLATE 32 Lesser Goldfinch, *Carduelis psaltria*
(photo by Greg W. Lasley)

Red Knot (*Calidris canutus*)

There has been a single report of this species from the Edwards Plateau. Two Red Knots were reported from Lake Buchanan on 16 November 1994. No details were provided with the sighting that would help confirm the identification.

Red Phalarope (*Phalaropus fulicaria*)

There is a single sight record of this species on the plateau. An experienced observer reported one at the Junction Sewage Ponds on 29 August 1987. This sighting was made prior to the delineation of review species. *Review Species*

Mew Gull (*Larus canus*)

This species was reported near Del Rio on 10 November 1984. Details were submitted, but the report was not accepted (TBRC 1985-10). *Review Species*

Common Tern (*Sterna hirundo*)

There has been only one report of this species from the Edwards Plateau. A single bird was noted at the Junction Sewage Ponds on 27 May 1973. Although Common Tern has undoubtedly occurred on the plateau, a well-documented sighting is needed to confirm its presence.

Green Parakeet (*Aratinga holochlora*)

Four Green Parakeets were carefully studied by multiple observers along the Guadalupe River in Kendall County on 14 September 1989. The original observers considered them escapees and that is likely correct, but a small flock of parakeets could potentially wander this far north.

Magnificent Hummingbird (*Eugenes fulgens*)

A male Magnificent Hummingbird was reported in northwestern San Antonio from 24 to 26 May 1959. This sighting has been included in most works that include the distribution of this species in Texas. The original description that had been submitted to the South Texas Regional editor of *Audubon Field Notes* was examined, and it is suggestive of a Green Violet-ear. Although the details are not sufficient to document Green Violet-ear, this may have been the first United States record.

Dusky Flycatcher (*Empidonax oberholseri*)

A single Dusky Flycatcher was reported as banded at Devils River State Natural Area on 16 April 1993. The bird may well have been correctly identified, but additional documentation is needed.

Cordilleran Flycatcher (*Empidonax occidentalis*)

This species has been reported numerous times on the Edwards Plateau. Cordilleran Flycatcher is potentially a regular migrant through the region, but this species has never been documented from the plateau. Despite the frequency in which they are reported, no photographs of this species have been published or deposited in the Texas Photo Record File. This species has never been reported as collected or captured in a mist net on the plateau.

Fork-tailed Flycatcher (*Tyrannus savana*)

Oberholser (1974) included a report of this species from north of Uvalde on 10 August 1946. No further information about the sighting is known. There are two documented records from eastern Travis County of this species (Lockwood 1999). *Review Species*

Yellow-green Vireo (*Vireo flavoviridis*)

This species was reported from Kerr County on 19 September 1976. Details were submitted, but the report was not accepted (TBRC 1977-2). There are three accepted records from eastern Travis County. *Review Species*

Black-billed Magpie (*Pica hudsonia*)

Oberholser (1974) included a report of two individuals from southwestern Uvalde County from early November 1849. No further information about the sighting is known. Up to three Black-billed Magpies were present in San Marcos between 3 and 18 April 1998. The record was not accepted by the TBRC because of questions about the origin of the birds. Eurasian and North American populations of the Black-billed Magpie were raised to species status with the forty-second supplement to the A.O.U. checklist (2000). *Review Species*

American Dipper (*Cinclus mexicanus*)

American Dippers have been reported four times from the Edwards Plateau. They have been reported twice each from Johnson Creek, Kerr

County, and the Llano River, Kimble County. The first Kerr County report was in July or early August 1919, and the second was on 19 August 1921. The Kimble County reports were on 6 May 1925 and 30 August 1937. The same individual, Bessie Reid, made all of these observations. There is one recent record from just beyond the region, in eastern Travis County on 5 March 1994 (TBRC 1994-51). *Review Species*

Aztec Thrush (*Ridgwayia pinicola*)

This species has been reported twice from the region: from near Del Rio on 11 October 1989 (TBRC 1989-256) and from Longhorn Cavern State Park, Burnet County, on an unspecified date in 1991 or 1992 (TBRC 1997-151). Details were submitted from both reports, but neither report was accepted. *Review Species*

Cape May Warbler (*Dendroica tigrina*)

There has been one report from the Edwards Plateau of this eastern warbler. A single bird was reported from Kerr County on 15 November 1984. No details were provided at the time of the sighting.

Red-faced Warbler (*Cardellina rubrifrons*)

Three Red-faced Warblers were carefully studied for an extended period by four observers near Bend, San Saba County, on 5 May 1973. Unfortunately, this sighting was not documented. *Review Species*

Black-chinned Sparrow (*Spizella atrogularis*)

This species has been reported twice on the Edwards Plateau. Single individuals were reported on the Del Rio Christmas Bird Count on 26 December 1949 and the Sheffield Christmas Bird Count on 2 January 1971. This species has not been documented east of the Pecos River in Texas.

Sage Sparrow (*Amphispiza belli*)

Oberholser (1974) includes winter sight records from Crockett and Val Verde Counties without details. Sage Sparrows are fairly common locally in the central Trans-Pecos during the winter.

Baird's Sparrow (*Ammodrammus bairdii*)

Baird's Sparrows have been reported at least 10 times from the Edwards Plateau. Details were provided with only one of those sightings. One, or possibly two, individuals were described from Kickapoo Cavern State

Natural Area on 3 and 13 February 1992 (TBRC 1992-158). The TBRC felt that the details provided were insufficient to eliminate Savannah Sparrow. Baird's Sparrows should occur on the plateau as a migrant and potentially as a winter resident. This species has been documented twice in Bexar and Tom Green Counties. Those records all involve spring migrants that occurred between 23 April and 11 May. *Review Species*

Nelson's Sharp-tailed Sparrow (*Ammodrammus nelsoni*)

This species has been reported, without detail, on five occasions within the region. Although Nelson's Sharp-tailed Sparrow migrates from the northern Great Plains to the Texas Coast each year, they are very rarely detected during migration. This species has the potential to be a rare migrant through the eastern half of the region.

White-winged Crossbill (*Loxia leucoptera*)

This species was reported from Llano County on 19 November 1993. Details were submitted, but the report was not accepted (TBRC 1994-26). *Review Species*

SPECIES EXPECTED TO OCCUR ON THE EDWARDS PLATEAU

The following list includes species that have been documented in areas close to the region covered in this book, but have not been reported on the plateau. Many of these species are migratory and undoubtedly have occurred on the plateau, but have been overlooked. There are others that are included based on probable migration routes that may, in fact, be less likely to find their way onto the plateau. The final group is of birds that would be out of range but have been found nearby in the past.

Clark's Grebe (*Aechmophorus clarkii*)

The population of winter Clark's Grebes in Texas has steadily grown over the past several years. This species is being found with increasing frequency on the reservoirs around San Angelo and is overdue at Lake Amistad. Any *Aechmophorus* grebe found on the plateau should be carefully examined to determine its specific identity, as both species are possible. Wintering Clark's Grebes are present in the Trans-Pecos from late September to early April.

Reddish Egret (*Egretta rufescens*)

Reddish Egret is accidental to casual to wetlands east of Austin and San Antonio and is accidental in the San Angelo area. Despite the rarity of this species in areas surrounding the plateau, Reddish Egrets have shown a pattern of wandering after the breeding season. There are at least four records from the San Angelo area and almost a dozen from Balmorhea Lake in the central Trans-Pecos. This species should be looked for between late July and early October.

Glossy Ibis (*Plegadis falcinellus*)

Glossy Ibis is a rare spring and fall visitor to Austin and San Antonio. The population of this species in Texas appears to be steadily climbing, and the records from areas adjacent to the plateau reflect that increase. There are a few spring records, mostly from late April and May, but most of the Glossy Ibis records involve postbreeding wanderers. These birds have been found between early August and late September.

Piping Plover (*Charadrius melodus*)

Piping Plover is a very rare spring migrant and a rare fall migrant through the Austin and San Antonio areas. Although this species is less likely to be found on the plateau than some of the other shorebirds listed here, Piping Plover is a regularly occurring migrant. Most of the spring records from just east of the escarpment are from late April and early May, and fall records are from between mid-July and mid-August.

Whimbrel (*Numenius phaeopus*)

Whimbrels have been documented at Austin, San Angelo, and San Antonio. Although this curlew is a very rare migrant at all three locations, it is a bird that can be expected to occur again. Most of the records from these areas are from the first half of May.

Hudsonian Godwit (*Limosa haemastica*)

This species is a regular, although rare to occasional, spring migrant through the Blackland Prairies physiographic region. They are found annually in the Austin and San Antonio areas and are a rare migrant at San Angelo. Hudsonian Godwits are very likely a rare spring migrant over the eastern third of the region. They should be looked for between mid-April and mid-May.

Common Pauraque (*Nyctidromus albicollis*)

Common Pauraque was reported from the Del Rio area in 1991 and 1992. In both cases, calling birds were noted in an area of dense brush. In an attempt to see the birds, it was determined that the calls were actually the dawn song of the Brown-crested Flycatcher. This species has been reported as close as along Quemado Creek in northern Maverick County. Pauraques have also been found as far north as Bastrop County to the east.

Gray Flycatcher (*Empidonax wrightii*)

An *Empidonax* was tentatively identified as this species in western Bexar County on 22 May 1999. The bird exhibited characteristics of Gray Flycatcher, including pumping its tail downward. Gray Flycatcher has also been documented during the winter in DeWitt County, southeast of San Antonio. This species could also occur as a rare migrant along the extreme western edge of the region. Gray Flycatchers breed throughout the Great Basin and southern Rocky Mountains, including the Davis Mountains in West Texas, and winter throughout the central plateau of Mexico.

Northern Shrike (*Lanius excubitor*)

A Northern Shrike was banded in Irion County on 11 December 1993. Although this is one of the southernmost documented records of this species in Texas, it does highlight the possibility that Northern Shrike could occur on the Edwards Plateau.

Virginia's Warbler (*Vermivora virginiae*)

This species has the potential to occur on the western Edwards Plateau as a migrant. The only record from near the region was a bird along Los Moras Creek in southern Kinney County on 16 November 1991.

Lapland Longspur (*Calcarius lapponicus*)

This species is probably a very rare or casual visitor to the live oak-mesquite savannas of the northern plateau. They frequently flock with Horned Larks and McCown's Longspurs farther north. Look for Lapland Longspurs during winters when they are being reported in large numbers on the South Plains or when McCown's Longspurs are unusually common on the plateau. They are generally found between early November and late February on the South Plains.

Bobolink (*Dolichonyx oryzivorus*)

This species is a casual or accidental spring migrant in the Austin, San Angelo, and San Antonio areas. Although quite rare, it is likely to be found again and should be looked for on the eastern plateau between late April and mid-May.

THE SEASONAL DISTRIBUTION OF EDWARDS PLATEAU BIRDS

The following checklist (Table 2, pp. 175–205) shows the seasonal distribution of the birds found on the Edwards Plateau. Because of the geography of the plateau and the east-to-west changes in avian populations, the distribution and relative abundance of species may be quite different from one location to another. Site-specific checklists may provide better information for a particular locality. For more detailed information on a particular species, please refer to the account found in the main list.

SPECIES OF SPECIAL INTEREST

Beyond the true Hill Country specialties, the Black-capped Vireo and Golden-cheeked Warbler, there are several species that may be of special interest to birders traveling in the region. This section is designed to provide some basic information about where to find some of these birds. For more detailed information about these birds and locations where they can be found, consult any of the bird-finding guides available for the area (Kutac 1998, Lockwood et al. 1999, Wauer and Elwonger 1998).

Black-bellied Whistling-Duck (*Dendrocygna autumnalis*)

This species has expanded its range to include much of the southern plateau. Black-bellied Whistling-Ducks have become a frequent sight from northwestern Bexar County west to Del Rio. They can usually be found at City Park Lake in Boerne, the Uvalde Fish Hatchery, or around any of the permanent bodies of water around Del Rio.

Zone-tailed Hawk (*Buteo albonotatus*)

This uncommon summer resident can occur almost anywhere in the southwestern quarter of the plateau, but can be easily missed. Look for them at Kickapoo Cavern State Park and along Ranch Road 674 between the park and Rocksprings, in the vicinity of Concan and Garner State Park, and around Lost Maples State Natural Area.

Montezuma Quail (*Cyrtonyx montezumae*)

Although this species occurs over a fairly large area of the southwestern plateau, it is almost never seen. The best bet, although still a very long shot, is at Kickapoo Cavern State Park. The population in the vicinity of the park appears to be growing, and the birds are being seen with increased frequency.

Eurasian Collared-Dove (*Streptopelia decaocto*)

As of this writing, the only reliable places to find this introduced species are Johnson City and Marble Falls. Small populations are established in both towns. In Johnson City, they are easily seen in the area around the post office. This bird will probably colonize other urban areas on the plateau in the coming years and eventually may be as common as Rock Doves.

Western Screech-Owl (*Otus kennicottii*)

Western Screech-Owls are most frequently found in Sutton, Schleicher, and Crockett Counties. Look for them around the campground at the Caverns of Sonora or other upland sites in the northwestern quarter of the region.

Elf Owl (*Micrathene whitneyi*)

Listen for this tiny owl around the campground and bunkhouse at Devils River State Natural Area. They can also be found, usually with great difficulty, at Kickapoo Cavern State Park and north along Ranch Road 674 toward Rocksprings.

Common Poorwill (*Phalaenopilus nuttallii*)

Present year-round throughout much of the plateau. Can normally be found by driving along rural roads in appropriate habitat just after dark. Look for them at Devils River State Natural Area, Colorado Bend, Guadalupe River, or Kickapoo Cavern State Parks.

TABLE 2

Seasonal Distribution of Edwards Plateau Birds

LEGEND

Abundance designations

Ab   Abundant: normally present and easy to find in proper habitat, often in large numbers

C   Common: normally present, and should be found, in proper habitat

U   Uncommon: normally present, but can be missed, in proper habitat in small numbers

R   Rare: not expected, annual although occurring only a few times per year

VR   Very Rare: occurs at irregular intervals, but not on an annual basis

Ac   Accidental: average of one or two records every 10 years

x*   Documented as a nesting species only once

?   Status uncertain

(ir)   Irregular in occurrence with numbers of individuals present fluctuating greatly from year to year

(L)   Local in occurrence

Geographic occurrence

E   Eastern half of the Edwards Plateau

W   Western half of the Edwards Plateau

S   Southern portion of the Edwards Plateau, generally referring to the Balcones Canyonlands subregion

SW   Southwestern portion of the Edwards Plateau—Val Verde and Kinney Counties in particular

NW   Northwestern portion of the Edwards Plateau—Crockett, Schleicher, and Sutton Counties in particular

NE   Northeastern portion of the Edwards Plateau

Seasonal occurrence

Sp   Spring (March, April, May)

Su   Summer (June, July)

EF   Early Fall (August, September)

LF   Late Fall (October, November)

W   Winter (December, January, February)

Species	Sp	Su
Red-throated Loon		
Pacific Loon		
Common Loon	VR	
Least Grebe	VR	Ac
Pied-billed Grebe	C-U	R
Red-necked Grebe		
Horned Grebe		
Eared Grebe	U	
Western Grebe		
Blue-footed Booby	Ac	Ac
American White Pelican	R	
Brown Pelican	VR	Ac
Neotropic Cormorant	R	R
Double-crested Cormorant	C-U	
Anhinga	VR	
American Bittern	R	
Least Bittern	VR	VR?
Great Blue Heron	C	C
Great Egret	R	
Snowy Egret	R	
Little Blue Heron	VR	
Tricolored Heron	VR	
Cattle Egret	C	
Green Heron	C	R
Black-crowned Night-Heron	R	
Yellow-crowned Night-Heron	U	U
White Ibis		Ac
White-faced Ibis	R	

EF	LF	W	Nesting status	Geographic occurrence
		Ac		
		Ac		
	VR-R	U		
VR	VR	VR		
R	C	C	x (L)	
		Ac		
		U		
	U	C		
		R		
Ac	Ac	Ac		
	R			
Ac		Ac		
R	VR		x (L)	
	U	C		
	VR			
	R			
VR				
C	C	C	x (L)	
R	R	VR		
R	R	VR		
R	R			
R	R	VR		
C	C			
R-C	C	R	x (L)	
	R			
U	U	VR	x (L)	E
Ac	Ac			E
R	R			

Species	Sp	Su
Roseate Spoonbill		Ac
Wood Stork		
Black Vulture	C	C
Turkey Vulture	C-Ab	Ab
Black-bellied Whistling-Duck	U	U
Greater White-fronted Goose	R	
Snow Goose	R	
Ross's Goose		
Canada Goose	R	
Tundra Swan	VR	
Wood Duck	U	U
Gadwall	C	
Eurasian Wigeon		
American Wigeon	C-U	
American Black Duck		
Mallard	U	R
Mottled Duck	Ac	
Blue-winged Teal	C	R
Cinnamon Teal	R	
Northern Shoveler	C	
Northern Pintail	U-R	
Green-winged Teal	U	
Canvasback	U-VR	
Redhead	U-VR	VR
Ring-necked Duck	U-R	
Greater Scaup		
Lesser Scaup	Ab-C	
Surf Scoter		

EF	LF	W	Nesting status	Geographic occurrence
Ac	Ac-VR			
VR	VR			
C	C	C	x	
Ab	Ab-C	U-R	x	
U	U	U	x (L)	E, S
	R			
	R			
		Ac		
	R			
		VR		
U	U	U	x	E, S
	C	C		
		Ac		
U	C	C		
		Ac		
R-U	U	U		
		VR	x*	
C	C-U		x (L, ir)	
	R	R		
C	C	C		
	R-U	U		
R	U-C	C		
		U		
VR	VR-U	U		
	R-U	U		
		R		E
	C-Ab	Ab		
	Ac	Ac		

Species	Sp	Su
White-winged Scoter		
Long-tailed Duck		
Bufflehead	C	
Common Goldeneye		
Hooded Merganser		
Red-breasted Merganser		
Common Merganser		
Ruddy Duck	C	U-R
Osprey	U	
Swallow-tailed Kite		
White-tailed Kite	R	R
Mississippi Kite	U	
Bald Eagle		
Northern Harrier	U-R	
Sharp-shinned Hawk	C	
Cooper's Hawk	U	R
Gray Hawk	Ac	
Common Black-Hawk	Ac	
Harris's Hawk	U	U
Red-shouldered Hawk	C	C
Broad-winged Hawk	U	R
Short-tailed Hawk	Ac	
Swainson's Hawk	C	
White-tailed Hawk	Ac	
Zone-tailed Hawk	U	U
Red-tailed Hawk	Ab-C	U
Ferruginous Hawk		
Rough-legged Hawk		

EF	LF	W	Nesting status	Geographic occurrence
		Ac		
		Ac		
		C		
		R		
		R		
		U		
		VR		
R-U	C	C	x (L, ir)	
U	U-R	R		
VR				E
R				
U				
		R		
R	R-U	C		
R	U-C	C		
U	U	U	x (L)	
	Ac			
U	U	U	x (L)	NW, S
C	C	C	x	E, S
U	U		x (L, ir)	E
C	C			
U			x (L)	SW
U	U-C	Ab	x	
		R		
		VR		

Species	Sp	Su
Golden Eagle	R	
Crested Caracara	R	R
American Kestrel	C-R	R
Merlin	R	
Peregrine Falcon	R	
Prairie Falcon		
Lesser Prairie-Chicken	Extirpated	
Wild Turkey	C	C
Scaled Quail	U	U
Northern Bobwhite	C	C
Montezuma Quail	R	R
King Rail		Ac
Virginia Rail	R	
Sora	R	
Purple Gallinule	Ac	Ac
Common Moorhen	R	
American Coot	C-U	R
Sandhill Crane	R-U	
Whooping Crane	VR	
Black-bellied Plover	R	
American Golden-Plover	VR	
Snowy Plover	R	
Semipalmated Plover	VR	
Killdeer	C	C
Mountain Plover	R	
Black-necked Stilt	R	VR
American Avocet	R	
Northern Jacana	Ac	Ac
Greater Yellowlegs	U	

EF	LF	W	Nesting status	Geographic occurrence
		R		
R	R	R	x?	NE, S
R	R-U	C	x (L)	
	R	R		
	R	R		
	Ac	R		
C	C	C	x	
U	U	U	x	W, SW
C	C	C	x	
R	R	R	x (L)	SW
			x*	
	R			
	R	R		
	R	R		
R-U	C	C	x (L)	
	U-R	R		
	VR			
R	R			
VR				
R	R		x (L)	
R	R			
C	C	C	x	
R	R	R		NW
R			x (L, ir)	
R	R			
R-U	U	R		

Species	Sp	Su
Lesser Yellowlegs	R	
Solitary Sandpiper	R	
Willet	VR	
Spotted Sandpiper	U	R
Upland Sandpiper	C	
Eskimo Curlew	Ac (1880)	
Long-billed Curlew	R	
Marbled Godwit		
Ruddy Turnstone	Ac	
Sanderling		
Semipalmated Sandpiper	R	
Western Sandpiper	R	
Least Sandpiper	C	
White-rumped Sandpiper	R	
Baird's Sandpiper	R	
Pectoral Sandpiper	U	
Dunlin	VR	
Stilt Sandpiper	R	
Buff-breasted Sandpiper	VR	
Short-billed Dowitcher	VR	
Long-billed Dowitcher	R	
Common Snipe	U	
American Woodcock	VR	
Wilson's Phalarope	U	
Pomarine Jaeger		
Laughing Gull	VR	VR
Franklin's Gull	C	
Bonaparte's Gull		

EF	LF	W	Nesting status	Geographic occurrence
R-U	U	VR		
R	R-VR			
VR				
U	U	U	x?	
C				
R				
	VR			
VR	VR			
VR				
R	R			
R-U	U	VR		
U-C	C	U		
Ac				
R	R			
U	U			
VR				
R				
VR				
R	R			
	U	U		
		R	x?	
U	U	Ac		
Ac				
VR	VR	VR	x (L)	SW
	R	VR		
		U		

Species	Sp	Su
Ring-billed Gull	C	
Herring Gull		
Black-legged Kittiwake		
Sabine's Gull		
Caspian Tern	VR	
Forster's Tern	U	R
Least Tern	R	R
Black Tern	R	
Rock Dove	C	C
Band-tailed Pigeon		
Eurasian Collared-Dove	U	U
White-winged Dove	Ab	Ab
Mourning Dove	Ab	Ab
Passenger Pigeon	Extinct	
Inca Dove	U	U
Common Ground-Dove	R	R
White-tipped Dove		
Monk Parakeet	U	U
Black-billed Cuckoo	R	
Yellow-billed Cuckoo	C	C
Greater Roadrunner	C	C
Groove-billed Ani	U	U
Barn Owl	R	R
Flammulated Owl	Ac	
Eastern Screech-Owl	C	C
Western Screech-Owl	U	U
Great Horned Owl	C	C
Elf Owl	U	U

EF	LF	W	Nesting status	Geographic occurrence
		C		
		R		
	Ac	Ac		
Ac				
VR	VR			
U	U-R	R	x (L)	
R	R	R	x (L)	SW
R	R			
C	C	C	x	
		Ac		SW
U	U	U	x (L)	E (spreading)
Ab	Ab	Ab	x	
Ab	Ab	Ab	x	
U	U	U	x	
R	R	R	x	S
	Ac	Ac		SW
U	U	U	x	E (Travis Co.)
	Ac			
C-U			x	
C	C	C	x	
R			x (L)	SW (Val Verde Co.)
R	R	R	x	
	Ac			
C	C	C	x	
U	U	U	x	NW
C	C	C	x	
U			x	SW

Species	Sp	Su
Burrowing Owl	R	
Barred Owl	R	R
Long-eared Owl	VR	
Short-eared Owl	R	
Lesser Nighthawk	R	R
Common Nighthawk	C–Ab	Ab
Common Poorwill	C	C
Chuck-will's-widow	C	C
Whip-poor-will	R	
Chimney Swift	C–Ab	Ab
White-throated Swift	R	
Green Violet-ear		VR
Broad-billed Hummingbird	Ac	Ac
White-eared Hummingbird		Ac
Buff-bellied Hummingbird	Ac	
Violet-crowned Hummingbird		
Blue-throated Hummingbird	Ac	
Lucifer Hummingbird	Ac	Ac
Ruby-throated Hummingbird	R	
Black-chinned Hummingbird	C–Ab	Ab
Anna's Hummingbird		
Costa's Hummingbird	Ac	
Calliope Hummingbird		
Broad-tailed Hummingbird	VR	
Rufous Hummingbird		
Allen's Hummingbird		
Ringed Kingfisher	R	R
Belted Kingfisher	U	R

EF	LF	W	Nesting status	Geographic occurrence
	R	R		
R	R	R	x	E, S
		VR		
		R		
R			x?	
Ab	R		x	
C	C-U	R	x	
R			x	E, S
R				E
Ab	C-U		x	
	R	R		SW (Val Verde Co.)
VR				
Ac	Ac	Ac		
Ac		Ac		
	Ac			
Ac	Ac			
Ac	Ac			
U	U			
Ab-U			x	
	Ac	Ac		
VR	VR	Ac		
R	R	VR	x*	
U	U	R-VR		
		Ac		
R	R	R	x?	
R	R-U	U	x (L)	

Species	Sp	Su
Green Kingfisher	U	U
Lewis's Woodpecker	Ac	
Red-headed Woodpecker	R	
Acorn Woodpecker	VR	VR
Golden-fronted Woodpecker	C	C
Red-bellied Woodpecker	R	R
Yellow-bellied Sapsucker	U	
Red-naped Sapsucker	R	
Williamson's Sapsucker		
Ladder-backed Woodpecker	C	C
Downy Woodpecker	U	U
Hairy Woodpecker	VR	
Northern Flicker	C	Ac
Pileated Woodpecker	Ac	Ac
Olive-sided Flycatcher	U	
Greater Pewee	Ac	
Western Wood-Pewee	R	
Eastern Wood-Pewee	U	U
Yellow-bellied Flycatcher	R	
Acadian Flycatcher	R	R
"Traill's" Flycatcher	U	
Least Flycatcher	C	
Black Phoebe	U	U
Eastern Phoebe	C	U
Say's Phoebe	U	
Vermilion Flycatcher	C	C
Ash-throated Flycatcher	U	U
Great Crested Flycatcher	U	U

EF	LF	W	Nesting status	Geographic occurrence
U	U	U	x	E, S
		Ac		
		R		
VR	VR	VR	x (L)	
C	C	C	x	
R	R	R	x (L)	
	U	U		
		R		
	Ac			
C	C	C	x	
U	U	U	x	E
		VR		
	C	C		
U				
R	R			W
U	U		x	
R				
R			x	
U	U-R			
C	C			
U	U	U	x	SW
U	C	C	x	
	U	U		W
C	C	R-VR	x	
U			x	
U			x	E, S

Species	Sp	Su
Brown-crested Flycatcher	U	U
Great Kiskadee	R	R
Couch's Kingbird	R	R
Cassin's Kingbird	VR	
Western Kingbird	C	C
Eastern Kingbird	U	
Scissor-tailed Flycatcher	C-Ab	Ab
Loggerhead Shrike	C-U	U
White-eyed Vireo	U-C	C
Bell's Vireo	U-C	C
Black-capped Vireo	U	U
Gray Vireo	R	R
Yellow-throated Vireo	U	U
Plumbeous Vireo	R	
Cassin's Vireo	VR	
Blue-headed Vireo	U	
Hutton's Vireo	Ac	Ac
Warbling Vireo	R	
Philadelphia Vireo	VR	
Red-eyed Vireo	U	U
Steller's Jay		
Blue Jay	C	C
Green Jay		
Western Scrub-Jay	C	C
Pinyon Jay		
American Crow	U	U
Chihuahuan Raven	R	R
Common Raven	U	U

EF	LF	W	Nesting status	Geographic occurrence
U			x	SW
R	R	R	x	SW
R	R	R	x	SW
C	R		x	
U			x?	
Ab	C-U		x	
U	U-C	C	x (L)	
C-U			x	
C-U	R		x	W
U	Ac		x (L)	
R			x (L)	SW
U			x	E, S
	R	R		
VR	?	?		
R-U	U	R-VR		
		Ac	x*	
R	R			
VR				
U			x	
	Ac	Ac		
C	C	C	x	
		VR		SW
C	C	C	x	
		Ac		
U	U	U	x	E
R	U	R	x?	
U	U	U	x	

Species	Sp	Su
Horned Lark	R	R
Purple Martin	U-C	C
Tree Swallow	R	Ac
Violet-green Swallow	VR	
Northern Rough-winged Swallow	U	R
Bank Swallow	U	R
Cliff Swallow	C	C
Cave Swallow	C	C
Barn Swallow	C	C
Carolina Chickadee	C	C
Tufted Titmouse	Ab	Ab
Verdin	U	U
Bushtit	U	U
Red-breasted Nuthatch	R	
White-breasted Nuthatch		
Brown Creeper		
Cactus Wren	C	C
Rock Wren	U	U
Canyon Wren	U	U
Carolina Wren	C	C
Bewick's Wren	Ab	Ab
House Wren	U	
Winter Wren	R	
Sedge Wren	R	
Marsh Wren	R	
Golden-crowned Kinglet	R	
Ruby-crowned Kinglet	C	
Blue-gray Gnatcatcher	C	U

EF	LF	W	Nesting status	Geographic occurrence
R	R	R	x	NW
C			x	
	U	Ac		
VR				
R-U	U	R-VR	x (L)	
U			x (L)	
C-U			x	
C	U-R	VR	x	
C	U-R		x	
C	C	C	x	
Ab	Ab	Ab	x	
U	U	U	x	
U	U	U	x	
	R	R		
	VR	VR		
	U	U		
C	C	C	x	
U	U	U	x	W
U	U	U	x	
C	C	C	x	
Ab	Ab	Ab	x	
	U	R		
	R	R		
	R	R		
	R	R		
	R	R		
U	C	C		
U-C	U-R	R	x	

Species	Sp	Su
Black-tailed Gnatcatcher	U	U
Eastern Bluebird	C	C
Western Bluebird		
Mountain Bluebird	R	
Townsend's Solitaire	R	
Veery	R	
Gray-cheeked Thrush	R	
Swainson's Thrush	U	
Hermit Thrush	C-U	
Wood Thrush	VR	
American Robin	C	R
Gray Catbird	U	
Northern Mockingbird	Ab	Ab
Sage Thrasher	U-R	
Brown Thrasher	R	
Long-billed Thrasher	R	R
Curve-billed Thrasher	U	U
Crissal Thrasher	R	R
European Starling	Ab	Ab
American Pipit	C	
Sprague's Pipit	R	
Cedar Waxwing	C	
Phainopepla	R	Ac
Blue-winged Warbler	R	
Golden-winged Warbler	VR	
Tennessee Warbler	U	
Orange-crowned Warbler	C	
Nashville Warbler	C	

ographic

urrence

(Crockett Co.)

Species

Northern Parula

Tropical Parula

Yellow Warbler

Chestnut-sided Warbler

Magnolia Warbler

Black-throated Blue Warbler

Yellow-rumped Warbler

Black-throated Gray Warbler

Townsend's Warbler

Hermit Warbler

Black-throated Green Warbler

Golden-cheeked Warbler

Blackburnian Warbler

Yellow-throated Warbler

Grace's Warbler

Pine Warbler

Prairie Warbler

Palm Warbler

Bay-breasted Warbler

Blackpoll Warbler

Cerulean Warbler

Black-and-white Warbler

American Redstart

Prothonotary Warbler

Worm-eating Warbler

Swainson's Warbler

Ovenbird

Northern Waterthrush

EF	LF	W	Nesting status	Geographic occurrence
U	U	U	x (L)	SW
C	C	C	x	
		VR (ir)		
	R	R (ir)		
	R	R (ir)		
VR				
	Ac			
VR				
	U	C		
	VR			
R	R-U	C-Ab	x (L)	
	U			
Ab	Ab	Ab	x	
		U (ir)		
		R		
R	R	R	x (L)	SW
U	U	U	x	
R	R	R	x?	NW (Crockett Co.)
Ab	Ab	Ab	x	
	C	C		
	R	R		
	C	C		
Ac		R		SW
R	R			
C	C	U		
C	C			

Species	Sp	Su
Northern Parula	R	R
Tropical Parula	Ac	Ac
Yellow Warbler	C	
Chestnut-sided Warbler	R	
Magnolia Warbler	U	
Black-throated Blue Warbler	Ac	
Yellow-rumped Warbler	Ab-C	
Black-throated Gray Warbler	VR	
Townsend's Warbler		
Hermit Warbler	Ac	
Black-throated Green Warbler	U	
Golden-cheeked Warbler	U	U
Blackburnian Warbler	R	
Yellow-throated Warbler	R	R
Grace's Warbler		
Pine Warbler	VR	
Prairie Warbler	VR	
Palm Warbler	VR	
Bay-breasted Warbler	R	
Blackpoll Warbler	Ac	
Cerulean Warbler	VR	
Black-and-white Warbler	U	U
American Redstart	U	
Prothonotary Warbler	R	
Worm-eating Warbler	VR	
Swainson's Warbler	Ac	
Ovenbird	U	
Northern Waterthrush	U	

EF	LF	W	Nesting status	Geographic occurrence
R			x (L)	
			x?	
C	C		formerly	
R	R			
	Ac			
	U	Ab		
VR				
VR	VR	Ac		
R	R	Ac		
R			x (L)	
VR	VR			
R			x (L)	
	Ac	Ac		
	VR	VR		
VR				
VR	VR			
VR				
U	R	VR	x	
R	R			
R			formerly?	
VR				
R	R			
R	R			

Species	Sp	Su
Louisiana Waterthrush	R	R
Kentucky Warbler	R	VR
Connecticut Warbler	Ac	
Mourning Warbler	U-C	
MacGillivray's Warbler	U-C	
Common Yellowthroat	C	R
Hooded Warbler	VR	
Wilson's Warbler	C	
Canada Warbler	U	
Painted Redstart	Ac	
Rufous-capped Warbler	Ac	Ac
Yellow-breasted Chat	C	C
Hepatic Tanager		Ac
Summer Tanager	U	U
Scarlet Tanager	VR	
Western Tanager	R	
Olive Sparrow	R	R
Green-tailed Towhee	R	
Eastern Towhee	R	
Spotted Towhee	C-U	
Canyon Towhee	C	C
Cassin's Sparrow	U	U
Rufous-crowned Sparrow	U	U
American Tree Sparrow		
Chipping Sparrow	C	R
Clay-colored Sparrow	C	
Brewer's Sparrow	R	
Field Sparrow	C	C

EF	LF	W	Nesting status	Geographic occurrence
R			x (L)	
R	R		formerly	
R-U	U-R			
R-U	U			
R-U	C	R	x (L)	
U-C	U			
R	R			
	Ac			
Ac	Ac	Ac	x?	SW
R			x	SW
U			x	
R	R	Ac		
R	R	R	x (L)	SW
	R	R		
	R	R		E
	U	C		
C	C	C	x	
U	U	U	x	
U	U	U	x	
		Ac		
R	C	C	x (L)	
U	U			
R	R			
C	C	C	x	

Species	Sp	Su
Vesper Sparrow	C	
Lark Sparrow	C	C
Black-throated Sparrow	U	U
Lark Bunting	C	R
Savannah Sparrow	C-R	
Grasshopper Sparrow	U	U
Le Conte's Sparrow	U	
Fox Sparrow	R	
Song Sparrow	U-R	
Lincoln's Sparrow	C-U	
Swamp Sparrow	R	
White-throated Sparrow	C-U	
Harris's Sparrow	R	
White-crowned Sparrow	C-U	
Golden-crowned Sparrow		
Dark-eyed Junco	U	
McCown's Longspur	R	
Smith's Longspur		
Chestnut-collared Longspur	C	
Northern Cardinal	Ab	Ab
Pyrrhuloxia	U	U
Rose-breasted Grosbeak	R	
Black-headed Grosbeak	R	
Blue Grosbeak	U	U
Lazuli Bunting	R	
Indigo Bunting	U	R
Varied Bunting	U	U
Painted Bunting	C	C

EF	LF	W	Nesting status	Geographic occurrence
	C	Ab		
C	C-U	R	x	
U	U	U	x	
R	U	C (ir)	x (L)	
	C	Ab		
U	R	R	x	
	U	U		
		U		
	U	U		
	U-C	C		
	R	R		
	U	C		
		U		
	U	C		
		Ac		
		C		
		R		NW
		Ac		
	R	R		NW
Ab	Ab	Ab	x	
U	U	U	x	
R	R			
R	R			
U-R			x	
U	U		x	E, S
U			x	SW
C			x	

Species	Sp	Su
Dickcissel	C–Ab	U
Red-winged Blackbird	Ab	Ab
Eastern Meadowlark	C	C
Western Meadowlark	C–U	U
Yellow-headed Blackbird	C	Ac
Rusty Blackbird	R	
Brewer's Blackbird	C	
Common Grackle	C	C
Great-tailed Grackle	Ab	Ab
Bronzed Cowbird	U	U
Brown-headed Cowbird	C	C
Orchard Oriole	U	R
Hooded Oriole	R	R
Bullock's Oriole	C	C
Audubon's Oriole	Ac	
Baltimore Oriole	U	
Scott's Oriole	U	U
Purple Finch		
Cassin's Finch		
House Finch	C	C
Red Crossbill		
Pine Siskin	U–R	
Lesser Goldfinch	C	C
American Goldfinch	C–R	
Evening Grosbeak		
House Sparrow	Ab	Ab

EF	LF	W	Nesting status	Geographic occurrence
U			x (ir)	
Ab	Ab	Ab	x	
C	C	C	x	
U	U	C	x (NW)	
C	C-U			
	R	R		
	C	C		
C	C	C	x	
Ab	Ab	Ab	x	
U			x	
C	U	U	x	
U			x	
R			x (L)	SW
C-U	U		x	
U	U			E
U			x	W, S
		R		
		VR		
C	C	C	x	
		VR		
		U (ir)		
C	C-U	U	x	
		C (ir)		
		VR		
Ab	Ab	Ab	x	

Ringed Kingfisher (*Ceryle torquata*)

The most reliable place to find this large kingfisher is along the Nueces River at Chalk Bluff. Other places worth checking are along the Guadalupe River around Kerrville and along the Medina River around Bandera.

Green Kingfisher (*Chloroceryle americana*)

This diminutive bird is locally common throughout most of the Balcones Canyonlands. It can be found along almost any clear stream. Look at Garner State Park, Neal's Lodge at Concan, the city park in Utopia, Devils River State Natural Area, along San Felipe Creek in Del Rio, Lost Maples State Natural Area, and almost anywhere along the Guadalupe River.

Acadian Flycatcher (*Empidonax virescens*)

Acadian Flycatchers can be found locally in riparian woodlands throughout the plateau. The easiest place to find this species is along the mesic canyons of Lost Maples State Natural Area.

Black Phoebe (*Sayornis nigricans*)

This species can be found along most of the rivers and streams of the southwestern plateau. Look along the Frio River at Concan, at Park Chalk Bluff, and at Devils River State Natural Area.

Vermilion Flycatcher (*Pyrocephalus rubinus*)

This attractive flycatcher of open habitats can be found throughout much of the plateau during the breeding season. It is more common in the south and southwest, where it can easily be seen around Concan or at Devils River or Hill Country State Natural Area or Chalk Bluff.

Cave Swallow (*Petrochelidon fulva*)

This bird has colonized the entire region in recent years. Although still present in the natural caves, such as Stuart Bat Cave at Kickapoo Cavern State Park or the Frio Bat Cave in Uvalde County, it can now be found in culverts and under overpasses throughout the plateau.

Western Scrub-Jay (*Aphelocoma californica*)

This widespread bird can be found in any Ashe Juniper–oak woodlands on the plateau. Look for it along roadsides or at any publicly accessible area with this habitat.

"Black-crested" Titmouse (*Baeolophus bicolor sennetti*)

As with the previous species, this is a common and widespread bird. It occupies almost all of the woodland habitats on the plateau and is usually easily located.

Bushtit (*Psaltriparus minimus*)

Although fairly common over the western two-thirds of the plateau, their nomadic nature often makes these birds difficult to find. They are frequently the only species that inhabits dense stands of juniper ("cedar breaks"). They are most often located by the incessant calling between members of family groups.

Long-billed Thrasher (*Toxostoma longirostre*)

This South Texas specialty can be consistently found on the southwestern plateau during the breeding season. Look for this bird at Chalk Bluff, around Concan, or at Kickapoo Cavern State Park.

Bell's Vireo (*Vireo bellii*)

Bell's Vireos are common and easy to locate on the western plateau, but become more local as one moves eastward. They primarily inhabit open shrublands on the plateau. They can be found at Devils River State Natural Area, Kickapoo Cavern State Park, and around Concan.

Black-capped Vireo (*Vireo atricapillus*)

The Black-capped Vireo inhabits the same types of habitats as the Bell's, but is a little more widespread through the southern and eastern plateau. Cowbird parasitism and habitat loss are taking heavy tolls on this endangered bird. Some of the more popular places to observe these birds are Balcones Canyonlands National Wildlife Refuge, Lost Maples and Devils River State Natural Areas, and Kickapoo Cavern State Park.

Gray Vireo (*Vireo vicinior*)

Gray Vireo reaches the easternmost extension of its range on the western plateau. They can be found in savanna-like habitats such as open shrublands with scattered mottes of trees. Perhaps the best places to look for this bird on the plateau are the Texas Department of Transportation picnic area near Sheffield in Crockett County and Devils River State Natural Area.

Golden-cheeked Warbler (*Dendroica chrysoparia*)

This Hill Country specialty is locally common in Ashe Juniper–oak woodlands throughout the Balcones Canyonlands and along the Colorado River drainage in the Llano Uplift. Golden-cheekeds can be found on several state parks, including Lost Maples State Natural Area and Garner, Colorado Bend, and Pedernales Falls State Parks.

Yellow-throated Warbler (*Dendroica dominica*)

Watch for this eastern wood-warbler in riparian woodlands dominated by Bald Cypress. They can be found along the Sabinal River in Utopia or along the Frio River at Garner State Park and around Concan.

Varied Bunting (*Passerina versicolor*)

Varied Buntings are found in densely vegetated canyons on the southwestern Edwards Plateau. The most accessible places to look for this bird are Devils River State Natural Area and Kickapoo Cavern State Park.

Olive Sparrow (*Arremonops rufivirgatus*)

As with the Long-billed Thrasher, Olive Sparrows can be found during the breeding season on the southwestern plateau. Look for them at Chalk Bluff, around Concan, or at Kickapoo Cavern State Park.

Black-throated Sparrow (*Amphispiza bilineata*)

This species is actually much more widespread than some people might think. They occur throughout the region, although they are quite local in the eastern third of the plateau. Look for them in arid habitats such as open shrublands at Devils River and Enchanted Rock State Natural Areas or Kickapoo Cavern and Colorado Bend State Parks.

Harris's Sparrow (*Zonotrichia querula*)

Look for this Texas winter specialty in brushy or weedy areas around the Highland Lakes. They can be fairly common along the county roads in western Travis, Hays, and Comal Counties. They are probably easier to find, and certainly more widespread, in the Blackland Prairies region to the east of the plateau.

Hooded Oriole (*Icterus cucullatus*)

This species is only likely to be found in the southwestern part of the plateau. The best places to look for this beautiful oriole are around Concan and at Kickapoo Cavern State Park. Another good place to look, but just outside the region, is the Judge Roy Bean Center in Langtry, operated by the Texas Department of Transportation.

Scott's Oriole (*Icterus parisorum*)

As with the Black-throated Sparrow, Scott's Orioles are far more common and widespread on the plateau than most people realize. They can be seen at Kickapoo Cavern, Garner and South Llano River State Parks, and Hill Country and Lost Maples State Natural Areas.

Lesser Goldfinch (*Carduelis psaltria*)

Lesser Goldfinch can be found almost anywhere on the plateau, although it is more common in the west. Look in weedy patches and listen for their distinctive call at Garner, Kickapoo Cavern, Lyndon B. Johnson, and Pedernales Falls State Parks and Enchanted Rock, Hill Country, and Lost Maples State Natural Areas.

SELECTED REFERENCES

Albers, R. P., and F. R. Gehlbach. 1990. Choices of feeding habitat by relict Montezuma Quail in central Texas. Wilson Bulletin 102:300–308.

American Ornithologists' Union. 1998. Check-list of North American birds. 7th ed. American Ornithologists' Union, Washington, D.C.

———. 2000. Forty-second supplement to the American Ornithologists' Union *Check-list of North American birds*. Auk 117:847–858.

Archer, S. 1981. Bird life of Lyndon B. Johnson State Park. Bulletin of the Texas Ornithological Society 14:10–12.

Attwater, H. P. 1887. Nesting habits of Texas birds. Ornithologist and Oologist 12:103–105, 123–125.

———. 1892. List of birds observed in the vicinity of San Antonio, Bexar County, Texas. Auk 9:229–238, 337–345.

Bailey, V. 1905. Biological survey of Texas. United States Department of Agriculture, Washington, D.C.

Baumgartner, F. M. 1949–1965. Southern Great Plains Region. Audubon Field Notes vols. 3–19.

Blair, W. F. 1950. The biotic provinces of Texas. Texas Journal of Science 2:93–117.

Booher, D. 1996. Birds of Pedernales Falls State Park: a field checklist. Natural Resources Program, Texas Parks and Wildlife, Austin, Texas.

Brown, N. C. 1882a. Description of a new race of *Peucaea ruficeps* from Texas. Bulletin of the Nuttall Ornithological Club 7:26.

———. 1882b. A reconnaissance in southwestern Texas. Bulletin of the Nuttall Ornithological Club 7:33–42.

———. 1884. A second season in Texas. Auk 1:120–124.

Bryan, K. B. 1999. Birds of Devils River State Natural Area: a field checklist. Natural Resources Program, Texas Parks and Wildlife, Austin, Texas.

Bryan, K., T. Gallucci, G. Lasley, M. Lockwood, and D. H. Riskind. 1999. A Checklist of Texas birds. Technical Series no. 32. Texas Parks and Wildlife, Austin, Texas.

Bryan, K. B., and M. W. Lockwood. 1993. Birds of Kickapoo Cavern State Natural Area: a field checklist. Natural Resources Program, Texas Parks and Wildlife, Austin, Texas.

———. 2000. Gray Vireo in Texas. Texas Birds 2(2):18–24.

Buechner, H. K. 1946. The birds of Kerr County, Texas. Transactions of the Kansas Academy of Sciences 49:357-364.

Casto, S. D. 1992. Texan contributors to the Mississippi Valley Migration Study of 1884-1885. Bulletin of the Texas Ornithological Society 25:51-63.

Cooke, W. W. 1885. A re-discovery for Texas. Ornithologist and Oologist 10: 172-173.

Diamond, D. D., D. H. Riskind, and S. L. Orzell. 1987. A framework for plant classification and conservation in Texas. Texas Journal of Science 39:203-221.

Dunn, J., and K. L. Garrett. 1997. A field guide to warblers of North America. Houghton Mifflin Company, Boston, Massachusetts.

Goetze, J. R. 1998. The mammals of the Edwards Plateau, Texas. Special Publications of the Museum of Texas Tech University no. 41.

Goldman, L. C., and F. G. Watson. 1951-1954. South Texas Region. Audubon Field Notes vols. 5-8.

Heideman, R. 1996. Birds of Lost Maples State Natural Area: a field checklist. Natural Resources Program, Texas Parks and Wildlife, Austin, Texas.

Highland Lakes Birding and Wildflower Society. 1999. Birds of the Highland Lakes area of Burnet and Llano Counties, Texas. Highland Lakes Birding and Wildflower Society, Burnet, Texas.

Jackson, N. 1991. Birds of South Llano River State Park: a field checklist. Natural Resources Program, Texas Parks and Wildlife, Austin, Texas.

James, P. 1963. Freeze loss in the Least Grebe (*Podiceps dominicus*) in Lower Rio Grande Delta of Texas. Southwestern Naturalist 8:45-46.

Jaramillo, A., and P. Burke. 1999. New World Blackbirds: the Icterids. Princeton University Press, Princeton, New Jersey.

Kincaid, E. B. 1956. Ringed Kingfisher at Austin, Texas. Wilson Bulletin 68: 324-325.

Kirn, A. J., and R. W. Quillin. 1927. Birds of Bexar County, Texas. Witte Memorial Museum, San Antonio, Texas.

Kramer, U. 1994. Birds of Inks Lake and Longhorn Cavern State Parks: a field checklist. Natural Resources Program, Texas Parks and Wildlife, Austin, Texas.

Kutac, E. A. 1997. Birds of Colorado Bend State Park: a field checklist. Natural Resources Program, Texas Parks and Wildlife, Austin, Texas.

———. 1998. A birder's guide to Texas. 2nd ed. Gulf Publishing Company, Houston, Texas.

Kutac, E. A., and S. C. Caran. 1993. Birds and other wildlife of south central Texas. University of Texas Press, Austin, Texas.

Lacey, H. 1903. Notes on the Texas Jay. Condor 5:151-153.

———. 1911. The birds of Kerrville, Texas, and vicinity. Auk 28:200-219.

———. 1912. Additions to birds of Kerrville, Texas. Auk 29:254.

Lasley, G. W., D. A. Easterla, C. W. Sexton, and D. A. Bartol. 1982. Documentation of Red-faced Warbler in Texas and a review of its status in Texas and adjacent areas. Bulletin of the Texas Ornithological Society 15:8-14.

Lasley, G. W., and J. P. Gee. 1991. The first nesting of Hutton's Vireo (*Vireo huttoni*) east of the Pecos River, Texas. Bulletin of the Texas Ornithological Society 24:23–24.

Lasley, G. W., and C. Sexton. 1984-1988. South Texas Region. American Birds vols. 38–42.

————. 1988-1994. Texas Region. American Birds vols. 42–48.

————. 1994-1998. Texas Region. Field Notes vols. 49–52.

————. 1999-. Texas Region. North American Birds vols. 53–.

Lloyd, W. 1887. Birds of Tom Green and Concho Counties, Texas. Auk 4:181–193, 289–299.

Lockwood, M. W. 1992. First breeding record of *Aechmophorus* grebes in Texas. Bulletin of the Texas Ornithological Society 25:64–66.

————. 1993. Infrequent flyers (Montezuma Quail). Texas Parks and Wildlife Magazine 51(1):24–27.

————. 1995a. Birds of Hill Country State Natural Area: a field checklist. Natural Resources Program, Texas Parks and Wildlife, Austin, Texas.

————. 1995b. A closer look: Varied Bunting. Birding 27(2):110–113.

————. 1996. Courtship behavior in Golden-cheeked Warblers. Wilson Bulletin 108(3):591–592.

————. 1999. Possible anywhere: Fork-tailed Flycatcher. Birding 31:126–139.

Lockwood, M. W., W. B. McKinney, J. N. Paton, and B. R. Zimmer. 1999. A birder's guide to the Rio Grande Valley. American Birding Association, Colorado Springs, Colorado.

Lockwood, M. W., and C. E. Shackelford. 1998. The occurrence of Red-breasted Sapsucker and suspected hybrids with Red-naped Sapsucker in Texas. Bulletin of the Texas Ornithological Society 31:2–6.

Lockwood, M. W., B. Zimmer, and P. Lehman. 1990. Birding the interstate highways: Interstate 10 from El Paso to Junction, Texas. Birding 22:79–87.

Lyndon B. Johnson School of Public Affairs. 1978. Preserving Texas' Natural Heritage. Policy Research Project Report 31:1–34.

Maxwell, T. C. 1975. Avifauna of the Concho Valley of west-central Texas, with special reference to historical change. Ph.D. dissertation, Texas A&M University, College Station, Texas.

————. 1977. Breeding status of the Least Bittern in the western plains of Texas. Bulletin of the Texas Ornithological Society 10:20–21.

————. 1979. Three men in Texas ornithology. Bulletin of the Texas Ornithological Society 12:2–7.

————. 1980. Significant nesting records of birds from western Texas. Bulletin of the Texas Ornithological Society 13:2–6.

McKenzie, P. M., and M. B. Robbins. 1999. Identification of adult male Rufous and Allen's Hummingbirds, with specific comments on dorsal coloration. Western Birds 30:86–93.

Mueller, K., and E. Mueller. 1998. Birds of Garner State Park: a field checklist. Natural Resources Program, Texas Parks and Wildlife, Austin, Texas.

————. 1999. Birds of Enchanted Rock State Natural Area: a field checklist. Natural Resources Program, Texas Parks and Wildlife, Austin, Texas.

Oberholser, H. C. 1974. The bird life of Texas. University of Texas Press, Austin, Texas.

Peterson, R. T. 1960. Field guide to the birds of Texas. Houghton Mifflin Company, Boston, Massachusetts.

Pulich, W. M. 1976. The Golden-cheeked Warbler, a bioecological study. Texas Parks and Wildlife, Austin, Texas.

Pulich, W. M., and J. E. Parrot. 1977. The occurrence of the Gray Vireo east of the Pecos River. Southwestern Naturalist 21:551–552.

Pyle, P. 1997. Identification guide to North American birds. Slate Creek Press, Bolinas, California.

Quillin, R. W., and R. Holleman. 1918. The breeding birds of Bexar County, Texas. Condor 20:37–44.

Raitt, R. 1967. Relationships between black-eared and plain-eared form of Bushtits (*Psaltriparus*). Auk 84:503–528.

Riley, C. M., ed. 1996. Texas Partners in Flight priority list for Texas bird conservation. Texas Parks and Wildlife, Austin, Texas.

Riskind, D. H., and D. D. Diamond. 1988. An introduction to environments and vegetation. *In* Edwards Plateau vegetation: plant ecological studies in Central Texas. B. B. Amos and F. R. Gehlbach, eds. Baylor University, Waco, Texas.

Schulze, A. E. 1902. The summer birds of Central Texas. A. E. Schulze, Austin, Texas.

Selander, R. K., and J. K. Baker. 1957. The Cave Swallow in Texas. Condor 59:345–363.

Sexton, C. W. 1992. Rare, local, little-known, and declining North American breeders: Golden-cheeked Warbler. Birding 24:373–376.

————. 1999. The Vermilion Flycatcher in Texas. Texas Birds 1(2):41–45.

Simmons, G. F. 1925. Birds of the Austin region. University of Texas Press, Austin, Texas.

Smith, A. P. 1916. Additions to the avifauna of Kerr County, Texas. Auk 33:187–193.

Sorola, S. 1999. Birds of Del Rio and vicinity: a field checklist. Wildlife Division, Texas Parks and Wildlife, Austin, Texas.

Stecker, J. K., Jr. 1912. The birds of Texas, an annotated check-list. Bulletin of the Baylor University Museum 15(1).

Stiles, F. G. 1972. Age and sex determination in Rufous and Allen's Hummingbirds. Condor 74:25–32.

Stringham, E. 1948. Kerrville, Texas, and its birds. Pacot Publications, Kerrville, Texas.

Texas Ornithological Society. 1995. Checklist of the birds of Texas. 3rd ed. Capital Printing Company, Austin, Texas.

Texas Parks and Wildlife. 2000. The guide to Austin-area birding sites. Texas Parks and Wildlife PWD BR W7000-328.

Thornton, W. A. 1951. Ecological distribution of the birds of the Stockton Plateau in northern Terrell County, Texas. Texas Journal of Science 5:158–177.

Watson, F. G. 1955. South Texas Region. Audubon Field Notes vol. 9.

Wauer, R. H., and M. A. Elwonger 1998. Birding Texas. Falcon Press, Helena, Montana.

Webster, F. S., Jr. 1956–1970. South Texas Region. Audubon Field Notes vols. 10–24.

———. 1971–1983. South Texas Region. American Birds vols. 25–37.

White, M. 1999. Inland occurrences of Nelson's Sharp-tailed Sparrow. Texas Birds 1(1):34–39.

Wiedenfeld, C. C. 1983. Lark Buntings (*Calamospiza melanocorys*) breeding in the Edwards Plateau of Texas. Bulletin of the Texas Ornithological Society 16:32–33.

Wiedenfield, S. 2001. Birds of Guadalupe River State Park and Honey Creek State Natural Area: a field checklist. Natural Resources Program, Texas Parks and Wildlife, Austin, Texas.

Williams, F. 1965–1971. Southern Great Plains Region. Audubon Field Notes vols. 19–26.

———. 1972–1988. Southern Great Plains Region. American Birds vols. 26–42.

Williams, G. G. 1949–1951. South Texas Region. Audubon Field Notes vols. 3–5.

Wolfe, L. R. 1956. Check-list of the birds of Texas. Intelligencer Printing, Lancaster, Pennsylvania.

———. 1965. Check list of the birds of Kerr County, Texas. L. R. Wolfe, Kerrville, Texas.

INDEX

Accipiter cooperii, 56
  gentilis, 166
  striatus, 55
Actitis macularia, 69
Aechmophorus clarkii, 170
  occidentalis, 38
Aeronautes saxatalis, 88
Agelaius phoeniceus, 158
Aimophila cassinii, 148
  ruficeps, 25, 148
Aix sponsa, 47
Ajaia ajaja, 44
Amazilia violiceps, 89
  yucatanensis, 89
Ammodramus bairdii, 169
  leconteii, 123, 151
  nelsoni, 170
  savannarum, 151
Amphispiza belli, 169
  bilineata, 150, 208
Anas acuta, 50
  americana, 48
  clypeata, 50
  crecca, 50
  cyanoptera, 50
  discors, 49
  fulvigula, 49
  penelope, 47
  platyrhynchos, 49
  rubripes, 49
  strepera, 47
Anhinga, 40, 176
Anhinga anhinga, 40
Ani, Groove-billed, 82, 186

Anser albifrons, 45
Anthus rubescens, 130
  spragueii, 131
Aphelocoma californica, 28, 112, 206
Aquila chrysaetos, 60
Aratinga holochlora, 167
Archilochus alexandri, 90, 91
  colubris, 90
Ardea alba, 41
  herodias, 41
Arenaria interpres, 70
Arremonops rufivirgatus, 146, 208
Asio flammeus, 86
  otus, 86
Asturina nitida, 57
Athene cunicularia, 84
Auriparus flaviceps, 117
Avocet, American, 68, 182
Aythya affinis, 52
  americana, 51
  collaris, 51
  marila, 51
  valisineria, 51

Baeolophus bicolor, 117, 207
Bartramia longicauda, 69
Basileuterus rufifrons, 144
Bittern, American, 40, 176
  Least, 40, 176
Blackbird, Brewer's, 160, 204
  Red-winged, 158, 204
  Rusty, 160, 204
  Yellow-headed, 159, 160, 204
Black-Hawk, Common, 57, 180

Bluebird, Eastern, 14, 125, 196
  Mountain, 125, 126, 196
  Western, 25, 125, 196
Bobolink, 173
Bobwhite, Northern, 9, 63, 182
Bombycilla cedrorum, 131
Booby, Blue-footed, 38, 176
Botaurus lentiginosus, 40
Branta canadensis, 46
Bubo virginianus, 84
Bubulcus ibis, 42
Bucephala albeola, 52
  clangula, 53
Bufflehead, 52, 180
Bunting, Indigo, 18, 157, 158, 202
  Lark, 150, 202
  Lazuli, 157, 202
  Painted, 9, 158, 203
  Varied, 13, 17, 22, 157, 202, 208
Bushtit, 118, 119, 194, 207
Buteo albicaudatus, 59
  albonotatus, 59, 174
  brachyurus, 58
  jamaicensis, 59
  lagopus, 60
  lineatus, 58
  platypterus, 58
  regalis, 60
  swainsoni, 58
Buteogallus anthracinus, 57
Butorides virescens, 42

Calamospiza melanocorys, 150
Calcarius lapponicus, 155, 172
  mccownii, 155
  ornatus, 155
  pictus, 155
Calidris alba, 71
  alpina, 72
  bairdii, 72
  canutus, 167
  fuscicollis, 72
  himantopus, 73
  mauri, 71

  melanotos, 72
  minutilla, 71
  pusilla, 71
Callipepla squamata, 62
Calothorax lucifer, 90
Calypte anna, 91
  costae, 92
Campylorhynchus brunneicapillus, 120
Canvasback, 51, 178
Caprimulgus carolinensis, 87
  vociferus, 87
Caracara, Crested, 60, 182
Caracara cheriway, 60
Cardellina rubrifrons, 169
Cardinal, Northern, 14, 155, 156, 202
Cardinalis cardinalis, 155
  sinuatus, 156
Carduelis pinus, 164
  psaltria, 164, 209
  tristis, 165
Carpodacus cassinii, 163
  mexicanus, 164
  purpureus, 163
Catbird, Gray, 128, 196
Cathartes aura, 45
Catharus fuscescens, 126
  guttatus, 127
  minimus, 126
  ustulatus, 127
Catherpes mexicanus, 121
Catoptrophorus semipalmatus, 69
Certhia americana, 120
Ceryle alcyon, 94
  torquata, 93, 206
Chaetura pelagica, 88
Charadrius alexandrinus, 66
  melodus, 171
  montanus, 67
  semipalmatus, 67
  vociferus, 67
Chat, Yellow-breasted, 145, 200
Chen caerulescens, 46
  rossii, 46
Chickadee, Carolina, 14, 117, 194

Chlidonias niger, 77
Chloroceryle americana, 94, 206
Chondestes grammacus, 150
Chordeiles acutipennis, 86
   minor, 87
Chuck-will's-widow, 9, 13, 87, 188
Cinclus mexicanus, 168
Circus cyaneus, 55
Cistothorus palustris, 123
   platensis, 123
Clangula hyemalis, 52
Coccothraustes vespertinus, 165
Coccyzus americanus, 82
   erythropthalmus, 81
Colaptes auratus, 98
Colibri thalassinus, 88
Colinus virginianus, 63
Collared-Dove, Eurasian, 78, 174, 186
Columba fasciata, 78
   livia, 78
Columbina inca, 80
   passerina, 80
Contopus borealis, 99
   cooperi, 99
   pertinax, 99
   sordidulus, 99
   virens, 99
Coot, American, 64, 65, 182
Coragyps atratus, 44
Cormorant, Double-crested, 18, 39, 40, 176
   Neotropic, 28, 39, 176
Corvus brachyrhynchos, 113
   corax, 113
   cryptoleucus, 113
Cowbird, Bronzed, 161, 204
   Brown-headed, 135, 161, 204
Crane, Sandhill, 65, 182
   Whooping, 65, 182
Creeper, Brown, 120, 194
Crossbill, Red, 164, 204
   White-winged, 170
Crotophaga sulcirostris, 82

Crow, American, 113, 192
Cuckoo, Black-billed, 81, 186
   Yellow-billed, 9, 82, 186
Curlew, Eskimo, 25, 70, 184
   Long-billed, 70, 184
Cyanocitta cristata, 111
   stelleri, 111
Cyanocorax yncas, 112
Cygnus columbianus, 47
   olor, 47
Cynanthus latirostris, 89
Cyrtonyx montezumae, 63, 174

Dendrocygna autumnalis, 45, 173
   bicolor, 166
Dendroica caerulescens, 136
   castanea, 139
   cerulea, 140
   chrysoparia, 137, 208
   coronata, 136
   discolor, 139
   dominica, 138, 208
   fusca, 138
   graciae, 138
   magnolia, 135
   nigrescens, 136
   occidentalis, 137
   palmarum, 139
   pensylvanica, 135
   petechia, 135
   pinus, 139
   striata, 139
   tigrina, 169
   townsendi, 136
   virens, 137
Dickcissel, 158, 204
Dipper, American, 168
Dolichonyx oryzivorus, 173
Dove, Common Ground-, 13, 15, 16, 80, 186
   Eurasian Collared-, 78, 174, 186
   Inca, 80, 186
   Mourning, 79, 186
   Rock, 78, 186

White-tipped, 80, 81, 186
White-winged, 78, 186
Dowitcher, Long-billed, 73, 184
Short-billed, 73, 184
Dryocopus pileatus, 98
Duck, American Black, 49, 178
Black-bellied Whistling-, 28, 45, 173, 178
Fulvous Whistling-, 166
Long-tailed, 52, 180
Mottled, 49, 178
Ring-necked, 51, 52, 178
Ruddy, 53, 180
Wood, 47, 178
Dumetella carolinensis, 128
Dunlin, 72, 184

Eagle, Bald, 55, 180
Golden, 60, 182
Ectopistes migratorius, 79
Egret, Cattle, 46, 176
Great, 41, 176
Reddish, 171
Snowy, 41, 176
Egretta caerulea, 41
rufescens, 171
thula, 41
tricolor, 42
Elanoides forficatus, 54
Elanus leucurus, 54
Empidonax alnorum, 100
flaviventris, 99
minimus, 101
oberholseri, 168
occidentalis, 168
traillii, 100
virescens, 100, 206
wrightii, 172
Eremophila alpestris, 114
Eudocimus albus, 43
Eugenes fulgens, 167
Euphagus carolinus, 160
cyanocephalus, 160

Falco columbarius, 61
mexicanus, 61
peregrinus, 61
sparverius, 61
Falcon, Peregrine, 61, 182
Prairie, 61, 182
Finch, Cassin's, 163, 204
House, 164, 204
Purple, 163, 204
Flicker, Northern, 98, 190
"Red-shafted," 98
"Yellow-shafted," 98
Flycatcher, Acadian, 22, 100, 190, 206
Alder, 100
Ash-throated, 13, 19, 22, 102–104, 190
Brown-crested, 13, 19, 103, 104, 172, 192
Cordilleran, 168
Dusky, 168
Fork-tailed, 168
Gray, 172
Great Crested, 13, 18, 19, 22, 102, 192
Least, 101, 190
Scissor-tailed, 9, 105, 192
"Traill's," 100, 190
Olive-sided, 99, 190
Vermilion, 9, 16, 102, 190, 206
Willow, 100
Yellow-bellied, 99, 190
Fulica americana, 65

Gadwall, 47, 178
Gallinago gallinago, 73
Gallinula chloropus, 64
Gallinule, Purple, 64, 182
Gavia immer, 35
pacifica, 35
stellata, 35
Geococcyx californianus, 82
Geothlypis trichas, 143

Gnatcatcher, Black-tailed, 13, 124, 125, 196
Blue-gray, 124, 196
Godwit, Hudsonian, 171
Marbled, 70, 184
Goldeneye, Common, 53, 180
Golden-Plover, American, 66, 182
Goldfinch, American, 165, 204
Lesser, 9, 27, 164, 165, 204, 209
Goose, Canada, 46, 178
Greater White-fronted, 45, 46, 178
Ross's, 46, 178
Snow, 46, 178
Goshawk, Northern, 166
Grackle, Common, 160, 204
Great-tailed, 160, 161, 204
Grebe, Clark's, 170
Eared, 37, 176
Horned, 12, 17, 18, 37, 176
Least, 36, 176
Pied-billed, 37, 176
Red-necked, 37, 176
Western, 38, 176
Grosbeak, Black-headed, 28, 156, 202
Blue, 156, 202
Evening, 28, 165, 204
Rose-breasted, 156, 202
Ground-Dove, Common, 13, 15, 16, 80, 186
Grus americana, 65
canadensis, 65
Guiraca caerulea, 136
Gull, Bonaparte's, 18, 75, 186
Franklin's, 75, 184
Herring, 18, 76, 186
Laughing, 11, 76, 186
Mew, 167
Ring-billed, 18, 75, 186
Sabine's, 76, 186
Gymnorhinus cyanocephalus, 112

Haliaeetus leucocephalus, 55
Harrier, Northern, 55, 180
Hawk, Broad-winged, 54, 58, 180

Common Black-, 57, 180
Cooper's, 56, 180
Ferruginous, 60, 180
Gray, 57, 180
Harris's, 57, 180
Red-shouldered, 58, 180
Red-tailed, 59, 180
Rough-legged, 60, 180
Sharp-shinned, 55, 56, 180
Short-tailed, 58, 180
Swainson's, 54, 58, 180
White-tailed, 59, 180
Zone-tailed, 13, 17, 59, 174, 180
Helmitheros vermivorus, 141
Heron, Black-crowned Night-, 42, 43, 176
Great Blue, 41, 176
Green, 42, 176
Little Blue, 41, 176
Tricolored, 42, 176
Yellow-crowned Night-, 43, 176
Himantopus mexicanus, 67
Hirundo rustica, 116
Hummingbird, Allen's, 93, 188
Anna's, 91, 188
Calliope, 92, 188
Costa's, 92, 188
Black-chinned, 9, 90, 91, 188
Blue-throated, 90, 188
Broad-billed, 89, 188
Broad-tailed, 92, 188
Buff-bellied, 89, 188
Lucifer, 90, 188
Magnificent, 88, 167
Ruby-throated, 90, 188
Rufous, 92, 93, 188
Violet-crowned, 89, 188
White-eared, 89, 188
Hylocharis leucotis, 89
Hylocichla mustelina, 127

Ibis, Glossy, 171
White, 43, 44, 176
White-faced, 43, 178

Icteria virens, 145
Icterus bullockii, 162
   cucullatus, 161, 208
   galbula, 162
   graduacauda, 162
   parisorum, 162, 163, 209
   spurius, 161
Ictinia mississippiensis, 55
Ixobrychus exilis, 40

Jacana, Northern, 68, 182
Jacana spinosa, 68
Jaeger, Parasitic, 75
   Pomarine, 74, 184
Jay, Blue, 95, 111, 192
   Green, 112, 192
   Pinyon, 112, 192
   Steller's, 111, 192
   Western Scrub-, 13, 17, 19, 22, 28,
      112, 192, 206
Junco, Dark-eyed, 154, 202
   "Gray-headed," 154
   "Oregon," 154
   "Pink-sided," 154
   "Slate-colored," 154
Junco hyemalis, 154

Kestrel, American, 61, 182
Killdeer, 67, 182
Kingbird, Cassin's, 104, 192
   Couch's, 28, 104, 192
   Eastern, 105, 192
   Western, 105, 192
Kingfisher, Belted, 94, 190
   Green, 18, 20, 22, 94, 190, 206
   Ringed, 19, 93, 188, 206
Kinglet, Golden-crowned, 123, 124,
   194
   Ruby-crowned, 124, 194
Kiskadee, Great, 104, 192
Kite, Mississippi, 55, 180
   Swallow-tailed, 54, 180
   White-tailed, 54, 180

Kittiwake, Black-legged, 76, 186
Knot, Red, 167

Lampornis clemenciae, 90
Lanius excubitor, 172
   ludovicianus, 106
Lark, Horned, 114, 155, 172, 194
Larus argentatus, 76
   atricilla, 75
   canus, 167
   delawarensis, 75
   philadelphia, 75
   pipixcan, 75
Leptotila verreauxi, 80
Limnodromus griseus, 73
   scolopaceus, 73
Limnothlypis swainsonii, 141
Limosa fedoa, 70
   haemastica, 171
Longspur, Chestnut-collared, 155,
   202
   Lapland, 155, 172
   McCown's, 155, 172, 202
   Smith's, 155, 202
Loon, Common, 12, 17, 18, 35, 36,
   176
   Pacific, 35, 176
   Red-throated, 35, 176
Lophodytes cucullatus, 53
Loxia curvirostra, 164
   leucoptera, 170

Magpie, Black-billed, 168
Mallard, 49, 178
Martin, Purple, 114, 194
Meadowlark, Eastern, 159, 204
   Western, 159, 204
Melanerpes aurifrons, 95
   carolinus, 95
   erythrocephalus, 94
   formicivorus, 95
   lewis, 94
Melanitta fusca, 52

nigra, 166
   perspicillata, 52
Meleagris gallopavo, 62
Melospiza georgiana, 152
   lincolnii, 152
   melodia, 152
Merganser, Common, 53, 180
   Hooded, 53, 180
   Red-breasted, 12, 18, 53, 180
Mergus merganser, 53
   serrator, 53
Merlin, 61, 182
Micrathene whitneyi, 84, 174
Mimus polyglottos, 128
Mniotilta varia, 140
Mockingbird, Northern, 128, 129, 196
Molothrus aeneus, 161
   ater, 135, 161
Moorhen, Common, 64, 182
Myadestes townsendi, 126
Mycteria americana, 44
Myiarchus cinerascens, 102
   crinitus, 102
   tyrannulus, 103
Myioborus pictus, 144
Myiopsitta monachus, 81

Nighthawk, Common, 87, 188
   Lesser, 86, 188
Night-Heron, Black-crowned, 42, 176
   Yellow-crowned, 43, 176
Numenius americanus, 70
   borealis, 70
   phaeopus, 171
Nuthatch, Red-breasted, 119, 194
   White-breasted, 119, 120, 194
Nyctanassa violacea, 43
Nycticorax nycticorax, 42
Nyctidromus albicollis, 172

Oldsquaw, 52
Oporornis agilis, 142

formosus, 142
   philadelphia, 143
   tolmiei, 143
Oreoscoptes montanus, 129
Oriole, Audubon's, 162, 204
   Baltimore, 162, 163, 204
   Bullock's, 162, 163, 204
   Hooded, 13, 17, 22, 161, 162, 204, 208
   Northern, 163
   Orchard, 9, 161, 204
   Scott's, 13, 17, 22, 162, 163, 204, 209
Osprey, 54, 180
Otus asio, 83
   flammeolus, 83
   kennicottii, 83, 174
Ovenbird, 141, 198
Owl, Barn, 82, 83, 186
   Barred, 22, 84, 86, 188
   Burrowing, 84, 188
   Eastern Screech-, 83, 84, 186
   Elf, 9, 13, 84, 174, 188
   Flammulated, 83, 186
   Great Horned, 84, 186
   Long-eared, 86, 188
   Short-eared, 86, 188
   Western Screech-, 13, 83, 174, 186
Oxyura jamaicensis, 53

Pandion haliaetus, 54
Parabuteo unicinctus, 57
Parakeet, Green, 167
   Monk, 81, 186
Parula, Northern, 16, 22, 133, 198
   Tropical, 134, 198
Parula americana, 133
   pitiayumi, 134
Passer domesticus, 165
Passerculus sandwichensis, 151
Passerella iliaca, 151
Passerina amoena, 157
   ciris, 158

cyanea, 157
versicolor, 157, 208
Pauraque, Common, 172
Pelecanus erythrorhynchos, 38
    occidentalis, 39
Pelican, American White, 38, 39, 176
    Brown, 39, 176
Petrochelidon fulva, 116, 206
    pyrrhonota, 116
Pewee, Eastern Wood-, 99, 190
    Greater, 99, 190
    Western Wood-, 99, 190
Phainopepla, 131, 196
Phainopepla nitens, 131
Phalacrocorax auritus, 39
    brasilianus, 39
Phalaenoptilus nuttallii, 87, 188
Phalarope, Red, 167
    Wilson's, 74, 184
Phalaropus fulicaria, 167
    tricolor, 74
Pheucticus ludovicianus, 136
    melanocephalus, 136
Phoebe, Black, 101, 190, 206
    Eastern, 19, 101, 190
    Say's, 101, 190
Pica hudsonia, 168
Picoides pubescens, 97
    scalaris, 97
    villosus, 98
Pigeon, Band-tailed, 78, 186
    Passenger, 79, 80, 186
Pintail, Northern, 50, 178
Pipilo chlorurus, 147
    erythrophthalmus, 147
    fuscus, 147
    maculatus, 147
Pipit, American, 130, 131, 196
    Sprague's, 130, 196
Piranga flava, 145
    ludoviciana, 146
    olivacea, 146
    rubra, 145
Pitangus sulphuratus, 104

Plegadis chihi, 43
    falcinellus, 171
Plover, American Golden-, 66, 182
    Black-bellied, 66, 182
    Mountain, 25, 67, 182
    Piping, 171
    Semipalmated, 67, 182
    Snowy, 11, 66, 67, 182
Pluvialis dominica, 66
    squatarola, 66
Podiceps auritus, 37
    grisegena, 37
    nigricollis, 37
Podilymbus podiceps, 37
Poecile carolinensis, 117
Polioptila caerulea, 124
    melanura, 124
Pooecetes gramineus, 150
Poorwill, Common, 13, 87, 174, 188
Porphyrula martinica, 64
Porzana carolina, 64
Prairie-Chicken, Lesser, 62, 182
Progne subis, 114
Protonotaria citrea, 140
Psaltriparus minimus, 118, 207
Pyrocephalus rubinus, 102, 206
Pyrrhuloxia, 22, 156, 202

Quail, Montezuma, 9, 63, 174, 182
    Scaled, 62, 63, 183
Quiscalus mexicanus, 160
    quiscula, 160

Rail, King, 63, 182
    Virginia, 64, 182
Rallus elegans, 63
    limicola, 64
Raven, Chihuahuan, 113, 192
    Common, 22, 113, 194
Recurvirostra americana, 68
Redhead, 51, 52, 178
Redstart, American, 140, 198
    Painted, 144, 200
Regulus calendula, 124

satrapa, 123
Ridgwayia pinicola, 169
Riparia riparia, 115
Rissa tridactyla, 76
Roadrunner, Greater, 82, 186
Robin, American, 128, 196

Salpinctes obsoletus, 120
Sanderling, 71, 184
Sandpiper, Baird's, 72, 184
    Buff-breasted, 73, 184
    Least, 71, 184
    Pectoral, 72, 184
    Semipalmated, 71, 184
    Solitary, 69, 184
    Spotted, 69, 184
    Stilt, 73, 184
    Upland, 69, 70, 184
    Western, 71, 184
    White-rumped, 72, 184
Sapsucker, Red-naped, 97, 190
    Williamson's, 97, 190
    Yellow-bellied, 95, 190
Sayornis nigricans, 101, 206
    phoebe, 101
    saya, 101
Scaup, Greater, 12, 51, 178
    Lesser, 52, 178
Scolopax minor, 74
Scoter, Black, 166
    Surf, 52, 180
    White-winged, 52, 180
Screech-Owl, Eastern, 83, 84, 186
    Western, 13, 83, 174, 186
Scrub-Jay, Western, 13, 17, 19, 22, 28,
    112, 192, 206
Seiurus aurocapillus, 141
    motacilla, 141, 142
    noveboracensis, 141
Selasphorus platycercus, 92
    rufus, 92
    sasin, 93
Setophaga ruticilla, 140
Shoveler, Northern, 50, 178

Shrike, Loggerhead, 106, 192
    Northern, 172
Sialia currucoides, 125
    mexicana, 125
    sialis, 125
Siskin, Pine, 164, 204
Sitta canadensis, 119
    carolinensis, 119
Snipe, Common, 66, 73, 74, 184
Solitaire, Townsend's, 126, 196
Sora, 64, 182
Sparrow, American Tree, 148, 200
    Baird's, 169, 170
    Black-chinned, 169
    Black-throated, 13, 21, 150, 202,
        208, 209
    Brewer's, 149, 200
    Cassin's, 9, 148, 200
    Chipping, 148, 200
    Clay-colored, 149, 200
    Field, 9, 13, 22, 149, 202
    Fox, 25, 151, 202
    Golden-crowned, 154, 202
    Grasshopper, 151, 202
    Harris's, 25, 153, 202, 208
    House, 165, 204
    Lark, 9, 150, 202
    Le Conte's, 11, 123, 151, 202
    Lincoln's, 152, 202
    Nelson's Sharp-tailed, 170
    Olive, 13, 19, 22, 146, 200, 208
    Rufous-crowned, 9, 17, 19, 25, 148,
        200
    Sage, 169
    Savannah, 151, 202
    Song, 152, 202
    Swamp, 152, 202
    Vesper, 150, 202
    White-crowned, 154, 202
    White-throated, 25, 152, 153, 202
Sphyrapicus nuchalis, 97
    thyroideus, 97
    varius, 95
Spiza americana, 158

Spizella arborea, 148
   atrogularis, 169
   breweri, 149
   pallida, 149
   passerina, 148
   pusilla, 149
Spoonbill, Roseate, 44, 178
Starling, European, 130, 196
Stelgidopteryx serripennis, 115
Stellula calliope, 92
Stercorarius pomarinus, 74
   parasiticus, 75
Sterna antillarum, 77
   caspia, 76
   forsteri, 77
   fuscata, 77
   hirundo, 167
Stilt, Black-necked, 67, 68, 182
Stork, Wood, 44, 178
Streptopelia decaocto, 78, 174
Strix varia, 84
Sturnella magna, 159
   neglecta, 159
Sturnus vulgaris, 130
Sula nebouxii, 38
Swallow, Bank, 115, 194
   Barn, 116, 194
   Cave, 9, 116, 194, 206
   Cliff, 116, 194
   Northern Rough-winged, 115, 194
   Tree, 114, 115, 194
   Violet-green, 115, 194
Swan, Mute, 47
   Tundra, 47, 178
Swift, Chimney, 88, 188
   White-throated, 88, 188

Tachybaptus dominicus, 36
Tachycineta bicolor, 114
   thalassina, 115
Tanager, Hepatic, 145, 200
   Scarlet, 146, 200
   Summer, 145, 200
   Western, 146, 200

Teal, Blue-winged, 49, 50, 178
   Cinnamon, 50, 178
   Green-winged, 50, 178
Tern, Black, 77, 186
   Caspian, 76, 186
   Common, 167
   Forster's, 77, 186
   Least, 77, 186
   Sooty, 77, 186
Thrasher, Brown, 129, 196
   Crissal, 130, 196
   Curve-billed, 9, 130, 196
   Long-billed, 13, 17, 19, 22, 129, 196,
      207
   Sage, 129, 196
Thrush, Aztec, 169
   Gray-cheeked, 126, 196
   Hermit, 127, 196
   Swainson's, 127, 196
   Wood, 127, 196
Thryomanes bewickii, 122
Thryothorus ludovicianus, 122
Titmouse, "Black-crested," 117, 207
   Tufted, 14, 117, 194
Towhee, Canyon, 9, 13, 14, 17, 147,
      148, 200
   Eastern, 28, 147, 200
   Green-tailed, 147, 200
   Spotted, 147, 200
Toxostoma crissale, 130
   curvirostre, 130
   longirostre, 129, 207
   rufum, 129
Tringa flavipes, 69
   melanoleuca, 68
   solitaria, 69
Troglodytes aedon, 122
   troglodytes, 122
Tryngites subruficollis, 73
Turdus migratorius, 128
Turkey, Wild, 9, 20, 62, 182
Turnstone, Ruddy, 70, 184
Tympanuchus pallidicinctus, 62
Tyrannus couchii, 104

forficatus, 105
savana, 168
tyrannus, 105
verticalis, 105
vociferans, 104
Tyto alba, 82

Veery, 126, 127, 196
Verdin, 117, 118, 194
Vermivora celata, 132
  chrysoptera, 132
  peregrina, 132
  pinus, 132
  ruficapilla, 133
  virginiae, 172
Violet-ear, Green, 88, 167, 188
Vireo, Bell's, 9, 17, 22, 107, 192, 207
  Black-capped, 1, 9, 11, 12, 16–18,
    20, 22, 107, 161, 173, 192
  Blue-headed, 109, 192
  Cassin's, 109, 192
  Gray, 9, 13, 17, 22, 108, 192
  Hutton's, 110, 192
  Philadelphia, 110, 192
  Plumbeous, 108, 192
  Red-eyed, 13, 18, 19, 22, 111, 192
  "Solitary," 108, 109
  Warbling, 110, 192
  White-eyed, 13, 22, 106, 192
  Yellow-green, 168
  Yellow-throated, 13, 18, 108, 192
Vireo atricapillus, 107, 207
  bellii, 107, 207
  cassinii, 109
  flavifrons, 108
  flavoviridis, 168
  gilvus, 110
  griseus, 106
  huttoni, 110
  olivaceus, 111
  philadelphicus, 110
  plumbeus, 108
  solitarius, 109
  vicinior, 108, 207

Vulture, Black, 44, 178
  Turkey, 44, 45, 178

Warbler, "Audubon's," 136
  Bay-breasted, 139, 198
  Black-and-white, 140, 198
  Blackburnian, 138, 198
  Blackpoll, 139, 198
  Black-throated Blue, 136, 198
  Black-throated Gray, 136, 198
  Black-throated Green, 137, 198
  Blue-winged, 132, 196
  Canada, 144, 200
  Cape May, 169
  Cerulean, 140, 198
  Chestnut-sided, 135, 198
  Connecticut, 142, 200
  Golden-cheeked, 1, 9, 11–16, 18,
    19, 25, 137, 138, 173, 198, 208
  Golden-winged, 132, 196
  Grace's, 139, 198
  Hermit, 137, 198
  Hooded, 143, 200
  Kentucky, 9, 142, 200
  MacGillivray's, 28, 143, 200
  Magnolia, 135, 198
  Mourning, 143, 200
  "Myrtle," 136
  Nashville, 133, 198
  Orange-crowned, 132, 198
  Palm, 139, 198
  Pine, 139, 198
  Prairie, 139, 198
  Prothonotary, 9, 140, 141, 198
  Red-faced, 169
  Rufous-capped, 144, 200
  Swainson's, 141, 198
  Tennessee, 132, 196
  Townsend's, 136, 198
  Virginia's, 172
  Wilson's, 143, 200
  Worm-eating, 141, 198
  Yellow, 135, 198
  Yellow-rumped, 23, 136, 198

Yellow-throated, 13, 15, 16, 18, 22, 138, 198, 208
Waterthrush, Louisiana, 9, 141, 142, 200
  Northern, 141, 200
Waxwing, Cedar, 131, 196
Whimbrel, 171
Whip-poor-will, 87, 188
Whistling-Duck, Black-bellied, 28, 45, 173, 178
  Fulvous, 166
Wigeon, American, 48, 178
  Eurasian, 47, 48, 178
Willet, 69, 184
Wilsonia canadensis, 144
  citrina, 143
  pusilla, 143
Woodcock, American, 74, 184
Woodpecker, Acorn, 95, 190
  Downy, 97, 190
  Golden-fronted, 14, 95, 190
  Hairy, 98, 190
  Ladder-backed, 9, 14, 97, 190
  Lewis's, 94, 190
  Pileated, 98, 190
  Red-bellied, 95, 190
  Red-headed, 9, 94, 190

Wood-Pewee, Eastern, 99, 190
  Western, 99, 190
Wren, Bewick's, 9, 13, 14, 17, 22, 122, 194
  Cactus, 21, 120, 194
  Canyon, 121, 194
  Carolina, 14, 22, 122, 194
  House, 122, 194
  Marsh, 123, 194
  Rock, 120, 194
  Sedge, 11, 123, 194
  Winter, 122, 194

Xanthocephalus xanthocephalus, 159
Xema sabini, 76

Yellowlegs, Greater, 68, 184
  Lesser, 69, 184
Yellowthroat, Common, 143, 200

Zenaida asiatica, 78
  macroura, 79
Zonotrichia albicollis, 152
  atricapilla, 154
  leucophrys, 154
  querula, 153, 208

DATE DUE

GAYLORD			PRINTED IN U.S.A.